THE
GLASS
HOUSE

THE GLASS HOUSE

THE LIFE OF THEODORE ROETHKE

BY ALLAN SEAGER

INTRODUCTION BY
DONALD HALL

THE UNIVERSITY OF
MICHIGAN PRESS

Ann Arbor

Introduction copyright © by Donald Hall 1991
Text copyright © Joan Fry 1968
All rights reserved
Published in the United States of America by
The University of Michigan Press
Printed and bound by CPI Group (UK) Ltd, Croydon, CR0 4YY

2011   2010   2009   2008   6   5   4   3

A CIP catalog record for this book is available from the British Library.

Library of Congress Cataloging-in-Publication Data

Seager, Allan, 1906–1968
    The glass house : the life of Theodore Roethke / by Allan Seager ;
introduction by Donald Hall.
        p.   cm.
    Reprint. Originally published : New York : McGraw Hill, 1968.
    Includes index.
    ISBN 0-472-09454-8 (cloth : alk.)— ISBN 0-472-06454-1 (paper :
alk.)
        1. Roethke, Theodore, 1908–1963—Biography.   2. Poets,
American—20th century—Biography.   I. Title.
    PS3535.039Z83   1991
    811'.54—dc20
    [B]
                                                                            91-11016
                                                                            CIP

Essays by Robert Heilman. Copyright © 1964 by *Shenandoah: The
Washington and Lee University Review.* Used by permission.

Theodore Roethke: Essays on the Poetry, ed. Arnold Stein. (Seattle:
University of Washington Press, 1965.) Used by permission.

Pictures from Brueghel and Other Poems by William Carlos Williams.
Copyright 1954 by William Carlos Williams. Reprinted by permission of
New Directions Publishing Corporation.

From *The Diary of Vaslav Nijinsky* edited by Romola Nijinsky. Copyright
1936, copyright renewed © 1963 by Simon & Schuster, Inc. Reprinted by
permission of the Publisher.

Reprinted by permission from *Twentieth Century Authors: First
Supplement,* edited by Stanley J. Kunitz. Copyright 1955 by the
H. W. Wilson Company.

The author had access to the Theodore Roethke manuscripts in the
University of Washington collection by permission of Mrs. Roethke and the
University of Washington.

ISBN 978-0-472-09454-7 (cloth : alk.)
ISBN 978-0-472-06454-0 (paper : alk.)

For Joan

Contents

Contents

Seager's Roethke: An Introduction

Donald Hall

The Glass House is a writer's book—work of a novelist, devoted to literature and its craft, writing about a dead friend who was a poet. Theodore Roethke and Allan Seager graduated from the University of Michigan a year apart. At that time, they scarcely knew each other, but their coincidence allows Seager to sketch out of memory the ambience of Roethke's Michigan. A decade later, when they had both started to publish, they met again at a writers' conference and became friends. Roethke suggested that Seager join him at Bennington College in Vermont, where they spent one year teaching together. They remained close until Roethke died at fifty-five in 1963. Allan Seager died five years later, at sixty-two, and this biography of his friend was his last work.

It was my luck to know both men. I knew Roethke only slightly, but for ten years I taught at the University of Michigan with Allan Seager. He was my senior by twenty years, and I had begun to read him in adolescence, saving my allowance when I was fourteen to buy his first novel, *Equinox*. Probably Seager's best novels were *Amos Berry* and *Hilda Manning;* there was also a fine book of short stories called *The Old Man of the Mountain*. (Eight of the stories had turned up in annual *Best* collections.) Seager's fiction was highly praised by Hugh Kenner, James Dickey, Robert Penn Warren... and it never won general recognition. Today one novel remains in print.

Allan considered us an embattled pair, as faculty members at the University of Michigan. We were Practitioners of the Word, islanded in a sea of Ph. D.'s who could not write an office-hours schedule without stylistic infelicity. Allan exaggerated; Allan enjoyed exaggerating. An erect, handsome, ironic figure, he strode the corridors of Haven Hall, where the English Department pastured itself, and popped his head into my office to tell a story; to quote a colleague's latest gaffe; to pass on writerly gossip. He told me stories about his friend Ted Roethke—whose work I had long admired—as cautionary tales or exemplary anecdotes for the edification of an apprentice. He spoke with affection about Ted's eccentricities, ambitions, habits of work—especially about Ted's professionalism, as we might have called it if Roethke had not been a poet.

When I was an undergraduate, I ran across Theodore Roethke's *The Lost Son*, and was immediately enthralled. After graduation, doing some time at Oxford in 1951, I lectured at the Poetry Society on "New American Poets"; I dwelt upon Lowell, Wilbur, and Roethke. Later I wrote a two-part piece for a magazine in London, telling about "American Poets Since the War," and praised Roethke again. During a brief stint at Stanford a year later, when I published a poem in a quarterly, Roethke telephoned from Seattle to congratulate me. (He knew I admired his work; he wanted to like mine.) He telephoned in December of 1953 while I was out Christmas shopping, and talked to my wife, telling her that he wanted to bring me to Seattle for a poetry reading—which was an absurd notion: I had published only two poems in American magazines, and no books. What else he said, I don't know, but he talked for an hour with enthusiasm and high excitement; much later, I learned that Roethke called from a hospital—and I understood the blood chemistry of his enthusiasm. Ignorant in 1953, I wrote him a note about the putative poetry reading, and a month later he answered that the university was out of funds; as for his own, "the Aga Khan phase is over for this year. . . ." In the spring of 1954 I heard him read at San Francisco State's Poetry Center—an ingratiating powerhouse of a reading, heavy on comic routines—and

talked with him at a reception the next day. It was nine years
before I saw him a second and last time.

Allan and his friend were men of their generation, courtly or flirta-
tious with women and cronyish with men, Prohibition-generation
drinkers, funny, and decent; these two committed their lives to
literature. Although Roethke was a poet, he aspired to the status
of a professional writer—like Allan who had edited at *Vanity Fair*
when he was a young man, who wrote serious novels and supported
them by stories in the *Saturday Evening Post*. Not all poets want
to be *writers*—not Shelley, not Blake, not Rilke—but a few poets
have been professional workers in literature, not above supporting
themselves by the pen: among others, Jonson, Dryden, Johnson,
Hardy, Lawrence, Graves, Plath. Suffering from the delusion that
fiction paid, Roethke collected books of advice on how to write it.
Doubtless, like Sylvia Plath, he looked into the *Writers' Digest*
from time to time; one cannot imagine Rilke reading *WD*'s list of
poetry markets.

But of course poetry for Roethke was more than a profession; it
was reason for living and breathing. He not only wanted to make
poems; he wanted to make the best poems, and he worked at his
art with utter diligence. Seager mentions the notebooks filled with
sketch-writing—drafts, observations, notes, tryouts. Every after-
noon outside his Washington house, Roethke sat with a notebook
on his lap, trying out lines and phrases, sentences, prose notes
about poetry, *generating language*—everything toward the goal of
great poetry.

Seager loves to speak of Roethke's notebooks, for *The Glass
House* is a book that takes pleasure in the life of writing. Seager is
continually intrigued by the creative process, although psychology
was not one of his obsessions. Doggedly he explores the relation-
ship between Roethke's mental illness and his genius. I find his
speculations suggestive and relevant still—on a subject under con-
tinual debate: bipolarity and literary achievement.

If *The Glass House* is not the ultimate exploration of Roethke's
mind or soul, it is appropriate to notice: For Theodore Roethke,
his mind and soul existed to provide material for poetry, like
Yeats's voices which spoke not to discover truth but to provide
metaphors for poetry. Even if we disapprove of Roethke's devotion

to art, his aestheticism, we must acknowledge that Roethke did not work at language in order to express himself; neither did he devote himself to Blake, Smart, Davies, and Yeats in order to promulgate doctrines or inculcate philosophies. Willy-nilly, his material was his own experience (which included his reading; which included a greenhouse and a father; which included madness) and the ideas or notions he had arrived at—but: *He wrote not in order to embody ideas; he wrote to make poems.* Out of love for the poetic art, he wrote to make objects of that art.

For Allan it was not poems; it was stories and sentences—maybe sentences more than stories. Although *The Glass House* is full of good writing, Allan was dying as he finished the book. If there are lapses, never mind: *The Glass House* is an exemplary biography accomplished under difficult conditions. Allan was not permitted to quote from Roethke's poems, a damning prohibition for a poet's biographer, yet *The Glass House* not only survives this prohibition, it profits from it. A descriptive writer's prose becomes better when he understands that his essay will not be illustrated. Seager relies on his own writing, not his subject's. Some of the handsomest language here describes natural history and establishes historical background, as Allan looks to the traditions of Parkman and de Tocqueville. In his narrative summary of Roethke's life, Seager finds a tone which is affectionate yet ironic where irony is appropriate. Compare his style to the language of the biographers of Roethke's contemporaries: bad or devious prose deployed to indicate that the biographer is superior to the subject.

Over my years at Michigan I visited Allan often at his big solid gloomy house on Michigan Avenue in Tecumseh—the Michigan house of a Michigan man. Allan derived from the small town of Adrian, not far from Tecumseh; he returned nearly to his place of starting, but in the meantime: At the University of Michigan he was a champion swimmer, and a Rhodes Scholarship took him to Oriel College at Oxford University. After some editing in New York he took to teaching (he taught part-time) while he worked at his fiction. He married Barbara and fathered two daughters, but then Barbara was crippled by multiple sclerosis, which finally took her life in 1966. After Barbara's death, and shortly before his own, he married a second time, his wife Joan. His last years were given over to *The Glass House*, for which he received a Guggenheim. This final work was his elegy for the friend he admired and his eulogy for the life of writing. The last time I saw Allan, at the hospital in Tecumseh with tubes up his nostrils, he had just proof-read *The Glass House*.

As it happened, I last saw Theodore Roethke not long before he died. I read my poems at the University of Washington in April of 1963—a decade after the manic invitation—and Roethke died in July without warning. When I began the reading, Roethke wasn't there—as I noted without pleasure. I had not seen him since San Francisco State. Frequently he sent me offprints with little notes, as he sent offprints to many admirers and critics under the impression that he was managing his career. Because his self-promotion was obvious, it was not shrewd—Robert Lowell was shrewder, with his strategic postcards—and I think no one took offense. Once he suggested to his publisher, in so many words, that they put the fix in, for the Nobel. Robert Frost—of all people—once complained to me that Roethke was too competitive. If Frost, Roethke, and Lowell (not to mention Yeats, not to mention Pope), were all operators, it seems that operating, albeit unattractive, suggests no inferior ability.

As I read my third poem—"Seattle, 1963"—Theodore Roethke bulked into the auditorium with his handsome wife, Beatrice. When I finished reading a poem Roethke would make a noise. Sometimes the noises sounded derisory, sometimes admiring; of course they were disconcerting but they were also funny. When I read a tiny poem about a Henry Moore sculpture, I heard Roethke's gangster-accent curl out of the corner of his mouth: "Read that one again. Read it slower this time." I did; and at a hundred poetry readings since, I have read the poem, told the story, and read the poem over again as "The Theodore Roethke Memorial Re-Reading." All in all, it was a crazy afternoon. When I was done Roethke came up to the podium, and David Wagoner showed us the graffito chalked on the classroom blackboard: "The teach blows horses."

Then we separated to go to the reception at George Bluestone's house. Roethke and I arrived early, and he led me by the arm to a corner where he sat me down. He sank his great hands into the

pockets of his suitcoat and pulled out sheets of galley proof which
he slapped together and pushed at me. "I got a new book coming
out," he said. "Read it. It's going to drive Wilbur and Lowell into
the *shadows*."

The Far Field is my favorite Roethke, even if it didn't drive
Wilbur and Lowell into the shadows. I sat in a corner reading
galleys until the party's noises took me over. Roethke was lively
and funny, wholly charming—while Beatrice sat unsmiling, look-
ing grim. (What a *prude,* I thought, not understanding that
Beatrice was grim because she saw mania coming on. Only manics
growl at poetry readings.)

Sitting in the corner, holding the long galley sheets, I read "The
Rose" for the first time. A little later, I read it again as it appeared
posthumously in the *New Yorker*. A month or two later still, at the
American Embassy in London, I read it aloud during a memorial
service for four American poets just dead: Cummings, Williams,
Roethke, and Frost. I read:

> Near this rose, in this grove of sun-parched, wind-warped madronas,
> Among the half-dead trees, I came upon the true ease of myself,
> As if another man appeared out of the depths of my being,
> And I stood outside myself,
> Beyond becoming and perishing,
> A something wholly other,
> As if I swayed out on the wildest wave alive,
> And yet was still.
> And I rejoiced in being what I was:
> In the lilac change, the white reptilian calm,
> In the bird beyond the bough, the single one
> With all the air to greet him as he flies,
> The dolphin rising from the darkening waves;
> And in this rose, this rose in the sea-wind,
> Rooted in stone, keeping the whole of light,
> Gathering to itself sound and silence—
> Mine and the sea-wind's.

This rose grew in the glass house. You who love the poetry—you
do not hold this book unless you love the poetry—now enter *The
Glass House*.

The Glass House

I

Roethke's Birthplace

We came upon a river nearly as large as the Seine at Paris, the Saginaw, which the prairie grass had hidden. In the evening toward sunset we come back alone in the canoe and go down a branch of the Saginaw, such an evening as one hardly ever sees. The sky was without a cloud, the atmosphere pure and still. The river watered an immense forest and flowed so gently that we could scarcely tell the direction of the current. The wilderness was before us, just as six thousand years ago it showed itself to the father of mankind. It was a delicious, perfumed, gorgeous dwelling, a living palace made for man, though, as yet, the owner had not taken possession. The canoe glided noiselessly and without effort: all was quiet and serene. Under the softening influence of the scene, our words became fewer, our voices sank to a whisper, until at length we lapsed into a peaceful and delicious reverie.

From entries for July, 1831, *Pocket Notebook, No. 2,*
Journey to America by Alexis de Tocqueville.

This landscape of the Saginaw Valley is the vision of a romantic who had grown up in the ambience of Rousseau and Chateaubriand, a vision to be supplanted a century later by that of another romantic, Roethke, and out of less facile materials. De Tocqueville, terrified but characteristically curious, had been guided through the forests from Detroit where he found Saginaw to be three log houses inhabited by fur traders. He mistakenly believed these men to have penetrated farther west than any white men on the continent and he returned to France happy in his error.

Earlier the Jesuits had probably passed through like ghosts, for there were few regions near the Great Lakes that were unknown to them, but the place must have seemed unpromising, for they left no mission.

The valley had been the home of the Sauks, one of the Algonquin tribes. They hunted the big woods and planted corn in their villages along the banks of the river, only sixteen hundred of them, tradition says, an ecologically sound distribution. They lived a soft life and they were annihilated. Their comforts excited the envy of the Chippewas to the north. The oral history of the Indians is definite about events, vague only as to the calendar. Two hundred, three hundred years before, the Chippewas scouted the Sauks' Eden and, after a council held on an island in the Straits of Mackinaw, formed an alliance with the Hurons from the east, the Pottawatamies from the south, and the Menominees from the west. They closed in, canoes coming down the shore line of Lake Huron into Saginaw Bay and up the river, other groups picking up the Sauk trails through the forests, no guns yet, tomahawks. The day they picked for the attack the Sauks were having a harvest festival in honor of a young chief, Raven's Eye. Their enemies waited until a big yellow moon came up in the evening. They gave their yell and fell upon the hapless Sauks, killing all they could find. A few escaped but in the weeks following they were harried through the woods until all were dead. Their memorial is "Saginaw," a version of an Algonquin word that means "the place of the Sauks." Eventually all that was left of the Indians in the valley was the sibilance of their place names, Saginaw, Shiawassee, Tittabawassee.

For after the fur traders came the soldiers, only a few at first so as not to frighten with too great a show of power, then the big councils with the barrels of whisky and speeches about The Great White Father in Washington, and the treaties, an early one signed in 1819 by "Lewis Cass and one hundred and fourteen Indians" ceding most of the Chippewas' land with certain reservations to the United States Government in consideration of one thousand dollars (in silver) to be paid to the tribe annually, and a government-supported blacksmith to serve the tribe "so long as the President of the United States may think proper." (One wonders how long he stayed. It is hard to imagine the elegant Monroe thinking properly of this distant blacksmith.) The Chippewas, a hunting people, were to be ground down and thoroughly tamed for they were to be furnished with farm implements and cattle, and the government was "to employ such persons to aid them in their agriculture as the President deems expedient."

In protest a young chief, Oge-maw-ke-ke-to, wearing on his breast a superb medal presented to him by this very government, addressed the treaty commissioners, "Our people wonder what has brought you so far from your homes. Your young men have invited us to come and light the council fire. We are here to smoke the pipe of peace but not to sell our lands. Our American Father wants them, our English Father treats us better. He has never asked for them. Your people trespass upon our hunting grounds. You flock to our shores. Our waters grow warm. Our land melts away like a cake of ice. Our possessions grow smaller and smaller. The warm wave of the white man rolls in upon us and melts us away. Our women reproach us. Our children want homes. Shall we sell from under them the spot where they spread their blankets? We have not called you here. We smoke with you the pipe of peace."

Of course, it did no good. Other encroaching treaties were foisted on them, providing, among other things, for resettlement in the West until, in 1855, the Chippewas ceded all their land to the government for $220,000 and a sawmill. They lingered on in the region for years, idle and debauched. One of their last chiefs, Shop-en-a-gons, permitted himself to be photographed in civilized garb, wearing a frock coat and holding a tall silk hat. It was all dreadfully usual and pathetic.

Emigration into the Saginaw Valley was slow because the climate was unhealthy. The mosquitoes were huge. The fevers were bad, and the fur traders, unwilling to see the trees go down because they made cover for the animals, discouraged settlers. De Tocqueville has left one of the few accounts of the equipment needed to pioneer this region. The untouched land never cost more than five shillings an acre, a day's pay. When he had chosen his plot, the settler would occupy it, bringing with him an axe, a gun, a tent, a salted pig, a barrel of corn meal, some seed corn, a bushel of seed potatoes and whatever cattle he had. He lived in the tent until he had felled enough trees to make a log hut. He planted his seed potatoes among the stumps. The potatoes, the meal, the pig, and whatever game he could bring down would keep him his first winter. As soon as he had built his hut, he would girdle all the nearby trees to kill them so that their foliage would not keep the sun from his crop of corn the second year. The first two or three years were the hardest. "Afterward comes competence, and later wealth," de Tocqueville said with prophetic serenity.

The few newcomers were chiefly New England farmers who, used to wresting crops out of the fourteen or fifteen inches of dirt covering their native rock, were delighted by the bottomless alluvial soil of the Valley; a few Irish who escaped from the potato famines of the Forties; and later a few Germans, Swabians, Bavarians, reluctant to do their military service.

The pioneers were aware of the vast forests surrounding them. How could they not be? Some of the gigantic pines did not put out a branch until they had risen eighty, even ninety feet above the ground. But they saw no particular value in these trees. They built a few sawmills in the Thirties to saw boards for houses but they had no notion that there would ever be more than a local market for lumber. The Maine forests were then judged to be inexhaustible and they were closer to the big eastern centers of population. And, worse, there was no transport for Michigan lumber, only a few lake steamers plying irregularly between Detroit and Saginaw. It was not until 1847 that a cargo of Saginaw lumber reached the market at Albany, New York.

All this changed very quickly when it was discovered that there were not going to be enough trees in Maine to keep pace with the growth of the country. Lake boats were built and against prodigious difficulties rail lines were put through the woods. For a shrewd man the opportunities for the investment of capital were almost limitless and the same names recur again and again as owners of timber land and sawmills, as executives of rail and steamship companies, as proprietors of banks and wholesale and retail mercantile companies. The lumber boom began. The history of the Saginaw Valley differs little from that of the rest of the Middle West except in this. It is its unique feature.

Statistics on the number of board feet of lumber were kept from 1851 when 92,000,000 feet were cut. In 1882, the zenith of the boom, the figure had risen to over a billion feet. This meant lumber camps on the Saginaw and all its tributaries, the Shiawassee, the Tittabawassee, the Flint, the Cass. (Today there is a little concrete bridge over the Tittabawassee. The stream is barely fifteen feet wide. The water itself seems to have gone with the timber.) The cut was made in the winter when the logs could be sledded over the snow to the riverbanks, piled there until the spring thaw, then skidded into the stream to let the current take them higgledy-piggledy down to the boom where they would be sorted. Each log had been struck at one end with a special hammer and it bore in intaglio the owner's brand. The booms were enclosures that stretched halfway across the stream. Lumberjacks guided the logs into the boom. At the sorting gap at the far end, each owner claimed the logs bearing his mark, made them into rafts, and floated them further down the stream to his sawmill.

There are winter photographs of the camps, the lumberjacks standing and crouching among the pines, the ground white all around them, burly men with mustaches, wide-awake hats, wearing mackinaws and short jackets, never overcoats to get in their way, and the plumes of their breaths show in the picture—the weather was often thirty below zero. Some of these men came from the dwindling Maine woods, arrogantly bringing their skills west "to show the Michiganders how to saw logs." Many were dark French-Canadians who spoke nothing but Canuck French. After the Civil War all kinds of unemployed soldiers found work in the woods or along the streams. They called themselves the "red-sash brigade."

When the winter was over they came to town, to Saginaw, with their winter's pay intact—there was nothing to spend it on in the woods. It would only be two or three hundred dollars but, full of lust, imaginings, and fresh air, they were ready to blow it all. They would take a lustral bath at one of the hotels, buy a new outfit of clothes and a red sash, and go down to Water Street or Franklin Street where the bars and the whorehouses were. And with a terrible physical exuberance that had not been sufficiently tested against mere axe helves or saw handles, they would fight with sheer male pleasure, drunken, gouging, kicking struggles where a river man still wearing his spikes would often leave the print of them in his opponent's face. The admiring police would fill the jail with them, turn them loose when they were sober, and they would go out and do it all over again. A week, ten days of this and they would be calm and penniless. They would meekly take summer jobs in the sawmills until the weather grew cold. Then back to the woods again.

By 1900 it was all over. A few stands of virgin timber were left, islands in a sea of stumps. Roethke was born in 1908 during what seems to have been a period of stunned assessment of what was left to keep a town going on. Beans had been planted to help feed the lumberjacks; they planted more until Michigan raised more navy beans than any state in the country. They had boiled water from salt springs and wells to get pure salt; they boiled more. They discovered veins of a damp, inferior grade of coal and mined that. As they cleared out the stumps, they planted sugar beets and a sugar industry grew up. (In my own childhood, Michigan sugar was bluish in color and the grains stuck together in lumps. This has now been corrected. The sugar is white and cannot be told from cane.) The factories that had supplied the mills and camps with hardware, boilers, and saws turned painfully to the manufacture of more suitable products or failed.

There was money there. A lot of capital had come from the East and it returned swollen with profit, but a lot of capital had been local and now with its increments it was cautiously invested in local enterprises or it went into trust funds in the vaults of Saginaw banks where it still lies, shedding beneficently its four or five per cent a year. Some of the lumber money and some of the lumber itself went into the splendid wooden houses of the rich, built in the style of the period with round towers topped by ornate finials, steeply pitched roofs, and porches running halfway around the house, set in the middle of wide lawns ornamented with beds of flowers. Many parks were laid out in what is now the center of the city and the well-to-do drove through them in landaus or victorias drawn by matched pairs of horses and later in the first Pierce-Arrows.

In 1889 the Saginaw Club was founded and, unlike many men's clubs, it had its own building where it still purveys quiet, a sound cuisine, and a sumptuous nude behind the bar for gaping at. In 1899 ten acres of farm land were purchased, turned into a nine-hole golf course, and the Saginaw Country Club was established. "An association of leading men and women" formed themselves into the Um-Zoo-Ee Club for the purpose of holding dancing parties. The Canoe Club was founded in 1904 facing the Titta- bawassee River "to promote an interest in canoeing, boating, and aquatic sports among the younger element of our best citizen- ship." A boat landing was provided, later a stand for shooting clay pigeons, and a tennis court. The insane romantic energy of the early years was gone but certain amenities of life had arrived, and it is pleasant to think of the quiet river, once crammed with ugly logs, now supporting the svelte canoes of the lumbermen's chil- dren, filled with spooning couples and occasionally a phonograph wafting the strains of "Moonlight Bay" or "Too Much Mustard" from its fluted horn.

What was happening was a consolidation of comforts natural enough, perhaps, after the hardships of the settlement and the lumber boom. The pace of life slowed and became peaceful, and lives tended to repeat themselves without much change from one generation to the next. As they were expected to do, young men went into business, the law, a few into medicine. What had been discovered to be convenient ways of doing things crystallized into habits so rigid that any departure from them could be sustained by a sense of actual guilt. The immigrants prospered, the Ger- mans, the Italians, and later Slavs of various kinds. The lumber boom became the subject of mural paintings on the walls of the Bancroft Hotel dining room. The capitalists, being already rich, hung on to their money. Why risk it? The old civic fire burned low.

It was into this placid town that Roethke was born. What does a man take from his community; what seeps in from roundabout? The first definitions, the fruits of the primary glances, can never be supplanted, for the trees of one's childhood are the touchstones of all later trees, the grass of the back yard the measure of all greenness, and other lights fail because they are not the true sun that brightens those trees, that grass. Man is, of course, Father, and Woman, Mother. All other definitions derive from these, how- ever tenuously. Since all take, we can assume Roethke took these. What else? As a man he had a furious energy all out of proportion to what was spent around him. How did he come by it? Is it a matter of psychology, of metabolism, or was there possibly some mysterious inheritance by rumor or example from an earlier time? It is so hard to tell that perhaps it should not even be mentioned.

A poet must take the materials of his imagery from somewhere, and it will help to describe him to see what he ignores. There is no memory of Roethke hanging around the old folks listening, like Faulkner, and his old folks were German, anyway. Their stories would have led him back to the Old Country which never interested him. He also ignores all the vivid racy tales of the lumber boom, tales that expressed courage, will, and cunning that might have engaged another man. Unlike Allen Tate or Robert Lowell, he ignores in his poetry the events of his region's history. He must have been aware of the Indians, for he collected a shoebox full of flint arrowheads in his rambles along the riverbanks. But, of course, many boys did that. There had been many Indians, many arrowheads, and they were not specially hard to find. Yet there may have been some impingement, for late in life he mentions Indians in one of his poems; and in his most recent notes, a long poem was projected based partly on the wrongs done to them. But, for the most part, he pays no attention to the history of the valley which expresses in modes of physical action an energy like his own. It is as if he had inherited the best part and did not need to acknowledge it.

Out of this prosperous region no poet, no painter or sculptor, no composer had ever emerged. When one did, a profound and innocent apathy surrounded, almost submerged him like a dune of sand on the lake shore. During his boyhood its countless, minute, unrecognized abrasions may have helped to form him both as a man and a poet and assisted unbeknown in their eventual identification.

II

Roethke's Family

About 1870 Wilhelm Roethke resigned his post as Hauptförster on the estate of Bismarck's sister, the Gräfin von Arnim, near Pasewalk in East Prussia. Pasewalk is one of the oldest towns in Pomerania, twenty-five miles from Stettin, which is far enough east to be now in Poland and spelled, Szczecin. Wilhelm's wife was the housekeeper for the von Arnim estate and there is a photograph of her, dressed in the black bombazine of the period, with a bunch of keys, her badge of office, hanging at her waist. A Chief Forester would have had to be learned about trees, shrubs, gardens of all kinds, the cutting of timber, and the reforesting afterward. His wife would have had to be an extremely capable woman to have managed the housekeeping for an estate as big as the von Arnims', who were a much older and wealthier family than the Bismarcks. The Roethkes would seem to have had the status of upper servants and as such enjoyed many privileges. Wilhelm's son, Otto, Ted's father, claimed even more. He said that the Roethkes were "poop-arse" aristocrats and implied that in the feudal past they had owned a couple of Pomeranian villages.

Wilhelm Roethke and his family moved westward at first to Berlin where he started a little flower shop near the Brandenberger Tor. (His daughter on her only visit to the Fatherland many years later saw the title deeds to this shop, signed by her father, and the shop was then still in existence.) After a short stay in Berlin, he moved west again in 1872 right out of Germany to America where he settled in Saginaw. At that time he had three sons, Emil, Karl, and Otto, who was still a baby in arms. He took

9

a second-class cabin for his wife and the baby but he and the
other two sons went steerage. His motives for the removal, one
that he felt strongly about, was the not uncommon one of taking
his sons out of a militaristic nation so that they would not have to
serve in the army. He seems to have chosen Saginaw, then attract-
ing the more *gemütliche* south Germans, because his older
brother, Karl, had already settled there.

Wilhelm acquired twenty-two acres in west Saginaw on what is
now Cratiot Avenue and he established a market garden. It was a
good time to start such a project. The lumber boom was just
beginning and there was a demand for fresh vegetables, fruits,
and berries of all kinds. The whole family, his wife, his sons, and
later, his daughters, worked in the fields as they would have done
in the Old Country. They prospered.

From the stories in the family, Wilhelm seems to have been less
Prussian than his wife. (I asked a German professor what Ger-
mans themselves thought of Pomeranians. He said, "They work
very hard. They drink very hard, and they have an enormous
sense of rectitude, not necessarily moral rectitude.") Wilhelm
liked to dress in his best black suit, take his gold-headed cane, and
lounge around Water Street; but his wife was always forestalling
him to make him take a load of fruit and vegetables into town.
She was an indomitably industrious woman, and one of the
Roethke cousins remembers her dinning into her family her
favorite command, *"Mach es tüchtig!"*, that is, "Do it right!"

When he had made enough money, Wilhelm did something that
was obviously close to his heart. He built a big greenhouse on his
property and started raising flowers. He Anglicized his Christian
name and called it, "The William Roethke Greenhouses." As he
grew older, it became clear that his eldest son, Emil, was not
interested in flowers. He took up other lines of work, became
County Drain Commissioner, and later, the head custodian of
Oakwood Cemetery. (He was the most "Prussian-looking" of the
three sons. He had an abrupt, somewhat stern manner, held him-
self very straight, and wore a small, clipped moustache.) The two
younger sons, Karl (now Charles) and Otto bought out his in-
heritance and took up the management of the property. Charles
was the business head, Otto the green thumb. They had been

carefully reared by their parents and there was little they had to learn about growing and marketing flowers.

The greenhouse has long been torn down and its place taken by a real-estate development called Roethke Court, but old photographs show that it was not one but many buildings, built parallel on an L-shaped plan, the original house having low brick walls, the later ones of concrete blocks, and the rest all glass. At first Wilhelm and his family lived in a kind of dormitory at the back of the original building to be handy to the flowers. Later, as the business expanded, they moved into a house. After the old man's death, Charles and Otto built houses side by side on Gratiot Avenue and the greenhouse was only a minute's walk from their back doors.

Charles Roethke's daughter, Mrs. Violet Mortensen, has vivid memories of the carnations. "We had two carnation houses. In the first one the carnations were planted in high concrete benches. The men in the greenhouse made them—they had the moulds for them—and every six or twelve inches were drainage holes. These were where the weeds came through and when Ted had to weed under the benches, they hung right down. In the other carnation house the benches were only about twelve inches high; they were flat on the ground. And these were beautiful and in that greenhouse, we grew sweet peas together with the carnations. The little fence to support the sweet peas ran down the center. It was a sight to behold! It would be below zero outside and about February, for St. Valentine's Day, the sweet peas started to blossom and here would be the beds for the pink, and white, and the red carnations. There must have been eight of them and I'd say they were a hundred and fifty feet long, each bed, and down the center the wires and strings going up for the sweet peas. Uncle Otto was artistic—the white sweet peas would be in the red carnations, and the lavender with the pale pink, and the pink would be in the dark pink carnations. I remember that Frau Bauman, Frau Zeiler, and Frau Schwarze strung—what do they call those beautiful curly— the tendrils? That's what they did because as the sweet peas grew, they would have fallen on the carnations. They stood there with their skirts billowed out, those horrible old woolen skirts. They were dirndls, those horrible old woolen things. They hung right down, and there they would be, those three old women straightening the sweet peas."

"Did these carnations have names?" I asked.

"*Enchantress* is the only one I can think of. I'm sure they all had names," she said.

"How hot did these greenhouses have to be?"

"Carnation greenhouses were cool and crisp. It was always a relief when you walked into them in the winter, this luscious coolness, and that's why they smelled so good. They must have had fertilizer on them but they didn't stink like some of the greenhouses. The high carnation beds, they were edged with radishes and parsley. We never knew what good living we had. When our parents would make vegetable soup, they'd say to the kids, 'Now you go out to the greenhouse and get me some parsley and tomatoes.' We'd have ten or twelve tomato plants that would bear fresh tomatoes all winter but you would have to go to another house and pick the bay leaves off the bay trees."

It was in this greenhouse that Otto Roethke, Ted's father, spent his life. He got up at six every morning, ate his breakfast, and went next door to his brother Charlie's and sat with him while he ate his breakfast, talking about the day's work. And this after a night when he might have gotten up two or three times to regulate the heat from the boilers or to check the ventilators, especially if it were windy. Early in this century, deliveries were made in a horse-drawn van. The horses, Sam and Sandy, were stabled at the rear of the greenhouse in space that later became a truck garage.

Many years later Ted wrote this account of his father and his work:

> My father's chief interest was the growing of the flowers. When the firm was at its height, it took up twenty-five acres within the city of Saginaw with a quarter of a million feet under glass. We lived in a frame house which was in front of the greenhouse and my uncle Charlie lived in a stone house which was next door. At one time the firm had three retail outlets, but a good deal of its business was wholesale. Its advertising created the slogan, "The largest and most complete floral establishment in Michigan" and undoubtedly it was, for it had its own ice-house, a small game preserve, and the last stand of virgin timber in the Saginaw Valley (mostly walnut and oak—not pine). In

spite of the fact that it was a working commercial greenhouse, a good deal of space, time and money was spent in experiment. Not only in flowers but also in determining what kind of wild game could be stocked in the game preserve which was seven miles outside the city, a plot of only one hundred sixty acres but completely fenced and very good natural cover for pheasant and partridge.

As a child I heard Europeans, Dutchmen and Belgians, say repeatedly that it was the most beautiful greenhouse in America. My father specialized in roses and orchids particularly. A good many of the items were never put on sale at all.

Some of the florists were wonderful men, trained in the botanical gardens, an absolute law unto themselves and who my father let alone but the working crew usually included a half dozen misfits, old punchy animal trainers, or people my father just liked to have around. The whole atmosphere was feudal and the book-keeping frequently chaotic.

Ted later wrote another account of his father and his professional preoccupation with fertilizer:

Fertilizer is a constant problem. My father literally spent weeks scouring the valley contracting with farmers for cow-dung. Whether he insisted on a particular breed of cattle, I can't say but even that could be possible. Such were the lengths to which Prussian perfectionism was carried. Sometimes I suspected he just bought from those disreputable cronies he liked, and a strange crew they were, but this was not so: he could not be corrupted. He insisted on richness, wetness, thick consistency, and above all, age. It got so I thought the only important part of the farm was back of the barn. And of course it had to be collected by one of our own men, personally shovelled into the back of the truck (usually a battered Model-T). Otherwise the material might turn up with hay, fodder, stones, dead cats, rubber tires, or even, God forbid, just ordinary muck, rich, valued, but useless for the manure machine. This was not just a contraption but a veritable Roman bath: about forty by twenty-five feet, with an assembly of pipes, faucets, steam-gauges, a cat-walk for the attending mixer of the brew, which was a special, I dare-say, scent-formula—such was the nature of the Roethkes' manure, lime, hot water, bone-meal, and God knows what else. Anyway, it grew roses.

I remember George Phoenix, a south Saginaw councilman,

offering him 32 loads of free manure if he would get the men to
vote his way. He got thrown out of the office, ours and the city's.
Not that buying votes was considered a crime, mind you, for my
father was a Michigan Republican: and to his mind the refusal
of the Senate to seat Truman Newberry for the mere spending of
three and a half million represented one of the grave miscar-
riages of justice in American history. George just had the mis-
fortune to touch on a sacred subject. Even so, I suspect that if
my father had thought the manure was really *good* manure, he
might have given the boys a hint or two.

The yearly holidays were the busiest times, Thanksgiving with
the fall flowers, asters and chrysanthemums, Christmas with poin-
settias and holly wreaths, New Year's and St. Valentine's Day.
(Otto raised violets for St. Valentine's Day on the property. It was
fashionable then to send one's sweetheart a bouquet of violets,
surrounded by paper lace, with a single red rosebud in the
center.) The family had been Lutheran in Germany so far as they
were religious at all but in Saginaw Charles Roethke affiliated
himself with the Episcopal and Otto with the Presbyterian
churches. Churches needed many flowers for altar pieces and
funerals, and with two churches in the family, the Roethkes in-
creased their business although there is no evidence that they
made these affiliations advisedly. During most of their association
the two brothers had a smooth relationship. It was almost neces-
sary that this be so if the business were to be run properly for they
saw more of each other than most partners.

Otto liked to hunt. His only vacation in the year was the two
weeks he took off during the hunting season. He would go with a
group of men, among them Congressman Joe Fordney, one of the
authors of the Fordney-McCumber Tariff Act, to the upper
peninsula of Michigan where they had a camp above the Tah-
quamenon Falls, a wild area with no roads whose only approaches
were by water. There is a photograph showing Otto standing
proudly with the other men beside fifteen deer hanging from a
rack in the snow-filled woods. He was a good shot.

A man six feet tall, blond, slender, he passed on to his son the
structure of his head. They would have resembled each other
closely if Ted had not been plumper. Otto's movements were slow
and deft. He was pleasant enough but seemed absorbed. The

children of the neighborhood thought him "cross," cross but not mean, but this was because he was always having to drive them out of the greenhouses. A greenhouse is a wonderful place for a child to play and they were always slipping in. His reading was the daily newspaper and the horticultural journals, all of them. If he loved flowers, the love did not show itself in his daily work. He was a professional. Many flowers had sapped any exuberance but not his care. His hired florists were men as expert as himself, Charlie Schwers and Max Laurisch, thorough, knowledgeable, and industrious. The love was revealed rather in the choice of the career itself and the artistry he had in little touches like the harmony of color between the sweet peas and the carnations. No customer would have seen this. He did it for himself because it seemed right, *tüchtig*. There were many German societies to join, the Germania, the Teutonia, which offered companionship, a social life among his own nationals. He joined none. He kept himself independent. In his way, he was a complete man, solid, grounded, having few questions to ask of himself.

In 1906 he married a Saginaw girl named Helen Huebner. She was slender, delicate, with very blond, almost white, hair. The Roethkes as a family were said to have "Ein Nagel im Kopf," (a nail in the head, an idiomatic expression for arrogant eccentricity). Emil Roethke, the eldest brother, referred to Helen Huebner Roethke all his life as "the Bay-Streeter." It was a term of contempt, implying that she had married above herself. Bay Street was filled with late-come German immigrants, unassimilated, clinging to the ways of the Old Country, speaking German in their homes. (None of old Wilhelm's sons spoke German in their homes nor did they have a trace of a German accent.) Helen Huebner had little formal education. She had gone to work early as a seamstress and she had hand-tucked many a blouse before her marriage. She was, however, beautifully prepared to be the wife of Otto Roethke.

Her week was run in the old style:

MONDAY: Wash day.
TUESDAY: Ironing day.
WEDNESDAY: Baking day. (She baked all her own bread, cakes, pies, coffee cakes, *schnecken*, which were strips of raised dough, baked and coming out in curls with cinnamon and

powdered sugar over them, and at Christmas, the usual
German cookies, *lebkuchen, Pfeffernusse,* and *Springerles.*)
THURSDAY: Upstairs cleaning.
FRIDAY: Downstairs cleaning.
SATURDAY: Baking day again. Kitchen cleaning.

Meals were served in the dining room with linen tablecloths and
sterling-silver napkin rings. It was felt to be lower class to eat in
the kitchen and Otto ate only snacks there. Dinner was at noon on
weekdays, a little later on Sundays, and was centered around meat
and potatoes. There was pie for dessert at Sunday dinners, cake on
Sunday night. Helen superintended the women greenhouse work-
ers, Frau Bauman, Frau Zeiler, Frau Schwarze, in the making of
sauerkraut every fall in a stone crock with a white plate upside
down as a cover, weighted down with a stone. They kept about a
hundred chickens. They had apple, peach, and pear trees on the
place. Each spring Otto and Charlie would buy two shoats apiece,
fatten them on garbage in the German way through the summer,
and butcher them in the first cold days of autumn. They cured
their own hams and bacon and smoked them in their own smoke-
house. The greenhouse women made sausage in the cellar of the
house where there was a wood stove, summer sausage, lung sau-
sage—the children held their noses when it was even mentioned
—and fresh pork sausage. They tried out leaf lard, fried quantities
of pork chops, laid the chops in a stone crock, and poured the
fresh lard over them to keep through the winter.

It must be clear that the center of Helen's life was her home.
She established a routine of domestic habit that she felt to be
beneficent and she stuck to it. Her house was clean. Her family
was well-fed and neatly dressed. Any moral problems she referred
to the Lutheran-Presbyterian elements in her nature, and with
these as guide there is no indication that she found them hard to
solve. She seems to have been aware of a refinement owed to her
new station in life and she practised it in speech and manner.
Years later her son wrote that his mother's favorite reading was
Dostoevsky and Jane Austen, but this seems to have been an
exaggeration, one of his characteristic bits of retroactive self-
inflation, although she did read a great deal. She had few visitors
except the family and the Roethkes did not go out socially, prob-
ably because Otto worked too hard to make social life seem attrac-

tive. Although she saw to it that her children went to the Presbyterian Sunday School and Christian Endeavor meetings, she joined no church activities herself. An occasional family picnic in the family's woods or a Sunday ride on the interurban car to Bay City were her respites from domesticity. It was the family circle that occupied her and to it she gave all her care, a strong, conscientious woman.

It was a good marriage. There are no memories of any of the quarrels that make children fear the end of the world has come. If Otto felt that his wife was pressing him too hard about something or other, he would laugh, shrug, and walk away. This probably engendered a certain resentment in her, never to be able to thresh a matter out openly, but it prevented bickering. If the Roethke household was, as many are, an arena that gave play to the profoundest human feelings, deep-set hatreds, frantic affections, it did not do so openly. Duties were set. Calm was maintained.

It is possible to see Otto Roethke as an artist whose fuller development was frustrated by the Prussian *Tüchtigkeit*. It is possible to see Helen Roethke as a woman who desired more acknowledged power than was ever put into her hands. But these are mere conjectures.

III

Childhood

Who records a childhood? Apparently none but the tutors of princes. In less exalted ranks of society, among the middle classes, a child intrinsically, a child as such is without importance. He appears as the guarantor of Daddy's manhood, the focus of Mummy's love. It takes a year or two for him to wail and stagger into a character of his own. His bright sayings, his severest accidents and illnesses will be remembered but hardly written down. He is kept clean to show that his mother is neat, well-dressed to prove that his father can afford it. He is a little donkey bearing reluctantly, sometimes even kicking at the weight of other people's plans for him, yet all the time he is looking, tasting, sniffing, listening, poking at things, fairly rolling in life on his own. The joys and terrors evoked by his activity are opaque to his parents who can only soothe him when he cries because he is too inarticulate to explain even the nature of his tremendous experiments. What is a childhood then? A thin sheaf of memories, a few adjectival flourishes from the mouths of aunts and cousins. The little creature grows and grows and that almost in secret.

Ted was born May 25, 1908, but not in his father's house. His Uncle Emil had a new house on Gratiot Avenue that for some reason he was unwilling to occupy at the time. He lent it to his brother, Otto, and it was in this house, ironically, that Helen Roethke was delivered. The boy was named but not formally christened Theodore Huebner Roethke. He lived in Uncle Emil's house with his parents for two and a half years before they moved into the new house Otto Roethke had built on the greenhouse

property at 1725 Gratiot Avenue. (The number was changed later
to 1805 Gratiot.) Ted lived there for the rest of his life in Saginaw.
Five years after Ted's birth, his sister, June, was born in the house
and she still lives there. It is a big square white clapboarded house
with a broad front porch, well-shaded by elms and maples.

His birth was perfectly normal. His father and mother had
married never doubting that they would have children, and when
their first-born was a son, they were naturally pleased. In those
days a child's first summer was a period of some danger because
of the incidence of cholera morbus which killed many infants.
(They were hopefully fed scraped apple but it was a useless
remedy.) Ted escaped this and the years of his babyhood seem to
have been without incident.

It was a time of almost unimaginable peace whose like has not
been seen since. For, while the hundreds of decisions that led to
the First World War were undoubtedly being taken in the chan-
celleries of Europe, few knew about them, few could care. The
vast complicated machinery for the purveying and interpretation
of information did not exist. There was no radio, no television.
Few houses even had telephones. Thus the daily budget of inter-
national alarm to which we are now fairly accustomed had few
means of entry. Our special *Angst* was foreign to that generation.
They could see the origins of their troubles or thought they could.
They did not consider themselves to be helpless puppets of malign
international forces that danced them from a distance. It may
have been an illusion but Otto Roethke working calmly in his
greenhouse could feel that he was a free-standing, independent
man, responsible only to himself and the forces of nature. It was
the last time.

It will surprise those who knew him as a man to learn that Ted
was thin, undersized, and sickly as a boy, obviously intelligent but
shy and diffident as well. Hardly a winter went by that he wasn't
laid flat by some infection, *la grippe* as most of what we call
influenzas was named then, bronchitis, or throat trouble. He had
what is now an archaic operation for mastoiditis very young, in his
fourth or fifth winter. His whole head was a mass of bandages.
The men who worked in the greenhouse sent him a big, painted,
papier-mâché turkey filled with candy—when you shook it, a
piece dropped out of the bottom like an egg. He stood at the

window looking out and all the children of the neighborhood came and played outside to entertain him, making angels in the snow, throwing snowballs, erecting a snowman. And this solemn little boy looked out at them, shaking a piece of candy out of the turkey new and then, and lifting it to his mouth.

When he was five years old, Ted was sent to the John Moore School on Court Street, named after one of the pioneers of the region. It was a mile and a half from his house and most of the time he, and later he and his sister, walked it four times a day. They were given street-car fare but they walked to save money. If this seems to be infant avarice, it must be remembered that a dime was as big as a cartwheel then. It would take you to a movie called *The Wolverine;* it would buy two big striped-paper sacks of popcorn or thirty wine-balls which, even assiduously sucked, should last a week. Occasionally the greenhouse delivery truck would pass them, stop, and the driver would give them a ride but he was not obliged to. The Roethkes had not yet bought a car and it is doubtful that his father would have driven one anyway. Children were regarded as somewhat muscular. June Roethke remembers that she always had to take big steps to keep up with her brother, and later he complained that she walked like a man, which she thought unjust. At this time Ted usually wore a thick red sweater, knickerbockers, black ribbed cotton stockings, and high black shoes.

The curriculum of the John Moore School would now be thought old-fashioned with its emphasis on reading, writing, and arithmetic. It had one unusual feature. Out of deference to the large German population of the district, one hour a day of the study of German was required of every pupil. Now Ted went to the John Moore School for the full eight years and received a certificate that admitted him to the Arthur Hill High School at the end of it. Clearly this means he had studied German for an hour every school day from the age of five to the age of fourteen, time enough to acquire a thorough knowledge, especially when he could ask either his father or his mother for help with any difficulties. Yet he seemed to resist learning it. He never spoke it except for a few idiomatic phrases he may have picked up in the greenhouse from the workmen; he could barely read it or write it. This may have been, with his parents' unspoken consent, some dim, attenuated hangover of the immigrant's rejection of the Old Country. Years later in Vienna he set down a list of common German words with their English equivalents, words that any beginner would have known, like "bread," "door," "window," "coat."

Ted's relations with his father had a basis that is almost unique —he saw what his father did for a living, followed him, watched, helped. How many boys know this and take it easily for granted? Most fathers leave in the morning for the office or the factory and return tired at night after a mysterious hiatus of eight or nine hours; and if the father attempts to explode the mystery by letting his son come to the office on a visit, the boy is often surprised and bewildered to find that Daddy does nothing all day but move papers around. Ted never suffered a shock like this. By absorption, the long, silent stares of a child, by a question now and then or a statement volunteered by his father, Ted learned the yearly seasons of the greenhouse, which flowers were planted from seeds, which from slips, which from bulbs; the various manures and fertilizers in extravagant detail; the flowers' diseases and their cures, the weeds that infested them—sour clover was one and the kids liked to eat it; the different periods of growth into maturity, and how fine the timing and the temperature had to be, for Easter lilies must bloom at Easter, not a week later, and there were no chemical retardants then; and, lastly, the marketing, the making of bouquets and flower pieces, the blending of the colors and textures of the flowers, and all the tissue paper and the boxes. Sometimes Ted rode on the truck with August Fischer, the driver, and scurried up to the door to deliver the flowers himself, full of pride and importance, pushing the doorbell and crying, "Flowers from Roethke's!"

It was clear to him that the end of all this patient calculation and labor was the sale of the bouquet—that was where the money came from—and the bouquet offered a few days of vivid color, of scent, of beauty to a church or someone's house. To make this possible, his father was not contending with the machinations of other men, it was rather with nature, imposing order upon its wild, raw, sumptuous growth, to make it *tüchtig*. His father seems to have let Ted pull weeds in the greenhouse and gather moss in the tract of virgin woods partly to give him something useful to do in his spare time—a boy could crouch under the concrete benches easier than a man—and partly, at ten cents an hour, to give him a source of pocket money. The greenhouse, then, was a place where he both worked and played. Although he could not have known it then, it was not a bad school for a boy who grew up to write poetry.

If the greenhouse was an Eden created and maintained by his father, there was for Ted another one untouched or touched very lightly beyond it. The word "field" occurs as often as any noun in Ted's work. It is part of the title of his last book, *The Far Field*, and there are lines in it where he seems almost to equate it with eternity. I asked his cousin, Mrs. Mortensen, if there were any place on the property that everyone called, "the field." She said, "Oh, sure. Out behind the greenhouse. Ted and I used to play there. When we said we were going back to the field, everybody knew you went down this road that ran around the side of the greenhouse, swung right for about a city block, turned left and there was the field. It was a good way in back. There were a lot of trees around the edges and there was about an acre of lilacs and they were as beautiful if not more so than the lilacs in the Arboretum at Ann Arbor because they were kept up so much better. That twenty-two acres was as flat as a board. And in front of these acres were seven poplars."

"But everybody called it 'the field,' " I said.

"Yes. I want to tell you of a little experience, one of the few really mystical experiences I ever had. Ted and I must have been very young. And it must have been an oat field that year because we raised food for the delivery horses. The oats weren't that wonderful gray-green; they were ripe and tall. And Ted and I went back there to play. We walked through into the oats and we couldn't see over the top so I think Ted must have been about four and I would have been six. I suppose the field held about five acres of oats and all we could see were the oats and the blue, blue sky, a very hot day. Then we said to each other, 'We're lost and nobody knows where we are.' It was a very wonderful happy feeling. I think this is when I first thought of Ted as somebody special because he was so little. We sort of played house there in the oats, talking, whispering really, what about I can't remember but we both thought it was so beautiful. And by this time, wandering around, we had tramped down a good piece of oats, about ten by ten. And, suddenly, like all kids, the play was over and we said, 'Gee, we'd better start home.' So we started but we couldn't find a way out. This seems silly but for two little kids who couldn't see over the top, it wasn't, and, all of a sudden, Ted began to cry. I wanted to cry, too, because I was scared but the thought came to me, 'No, I mustn't cry in front of Ted. He's so little.' I felt big, you see, two years older. 'I've got to get him out of here.' So I said, 'Now, Ted, don't cry. We'll get home all right.' And of course eventually we did. I can remember what he had on that day. It was a little seersucker suit, blue and white stripes, all in one piece, buttons all down the front and a little belt around the waist. So we got home and I don't suppose we said anything about getting lost in the field but the next day we really caught it because we'd tramped down so darned many oats."

Beside the greenhouse and the field, there was a piece of woods his father and uncle owned further west out Gratiot Avenue, what Ted called in a BBC broadcast in July, 1953, ". . . a wild area of cut-over second-growth timber, which my father and uncle had made into a small game preserve. As a child, then, I had several worlds to live in, which I felt were mine. One favorite place was a swampy corner of the game sanctuary where herons always nested." Except for the greenhouse, few buildings, few people in his little worlds, herons rather.

Ted has left some accounts of his childhood and of his relations with his father then. This first one seems, from the unformed handwriting and the bugs in the grammar, to have been written in high school, probably shortly after his father's death when Ted, shocked beyond his own comprehension, was trying to sort out the threads of the tie that bound him to his father. (In this essay, Ted calls himself "John."):

PAPA

Papa and the man were fixing the well. They had the top off. You could lie on your stomach and look way deep into the black water. He thought it would be wonderful to spit down there. He did. It went floating down like foam, then bobbed like a paper boat. Just when he felt so nice and dreamy, Papa grabbed him by the collar and boxed his ears until his head reeled. "You dirty boy!" he yelled. "*Schreckliches Kind!*" echoed Bob, the foreman, who always agreed with Papa.

No, Papa didn't like him much. He always gave Bud everything. Bud had a whole pot shed for a pirate's den and wouldn't even let him play. "Don't be such a whiner," Papa said.

But Bud didn't always talk nice about Papa. When John said that his father used to be the best old pitcher around, Bud would whisper to the other fellows like some smarty. "Aw," he said one day, "My dad says that Uncle Otto may be the president of the company but he's really nothin' but a watchman and coal-driver."

That made John good and mad. He walloped Bud, and tore his shirt, and made him eat dirt. It wasn't often that he licked him, either. Just when he'd flopped Bud over after he'd wiggled away a little, Papa came up, swearing like everything. "My God, Otto, you shouldn't shake that child so," Mama said.

Sometimes he dreamed about Papa. Once it seemed Papa came in and danced around with him. John put his feet on top of Papa's and they'd waltz. Hei-dee-dei-dei. Rump-tee-tump. Only babies expected dreams to come true.

There must be something wrong with himself, he thought. He often looked in the mirror to see if he looked funny. Mama loved him all right. But even old Mrs. Wilson next door called her kid, "Honey-boy," and he was "Monkey-face" to everyone else."

One afternoon, John slept on the bed in Grandpa's house. Grandpa had swords and things. He knew lots of stories. Grandpa would start telling a story about Bismarck and John would fall asleep. Then Grandpa would go to sleep, too.

This time Grandpa was gone when John awoke. There was laughing in the next room. When he looked through the door, he saw Grandpa's maid in Papa's arms. He gasped and stared. The world seemed to spin around.

Then he crept out the back door, feeling quite happy. He wouldn't have to worry any more. He hated Papa.

(The "Bud" mentioned is Charles Roethke's son, his cousin, six months older than Ted.)

A second essay seems to have been written for a Rhetoric course at the University of Michigan:

FISH TALE

There is a supreme thrill in life that comes only to stupid people. It comes when they blunder into good fortune.

As a small boy, I was always awkward and lubberly. If we went fishing, I rocked the boat; if we hunted, I stumbled and flushed the game too soon. I was awkward of mind as well as body. I asked thousands of questions. I always imagined myself fearfully hungry. All these things irritated my father who wanted, above all, to make me a wise fisherman and a self-reliant woodsman.

One day while we were casting for pike and bass on Houghton Lake, I was particularly exasperating. I got up late, forgot part of my tackle, rowed my turn poorly, and, to climax it all, knocked his hat into the lake! The next day I wasn't asked to go along.

It was a hard blow. But with the courage of despair I went still-fishing alone in an old scow, using my father's new jointed bamboo pole.

Only a few miserable sunfish and bluegills chewed on my lovely night-crawlers. The sun beat down relentlessly. The seat grew harder. The bottom of the boat reeked noiseomely of fish scales and dead worms. It was worse, I believe, than Thoreau's "foul juice" in the bottom of the mackerel boats. But the bitterness in my heart wouldn't let me go back.

At last I noticed that the sun was casting mile-long shadows on the water and the lake had turned into quivering oil. Soon I would be forced to go in on account of darkness. I pulled in my line and put on a big hook with two enormous worms. Then I pulled up the anchor and let the boat drift.

As the sky turned from a mellow gold to a dusky purple, the wind began to shift and veer in little puffs. The waves slapped against the sides. The sun, a bloated orange, had almost disappeared. I felt dejected and lonely. Suddenly a furious tug jerked the pole from my hands! It completely disappeared! Consternation siezed me. It was my father's best pole. However, fifty feet away I saw it again, skimming a zig-zag course on the water. It slid about like a giant water beetle. As soon as I got near enough to snatch it, away it would dart. Then a great thought came to me: I would wait until the fish tired itself out and then snatch it guilefully. So I settled down to the business of escorting the pole about the lake. The fish seemed possessed of the devil's energy. Finally, the pole became quite still near the shore. I snatched at the line and pulled hand over hand like mad. When I looked over the side, I saw leaping and lashing like fury, the largest and most evil-looking pike I'd ever seen. I gave one more fierce jerk and by some miracle got my fingers behind the gills. Then I pulled him into the boat and fell to thumping him with an oar.

Never will I forget that triumphal return. I felt the glorious peace that comes after fierce conflict, the calm after the storm. My hands dripped blood but I never noticed them. I rowed leisurely, for I knew that with such a fish I would never be scolded. I even contemplated staying out until midnight to make the effect more dramatic.

When I reached the dock, my father, his face black with anger, was getting ready to go out after me. "Where have you been?" he roared.

Then he saw the fish. "How did you get him?" he asked beaming.

"Well, I let your pole fall in the water."

"By God, Otto!" said old Kearns, the guide, "That's an old trick, throwing your pole in the water. It's the only way to tire a big fish out when you aint got a reel. There aren't many people would know enough to do that!"

And that was the sweetest moment in a day filled with glory, far more thrilling than the first tug of the pike, or the horrible first glimpse of him, or the hand-to-hand struggle, or the calm peace that followed. I had been adjudged clever of hand and mind for the first time in my life and I hadn't deserved it.

From the first piece, Ted seems to have remembered his father as a stern, short-tempered man whose love he doubted. When he says he hated him, it can, I think, be taken as an honest statement but it is one that nearly all boys have made one time or another and then forget. It is somewhat different with Ted; his sensitivity was greater than the average boy's and this hatred, however temporary it was, seems to have stayed in his mind and secreted guilt. In the second piece, Otto is still stern and short-tempered but he is remembered as a teacher whose irritation is caused by Ted's awkwardness, and this is a more mature view. But the most interesting thing is that Ted felt compelled somehow to write about his father. All his life the memory loomed over him.

Ted and his sister went regularly to the Presbyterian Sunday School and June remembers Ted driving her there in the family car, which means that he continued to go to Sunday School until he was nearly ready for college. He seems not to have objected as many boys did, rather he took it for granted as the thing to do. On Sunday nights he went to Christian Endeavor meetings and one of his friends believes that this is where Ted first began to notice girls. How charming this is, how quaint, like an old-fashioned paper-lace valentine, to notice girls first at Christian Endeavor meetings.

Evenings and Sunday afternoons the family usually kept together (it seems to have been hard for Ted to get out at night with other boys), Otto reading the paper, Helen sewing perhaps, June and Ted reading. He began to read very early and they were books of his own choice, his choice, that is, out of the public library—there were few bookstores in Saginaw then and there are few now. He had a set of books with leatheroid bindings that stank in wet weather, *Birds of Michigan, Wild Flowers of Michigan,* and so on through the animals and insects. He liked to watch birds but, later, he hated birdwatchers in groups—they were too highly organized. Like many boys in America who are intelligent and sensitive, more so than the people around them, he read beyond his years, indiscriminately but with great concentration. He was also good at indoor games and contests. Often his cousins would come in and they would play Rook. Ted nearly always won and he could always join the dots with a pencil line to make the picture in the contests in the Sunday paper where the prize was a live Shetland pony, but no matter how well he did it, the pony never seemed to materialize.

There is no evidence that Ted was a lonely child but such evidence is hard to get. No child comes up and says, "I'm lonely." If he is, he endures the condition and does not put a name to it. There is some evidence however, that he considered himself later to have been an unhappy child. In his notebooks there is an entry for November 6, 1930:

> He remembered his youth, his childhood, but most of all he remembered his childhood. Somehow this stood out more strangely than anything. There was something very fine in the suffering young boy. He had led a hideous life but everything was natural then. His courage then was a fine moral courage— physically he had been afraid of everything, of dogs, of thunder. Now he was afraid of none of these things. But he was afraid of the very idea of life. Sometimes he almost hated to be alive.

And on November 17, 1930, he writes:

> He was like one who had carefully preserved himself from
> being a sissy.

Ted was twenty-two years old when he wrote these entries. Are
all young men that age romantically, hyperbolically gloomy? In
the light of the amenities that his parents provided, and his later
views, to say that he had led "a hideous life" may seem exces-
sive, yet his despair seems to prove that he already had the prime
requisites of a poet, a tingling sensitivity as if he lacked an outer
layer of skin, and some sort of compulsion to elevate his life, his
emotions into words.

Ted was not a leader, the head of a gang of boys, but he seems
to have played with all the neighborhood children who were
suitable. But the Browns next door were not suitable. First of all,
they were Catholics and there was a widespread Middle-Western
prejudice against them. Secondly, they had twelve children and
Helen Roethke probably did not want them all traipsing through
her house and yard. Also, such abundance may have seemed
vulgar with probably reprehensible sexual overtones, the simple
pleasures of the poor. Thirdly, it was believed that Mr. Brown
"drank." A high board fence stretched between the Roethkes' and
the Browns' and Ted's Aunt Margaret, Charles Roethke's second
wife, can recall Ted and June sitting on their back porch all
dressed up. "Helen kept those children spotless." Every now and
then one of them would find a knothole in the fence and stare
through it at the happy moil of the Brown children playing.

Certainly one of Ted's playmates was his cousin, Bud, whom he
mentioned in *Papa*. He was Charles Roethke's son, William A. C.
Roethke. He was six months older than Ted and for many years
seems to have been bigger and stronger. Whenever there was
mischief afoot in the neighborhood, mothers would say, "I'll bet
it's that Bud Roethke." Six months' size and experience would
have been crucial and he may have bullied Ted. Anyhow Ted
hated Bud Roethke with a passion that lasted nearly all his life. I
myself have heard Ted when he was past forty inveighing against
"that bastard, Bud Roethke." He wrote and published a poem that
began, "My dim-wit cousin . . ." He accused him to me of having
had the effrontery to come back to Saginaw during the impover-

ished Thirties with a brand-new Duesenberg to drive down the street. When I talked to Bud Roethke, he said, "I didn't own a Duesenberg in the Thirties. I was too poor like everyone else. I never owned a Duesenberg in my life." The story seems to have been a little fantasy Ted concocted—he felt that it would have been a characteristic thing for his cousin to do, if he had done it.

Envy may have been partly the origin of his later hatred. Bud Roethke was graduated from the University of Michigan Law School and he went west to Hollywood, California, to practise. He married well. He made money and drove a Cadillac. He lived in a beautiful house in Beverly Hills on Coldwater Canyon Drive where George Raft was a neighbor. At one stage of his career he seems to have represented the well-known gangster, Bugsy Siegel. To Ted it was unforgivable that blood kin of his should get rich and be a friend of gangsters because, if Ted had had other lives to live, this would have been the type of one of them. Bud Roethke never saw Ted after 1931 and he recalled hardly anything of their childhood, which may indicate that they never played much together or that Ted had not been important to him.

There is one incident that may have terrified Ted and so been the primary source of his hatred. When they were about six or seven, they went to a vaudeville show where they saw a magician. This man laid his assistant down on a block, struck off his head with a broad-bladed axe, and the head, after rolling across the stage, had flown through the air, rejoined its neck. The assistant got up smiling and bowing. Later that afternoon Ted's mother happened to look out of her kitchen window. She saw Ted laid face down with his head on a stump and over him stood Bud with an axe he had pinched from the greenhouse raised high, ready to bring down. Helen Roethke gave a shriek, rushed out, and stopped the vaudeville. But this hardly suffices for a source of hatred, for unless Ted was already so scared of Bud that he didn't dare disobey him, why did he lie so still? And if he were that scared already, the source lies further back. It may be that Ted, caught up in the play, was naïvely unafraid. At any rate the hatred was real enough to Ted, as anyone who knew him well can testify, and it was only toward the end of his life when he was able to reconcile a great many things one to another that he seems to have forgiven Bud. He sent him an autographed copy of *Words for the*

Wind and in 1959 he telephoned Bud from Seattle at three o'clock in the morning and said, "Come on up here, you son-of-a-bitch, and let's talk."

During Ted's boyhood, it was a custom evaded only through poverty for mothers to give their children dancing and music lessons, usually on the piano, in the fervent hope of making them genteel and accomplished. Ted was not let off. At the age of six, he was given dancing lessons at the Masonic Temple.

The turkey trot, the bunny hug, the fox trot, and the Castles with their more refined Castle Walk were still dances of the future. What these reluctant children were instructed in were usually the schottische, the polka, and the waltz or *valse* as hip teachers sometimes called it. There was the dreadful business of stuffing one's dancing pumps into one's coat pocket for the ride on the streetcar, the being restrained from sliding on the vast slippery waxed floor, the agonizing selection of some little girl as partner— a bow from the waist was required—and then the endless "a heel and a toe and a one, two, three" to the clatter of the teacher's piano. Ragtime was extant but it was what came out of player-piano rolls and was vulgar while jazz was still buried in New Orleans. One of Ted's partners remembers him as small "because I was small then and he was no bigger than I was. I was glad because I was scared of boys and if he had been bigger, I would have been scared worse but Ted was always kind and gentle with me. I'll never forget that." Later in life, like many big men, Ted became a good dancer but whether his ability was taught him in the corvée of dancing school is problematical.

For many years Ted took piano lessons from a Mrs. Emma Martin, a vivid, lively woman who wore the shirtwaists of the period with high, boned net collars and a chatelaine watch on her bosom. She played beautifully and she seems to have infected Ted with her enthusiasm for he seems actually to have liked the detestable chore of practising. Hundreds of little boys in the republic were hailed from their healthful play, plumped down on piano stools (which sometimes could be made to whirl around until the top flew off), and set to clobbering the interminable Czerny études, then slyly lured as far as *To a Wild Rose* and the teetering arpeggios of *The Scarf Dance*, a depressing picture into which Ted does not fit. Not only did he like to practice but he learned to play rather well and doubtless made hosts of enemies among his con-freres because he became a byword. Mothers said to their wretched little sons, "If you'd practise the way Ted Roethke does, you could play like him." Eventually, in fact, he became Mrs. Martin's star pupil and by the time he had reached high school had progressed as far as the intricacies of Liszt's *Rhapsodies*. Jazz was beginning to be heard then and he tried to play it but he did not go far. Few properly instructed boys did.

It is curious that when he went away to college he dropped the piano completely. Only one or two people ever saw him play again or heard him acknowledge that he ever had. And a Faculty Profile, published in *The Washington Alumnus* in the spring of 1962, says, "Most surprising are his hands with long, firm, but delicately-shaped fingers—a pianist's hands although Roethke does not play the piano." If he had hated it like most boys, this would have been easily understandable but he did not. It seems to have been one of the rejections he made as part of the break with Saginaw, his home, and his mother's influence when he went away.

Later in life, Ted said that he had also taken painting lessons from Albert Fuchs, "a member of the Dutch Impressionist School," but this is one of his exaggerations. Albert Fuchs was a German who worked for the City as a draughtsman. He was a Sunday painter and did several competent canvases, mostly of harbors. His wife, "Tante Emma," became the Charles Roethkes' house-keeper for a while, and on weekends, Albert used to amuse the children, Violet, Bud, and sometimes Ted by showing them how to use a compass or T-square or occasionally making little drawings. Ted was about six at this time.

When Ted was eleven and his sister six, they were christened together by the Presbyterian minister one morning in the living room of their house. Otto Roethke either did not know about it or had forgotten because they had to send to the greenhouse for him. He removed the big rubber boots he always wore and put on proper shoes in the kitchen. When the little ceremony was over, Otto said, "Aren't we going to have something to eat?" A question like this did not perturb Helen Roethke in the least. She went out to the kitchen and shortly returned with sandwiches and straw-berry shortcake for all. The minister's son had been waiting outside in the car. He was sent for to take part. After a busy silence, his father said to him, "How many of these sandwiches have you eaten?" and the boy replied, "Four—one more than you."

In 1918, a well-remembered date, the Roethkes, Charles and Otto, jointly bought their first automobile. It was a big Buick touring car, painted a dark blue, and it did not have carbide but electric lights, a rather unusual feature for the time. It was not driven casually as mere transportation. It was still a thing of wonder, and, to savor the newness of the contraption, it was taken out only on Sunday afternoons, Otto having it one Sunday, Charles, the next. Otto would drive, Helen next to him, and the children would ride in the back seat, and slowly and solemnly, they would go jouncing a few miles over the gravel roads of the countryside. The children, unawed, found this fairly dull and they used to play a game in the back seat. Ted would cover June with a lap robe so she couldn't see, and he would ask her, "Where are we now?" and she would guess. She still remembers once when they had gotten home and the car was standing in the horse barn, he asked her and she got it right.

In the BBC Broadcast on The Third Programme in July, 1953, Ted said of the greenhouse and the land he had to play on, "It was a wonderful place for a child to grow up in and around." It is perhaps significant that he mentions the place but not the child who is doing the growing. We get that child in the notebook entries when he said he had lived "a hideous life." Perhaps both statements are true, the calm judgment made at forty-five and the emotionally inflated one made at twenty-two. Then we have the unhappy child at play in "wonderful" surroundings. Certainly it seems that Ted very early acquired the burden of fears that haunted him the rest of his life, but equally certainly the flowers, both wild and cultivated, and the cultivation itself, the trees and shrubs and weeds, the marvellously changing light (no one has ever made anything of the light in Michigan—it deserves as much attention as the sun of Andalusia). All the birds and the little animals in the grass formed him and, willy-nilly, became a part of him. To be exact we must say he "remembered" them when he came to write his poetry but they do not seem to be drawn from any past. It is more as if they were all there, complete and shining, like his head and hands. To live at all, you have to take something for granted around you, so he took them, and what you take for granted, you trust.

As a child he was not specially precocious. He did not attract the town's or even the neighborhood's attention. One of his teachers at the John Moore School said, "Yes, he was smart but no smarter than a couple of others in the class." Was he fortunate? In a moment of Presbyterian anger, he could say he hated his father but he also knew that his father was trying to teach him to be a "wise fisherman" and a competent woodsman. Except for their angers, the Roethkes do not seem to have been emotionally demonstrative. His mother did not lavish the treasures of her affection on him so much as that she brought him up, as she would have said, "in the way he should go," to make him, in fact, a Christian gentleman. Far more than most children, Ted lived in the worlds his parents had made, offshoots of his father's pride in his craft and his mother's in her housewifery, and they dutifully brought him up as well as they knew how. No parent can know, although he may think he does, what goes on inside his child, and neither Otto nor Helen Roethke could imagine the depth of their son's raging sensitivity where an unregarded kindness or reproof could swing him in a moment from ecstasy to terror, and when this showed in his behavior, how could they think it anything but excessive? They did their best for him but nothing could prepare him for catastrophe.

IV

His Father's Death

In 1921 Ted was ready for high school and it was about this time that he put on his first pair of long pants. These were events in a boy's life then, almost puberty rites, certainly thrilling signals that it was time to stop being a boy and by peeping at one's elders and the ritual imitations of them to begin the slow, frightening, glorious process of becoming a man.

Two big public high schools were available to him, Saginaw High and Arthur Hill. Since his mother exerted an effective pressure on him four years later to make him go to the University of Michigan instead of Harvard where he wanted to go, it may be that he did not choose Arthur Hill himself; rather it may have been a decision of his family's. The pupils of Saginaw High were in the main the children of the older, wealthier lumber families of the town. (There were no non-Catholic private schools in the area and it is doubtful if they would have been successful if there were. It would have taken a kind of daring to send a boy to a private school then. The Saginaw rich had not yet acquired that kind of savoir-vivre.) Arthur Hill was filled with the children of the more lately arrived, the industrial money, the poorer families. In the words of one of Ted's contemporaries, "Saginaw High was the Gold Coast; Arthur Hill, the hard-noses. No Saginaw High girl would date an Arthur Hill boy. The two schools kept apart except before the Thanksgiving football game when they would meet and have a fight." In sports Arthur Hill produced, and still does, some of the best teams in the state and its pupils had on the whole better scholastic records. It was said then that their top ten pupils could enter any university in the country without having to take College Board examinations.

When he was a freshman, Ted gave a speech he had written at the John Moore School before the Red Cross Chapter in Saginaw. It was a great success. It was translated into twenty-six languages and got a wide international circulation. Ted was always a little sheepish about it in his later years but he seldom failed to mention it. Since it is the first time he received notice as a writer, it will be worthwhile to give it in full:

A JUNIOR SPEECH BY A JUNIOR

The Junior Red Cross is a league of boys and girls organized for unselfish service, a league born during the World War, a league which has a great and wonderful, past and whose future will be greater and even more wonderful.

When a group of boys and girls decide to join this organization they agree in substance to the following:

"We will seek in all ways to live up to the ideals of the Junior Red Cross and devote ourselves to its service.

"We will strive never to bring discredit to this, our country, by any unworthy act.

"We will revere and obey our country's laws and do our best to inspire a like reverence and obedience in those about us.

"We will endeavor in all these ways, as good citizens, to transmit America greater, better, and more beautiful than she was transmitted to us."

This is the bond of five million American children. Upon its ideals, the great future America—a great future world, in fact, must depend.

By "Junior" is usually meant something smaller, younger than its superior. Yes, the American Red Cross is much older, and our members are diminutive in size, but we hope to rival our affectionate parent in achievements at least.

In the Junior Red Cross program there are two divisions of service, the home and the foreign. Both are equally important. One advances American ideals in America; the other advances these same ideals in the rest of the world. The program is a broad and varied one. It contains practically every form of relief and educational activity for children, thus enabling each chapter to choose the service best fitted to its community.

I am taking a few of the accomplishments of the Juniors in the

Saginaw Chapter as examples of these activities. When I speak of the Saginaw Chapter I am speaking of the hundreds of other chapters in America doing like work. Last winter over five hundred garments were collected and distributed by the Juniors to keep rural children in school. Shoes were furnished country children, $110 being spent. Sewing classes made over two hundred dresses out of sheets which were apparently of no further use. We found crippled children needing braces mended, other children needing eye-glasses. Simple plays and pageants, presented by Juniors were witnessed by 15,000 people in Saginaw. Over four thousand Christmas boxes, also clothes, were sent to European children.

A member of the newly organized Junior Red Cross in Italy writes:

"Friends from over the sea:

You wish then to build a bridge between America and Europe to open a relationship with us."

"A bridge between America and Europe!" Yet that is exactly what is being done through the Junior correspondence. The letters being sent to American juniors, besides being very interesting, are very valuable. Geography and history are contained in their magical pages. Foreign language classes may receive practical experience in translating by using them. But the biggest thing derived from them is the true idea of the people of other lands.

There is no greater thing in life than to be able to think and act first in the aid of others. But in whatever service the Junior renders he is amply repaid. His outlook on life is broadened, his character is enriched, and he cultivates an understanding and sympathy for other people which he has never before possessed.

The children of the civilized nations united under the junior Red Cross Banner of Service! Such will be the Junior Red Cross of the near future. A league of children promoting good will and friendliness and abolishing prejudice and ignorance, man's greatest enemies. The purpose and spirit of the Junior Red Cross are beautifully described in this quotation from S.R. Oldham:

> "Why stand still
> In a world that goes on forever?
> What is an education
> But the continual expansion
> Of the mind and powers

That should go on from year to year?
And is it an education
In school or out,
Unless it brings to life
A voice that says, 'Step out!
Step out of self,
And serve your fellow men?' "

This is a very able piece of work for a thirteen-year-old boy and while Ted was sharp enough even at that age to tell the Red Cross what they wanted to hear, it is cynical to suggest that he did. It is much more likely that he believed every word of it. As an indication of his future thinking, it will be noticed that he takes the high line of idealism and tempers it almost at once with practical benefits as rewards.

In high school he took the college-preparatory courses and, since he had already done a great deal of reading on his own, they seemed to be easy for him but the society of his peers had no place for intellectuals. It was dangerous to be known as a "brain"—you were called a sissy, and if you were, you had to take cruel, often violent ridicule and no sensitive boy wants to endure that. He was not a well-known athlete although he was a substitute on the basketball team for a season or two and he injured his knee—the first of a long line of knee injuries—in a track meet. He also wrote pieces for the school newspaper. These were not big enough achievements to protect him. If he had been a varsity tackle, he could have gotten any grades he pleased, high or low. Since learning was a pleasure to him and he was still young enough to identify learning with high grades and he could get these grades pretty easily, he had to find a way to get himself accepted if he were going to indulge himself in this pleasure. He was not yet old enough to criticize the society he moved in, and, with the courage the making of the criticism would have given him, to stand alone as an individual person. He wanted to belong.

Most high schools then and many now have illegal fraternities. Arthur Hill had one called Beta Phi Sigma whose members were mostly athletes. New pledges were usually taken in at the end of the freshman year. Ted was invited to join and he did. While drinking whisky does not seem to have been an actual part of the initiation rites, nearly all the members drank. It must be remem-

bered that this was during Prohibition. Half the populace were
engaged in a massive protest against what they regarded as re-
strictive legislation unworthy of a free people; that is, they drank
like fishes. Ted began to drink and, doing it, he had the double
pleasure of simultaneous conformity and protest.

The so-called whisky of the Saginaw Valley, like most bootleg
whiskies, was frightful stuff to imbibe. It could hardly be said to
have been distilled in any proper sense of the word; rather it was
a boiled fermentation of corn or rye or possibly potatoes, some-
times pinkish in color, sometimes as clear as gin. It was sold in
quart Mason jars and cost three dollars a jar. It was called "Sag-
inaw Butch" after Butch Kondinger who owned a place with a
restaurant above and a hamburg joint downstairs where the whisky
was sold. In South Saginaw the Poles made it and sold it also, and
Ted sometimes bought it from them. It was very strong.

It is not remarkable that Ted drank and very likely he did not
drink much in high school, although the archaic protocol of the
period demanded that you accept any drink that was offered. It
was unmanly not to, especially for a high-school boy making his
first tentative forays into a larger world than his home. While his
father regularly took a schnapps or two, he could hardly be called
a drinking man in spite of Ted's later statement that he came from
a long line of drunks. And his mother never took a drink in her life.
Certainly, in the years after the First World War, Victorian morals
were crumbling, but the rules of Ted's house were stricter than
most and as long as his father was still alive, he would probably
have been afraid to come home even smelling of whisky.

In his later years, as we all do, Ted liked to tinker with his past,
rectify it by selections and suppressions, true it up to fit a mature
notion of himself or it may be that he was unaware that he was
rectifying, that he really remembered his youth in this way. In a
class lecture at the University of Washington he said, "My mother
was looking through an old 1918 Buick we had, and there in the
side pocket was a pint of whisky and a blackjack. She was a little
taken aback. Sometimes when you go to the Polish hall and three
or four guys jump you, you got to get a-hold of that blackjack and
work them over a little before you proceed to the floor." In this
lecture he was giving a short sketch of his life and the incident of
the blackjack and the Polish hall is the only thing he mentions of

his high-school years. It leaves the impression of a burly, virile, commanding personality, a genuine tough guy. Yet two of his contemporaries at Arthur Hill remember him as "well-liked by those who knew him. He never tried to make himself popular. You took him as he was." In *Twentieth Century Authors,* he writes, "I really wanted, at fifteen and sixteen, to write a beautiful, 'chiseled' prose as it was called in those days. There were books at home and at the local libraries (and very good ones they were for such a smallish town); I read Stevenson, Pater, Newman, Tomlinson, and those maundering English charm boys, the familiar essayists. I bought my own editions of Emerson, Thoreau, and, as God's my witness, subscribed to *The Dial* when I was in the seventh grade. I was strong for anthologies of great thoughts, including Elbert Hubbard; and had such deep interest in the short story that I started buying the O'Brien anthologies in 1920 when I was twelve. (You could make money in the short story!)"

The roisterer and the scholar. Or if not the scholar, the avid reader feeding indiscriminately a growing sensibility alone, in secret, on literature while occasionally getting drunk with the boys. In this curious double life appears for the first time the signs of his furious energy. Although adolescence had brought with it a monumental case of hay fever every year when he would sneeze three hundred times a day and startle the neighborhood, it seems to have eradicated the petty illnesses that plagued his childhood and cut loose the enormous vitality that inspired him the rest of his life. And if the drinking and playing around with boys who were his intellectual inferiors were concessions he made to ward off their sneers, he was too young to know they were concessions. His public manner seems to have been the beginning of an effort to shield the best part of himself, to protect it from the rigors of a rough climate. He seems to have had no real friend, no one he could talk to.

In 1922, when Ted was fourteen, friction began to develop between his father and his father's brother, Charlie. Family quarrels are the bitterest of all. Each side has its own story. The very blood tie extinguishes even an attempt at impartiality and the truth is hard to come by. The upshot of the quarrel was so important in Ted's life that it is certainly apropos to have Ted's version of the whole affair. He submitted a paper in a Rhetoric class in his sophomore year at Michigan with a note appended to the instructor:

> Mr. Mallory,
> I hand this in with misgivings. Probably I've stepped beyond the bounds of good taste. It isn't a story, yet I think it's effective in its own way. My mother thought so and she is a harsh critic.

PILOT MATERIAL

In literature a great love of one man for another, of one brother for another, always triumphs beautifully over all obstacles. I have yet to see that happen in life. I have found that whenever a man puts complete trust in another, he was bitterly disappointed or betrayed. When I say this I am thinking of my own father and his brother.

I suppose that I ought not to write about such things. To pour out one's heart in a Rhetoric theme is not a customary practice perhaps. But when one is tired of life, when the fools with whom you (sic) live nearly drive you mad, when one has racked (reached?) for something strange and beautiful in his experience and can think of only ugliness and evil, it is natural that he should clutch more desperately at the fine, futile things in his life. Therefore, I'm going to write soberly and without sentiment about my father.

I never saw a devotion more beautiful and splendid than that of my father for his brother, Charles.

Uncle Charlie was a person for whom it was extremely difficult to express a real regard.

When he liked, he could be the most charming and agreeable person in the world. Then his sly, provocative manner would put everyone in good spirits. But he never kept the same mood or attitude toward any person or thing. One day he would eulogize someone until he appeared almost god-like, the next, curse him until even the workmen shivered.

Uncle Charlie was horribly jealous. When my father got invitations not sent to him, he would say, "Otto, you know we mustn't waste our time on such *Schweinerei*." Often when he later got the same invitation, he would accept with alacrity. "Well, Otto, you can't bump everybody on the head like you do."

No matter how exasperating, fickle, deceitful, or inefficient Uncle Charlie was, my father never, to my knowledge, gave him a word of reproof. Instead he always savagely attacked anyone who criticized him. Uncle Charlie squandered money on one of the stenographers, finally married her, and then began to lavish more money on her relatives. "But Charlie had money of his own, mother."

Some of the things my father permitted his brother to do were idiotically ridiculous. Since Uncle Charlie possessed 54% of the stock and my father 46%, profits were divided on that basis, but all debts were divided (equally?). "We'll fix that up next year. Don't row so. Charlie's honest."

Some of the things were cruel. My Uncle Gustave had managed the East Side Store for over thirty years. His sales were double those of Uncle Charlie. Uncle Gus was fired. "Well, mother, Charlie and Gus couldn't get along."

After his marriage Uncle Charlie began a new practice. He bitterly criticized everything my father did. He spoke to him very condescendingly. "You're worse than Gus," he screamed one day. "A poor fool!"

"All right, Charlie," my father said. "I'll give you the business."

My mother refused to sign until my father had looked at the books and had taken some money for the stock. He examined the books for just the previous year. He found that some funds were entirely gone, that Uncle Charlie had overdrawn the account by thousands of dollars and was loaning money back to the company at 6%. All my father ever said was, "If you'd only spoken to me about it, Charlie."

The business didn't fare well under the new management. Uncle Charlie begged my father to come back. "You, Gus, and I can all be together again, Otto."

"I'm afraid those days are over, Charlie," my father replied.

My father became very ill. Doctors couldn't understand the nature of his disease. They pronounced his constitution perfect.

Then Uncle Charlie shot himself. Three months later my father died—of a "kink in the bowels," the doctors said.

Have I only been reciting a drab and sordid family history? I think not. It *is* intense and bitter human drama. A good deal has been left unsaid. A great story could be written about my father for in many ways he was a truly great man. I have never found anyone remotely like him in life or literature.

Now this account may not be the truth as God would see it with absolute justice in all its details. What matters here is that it is the truth as Ted saw it. This was written in 1926, when Ted was eighteen, four years after the quarrel, so it cannot be said to have been done in the first heat of his anger, but it rankled. It is obvious that he was still filled with bitterness against his uncle and his admiration for his father almost reaches the pitch of adoration.

The negotiations for the sale of the greenhouse were completed in October, 1922. Since all the principals are dead, the exact amount of the sale price is impossible to unearth. I have heard it was ninety thousand dollars and it is probably safe to say that the Otto Roethkes received somewhere between fifty and a hundred thousand dollars, a lot of money in those days.

It was about this time that Otto Roethke began to sicken. At first the doctors were, as Ted says, baffled. They suggested that he go to the Ford Hospital in Detroit for a complete examination. He spent two weeks there and it was recommended that he have an exploratory operation. It does not sound like a medical diagnosis but the phrase "a kink in the bowels" was used by his family. He returned to Saginaw, went into a hospital, and the first operation removed one "kink." At what point in Otto Roethke's decline cancer was discovered is not clear, and it is probable that he was not told. A second and unsuccessful operation was performed in Saginaw in 1923, and Otto and Helen Roethke were formally received as members of the Presbyterian Church. In a pathetic effort to retain some of his old independence of mind, he said, "You understand, I am not creeping to the Cross."

In February, 1923, Charles Roethke committed suicide.

What effect his brother's death had on Otto Roethke is not known—he was very ill at the time—but he would undoubtedly have been shaken by it, for he was a forgiving kind of man.

It then became certain that Otto was going to die and it would be a bad death for him and those who watched it. He was a man of indomitable will and he persisted in dressing himself although he was very weak, and coming downstairs. Later, when this was beyond him, he would be taken to the back porch on sunny days in a chair and sit there looking out toward the greenhouse.

As many cancer patients do, he wore out morphine and the pain came flooding in on him with all its strength. He became unable to suppress his cries of agony. Toward the end Ted and June used to stand in the doorway of his bedroom and watch his blankets to see if he were still breathing. He died in the spring, in April, and the death certificate read, "Cancer; obstruction of the bowels." He was buried in Oakwood Cemetery where his brother Emil had been superintendent.

Ted did not grieve openly. On the day of the funeral, after the family had come home from the burial, he sat in the living room reading the *Atlantic Monthly*. "We didn't subscribe to it," his sister said. "He must have bought it." That night he took his father's place at the head of the table and he sat there from that day on.

For a while every boy's father is a god to him. Then, slowly, as the boy makes his own discoveries, he dwindles into a man. For better or worse, Ted was spared this gloomy declension. Otto Roethke died when he was still the untainted source of power, love, and the lightnings of his anger. Once the numbness of shock had worn away, it must have seemed to Ted that the stays and props of his whole life were broken. In the space of three months, the greenhouse was gone, his uncle was gone, his father was gone. The stage where he had played out his childhood was no longer his. The object of his hatred was removed and nothing is so foolish as to hate the dead, and what he lost when the dirt fell in his father's grave was going to take him the rest of his life to learn.

It was noticed that Ted became very quiet in the year that followed. He had assumed his father's seat and with it perhaps a ghostly burden that seemed heavier than it was. It is his mother who solicits our sympathy here. She was a dutiful German woman who was naturally subservient to the men of her family. With a kind of double vision she could accept Ted as head of the house; the son, who else would it be? But she knew that he wasn't actually. She held the purse and he was only a fifteen-year-old boy whom it was her responsibility to raise, yet she recognized his new position far enough to voice complaints of his predecessor. This could not but trouble Ted deeply and it seems to be the basis of the uneasy, resentful relationship he had with her ever afterward. He respected her, he admired her courage, but the old candor and affection was finished. In spite of his grief the inertia of the accumulated habits of his upbringing exerted their repetitive, perhaps consoling, power and kept him going.

On July 21, 1923, he was awarded a certificate by the Presbyterian Training Conference at Alma, Michigan for "having completed the required class work in Bible Study—Stewardship,

Home Missions, Essential Christian Doctrine." Personally I find it
hard to believe that Ted was ever a big shot in a Bible camp but
the evidence is incontestably there. His mother must have been
proud of him.

During the Training Conference he filled out a questionnaire
called Life Work Choice. His answers to some of the questions are
interesting:

> Q. Name three or four of the commonest considerations that
>   most influence Life Work Choice.
> A. Parental influence, compensation, inclination.
> Q. When is self-discovery complete?
> A. When one is a success.
> Q. What are some of the other difficulties in Life Work Choice?
> A. Whether sufficient money will be made.

When he was about sixteen, he joined the Canoe Club. There
he made the acquaintance and soon a firm friend of Burrows
("Buzz") Morley. The Morleys are an old mercantile family in
Saginaw. They own a city block of different kinds of stores and
have large interests in the Second National Bank. At the time he
met Ted Buzz was going to Saginaw High School from which he
went to Dartmouth, and he was an avid tennis player.

It is hard to tell whether Ted joined the Canoe Club so he could
play tennis or whether he played tennis because he joined the
Canoe Club. The Canoe Club was the country of the rich. Ted was
fascinated by them, not that he thought, like Fitzgerald, that the
rich were different from you and me, and so let himself in for
gnawing pangs of envy. It was more that he believed he had a
mysterious right, if he could only come by it, to the rich's only dis-
tinction, money. When he was young and had little, he wanted the
luxuries it could buy. He had not had many. When he was older
and had more, his mind penetrated to the mystic equivalent of
money, enough money that is, power. Considering his vivid in-
terest, it is a wonder he didn't go where the money was, into law
or banking instead of writing poetry. Poetry, as any serious poet
knows, has many rewards, but money, big rolls of coarse, folding
money, is not one of them. Years later, however, Ted came to take
a larger view. He expended the peripheral effort, the residue that
the writing of poetry did not use, in trying to make poets, himself

as one, into rich, powerful civic figures, and this *because* they were poets. He said to me once, "Hell, a poet ought to be as big a guy in a town as a banker." But at sixteen he was making his first entry into this terrain and he seems to have used tennis as a passport.

He was not a natural athlete. Buzz Morley said that he had hardly any talent for the game at all. He was split high; his legs were thin; he moved in a series of lunges but he covered the court. Morley said, "He had this Prussian thoroughness. We had a practice board. If any of us did ten minutes on it, we had had enough, but I have seen Ted out there going bang! bang! bang! for three hours at a time. Pretty soon he was trying shots that only Tilden could have made." He played to win and, if he made a bad shot, he would fly into a rage at himself and heave his racket into the Tittabawassee River which was just over the fence. He even developed the skill—although this sounds implausible—of bursting an offending tennis ball by stamping on it. One of the members said he never liked Ted because of his manners on the court.

"In an important match, tournament play, he was not above psyching an opponent," Morley said. "He would come limping out on the court and say his foot was sore, or cough and hack and sneeze—had the flu—, and before his opponent realized it, Ted would be several points ahead. Once in a match with a guy named Doug Kimball, Ted brought out a little camp stool and set it down at the end of the court just out of bounds. And he had a big bath towel with a little bottle of wine hidden in it. Between sets he would sit down on the stool to rest and sneak drinks of wine while he pretended to mop his face. This Kimball was a stickler for the tennis proprieties and Ted's antics got to him so bad that he lost the match. Which is how Ted planned it, of course." In time Ted got to be a pretty good tennis player and he took part in city and state tournaments.

He continued to get good grades in high school (in his senior year he made A's in both chemistry and English literature—this indicates a certain breadth of mind) but he missed the top senior student's award, the Arthur Hill Scholarship, which would have almost paid his way through college. The confidence and the local fame given him by his Red Cross speech seems to have released in him the first faint stirrings of literary ambition, but he confined his work to class assignments. He wrote nothing on his own. There was no one to encourage him. Even the study of literature was strange in his family, and there were no writers or artists in the community who might have served as models. He did not have the luck to run into a teacher, one of those intelligent, untidy, generous-minded maiden ladies with taste sometimes found withering in the public schools, who might have stimulated him. And he did not have the precocious arrogant confidence of Rimbaud at Charleville. It is hard to convey how strange, how foreign the wilful making of a poem would have been in a society like his, the inert weight of custom that not only did not have room for any original work in the arts but feared and hated it. His only resource was the shadowy figures of the great he read about in his textbooks but, the way literature is taught in high school, they remained remote, unhelpful, mere plaster figures who had never lived or lost a father.

Buzz Morley was with Ted the night he told his mother he wanted to go to Harvard but she was firm—he had to go to Michigan. (Harvard was far away, in the mysterious East.) Ted blew up. "I'll work in the pickle factory first!" he shouted. It may have been a mere threat, a threat because such work seemed a degrading occupation, but he made good on it.

After he had finished at Arthur Hill, at the beginning of the summer vacation, Ted was taking June back to her Girl Scout camp. They were hitchhiking, which was both rare and daring then. A man in a car picked them up and got to talking. Ted said he was looking for a summer job and the man offered him one. He was manager of the Heinz pickle factory. Ted's first job was picking the cucumbers, dirty, messy work. Later he was given a receiving station at the edge of town. He was so young he had to be bonded. He complained that the farmers tried to cheat by hiding the big ones under the little ones.

In the fall he went to Ann Arbor, the first of his family to go to a university.

V

College

In 1925 Ann Arbor was a pretty little town of about twenty thousand people. There was hardly any industry. Its streets were lined with superb elms and maples and most of the University buildings occupied the original forty-acre campus in the center of the town. The climate was and still is abominable, hot and damp in summer, bitingly cold and damp in winter largely because the town is sited in a pocket of the Huron Valley where the air hangs for days without much movement. Instead of the present honky-tonk string of filling stations, bars and grills, body shops, and shopping centers there was thirty-five miles of open farm land between Ann Arbor and Detroit.

In spite of its claim to be the "Harvard of the Middle West," the University was a provincial institution, a good one, probably the best in the region except Chicago and Wisconsin but much more limited in its purview than it is now. Its law and medical schools were regarded as excellent and a few of its faculty members were genuinely learned, genuinely educated, men with national and even international reputations like Dr. Frederick Novy of the medical school, who was the model for Dr. Max Gottlieb in Sinclair Lewis's *Arrowsmith*, W. W. Kelsey in classics, or Mark Wenley in philosophy. Far too many, on the other hand, were mere specialists who had struggled up from small colleges, brandishing their degrees, arrogantly and ignorantly insisting on the importance of their study without any very clear notion of its connections with others in the field or with the great body of knowledge as a whole. A new president, Clarence Cook Little, had just been installed. Changes were expected and they were awaited with interest and trepidation.

There were about twelve thousand students. Most of them, like Ted, came from high schools in the state. There were only the forerunners of the present cosmopolitan horde—a few Chinese supported by the Boxer Scholarships and I remember a splendid Sikh with a parted beard and a big, intricate, lavender turban. Living was cheap. The yearly tuition charge for Michigan students was ninety-three dollars, and for one month Ted paid a bill, for board, lodging, and a ten-dollar fine at his fraternity, of sixty-nine dollars and ninety-three cents. A thousand dollars a year would see a student through without any hardship.

There was no tradition of hard, grinding work like that of a French lycée or the University of Edinburgh. A student was expected to put in fifteen hours a week in the classroom and a "C" was a gentleman's grade. (Many of the gentlemen showed up for Saturday morning classes in the dinner jackets of the night before.) A student's time was solicited, as it is now, by dozens of legitimate extracurricular activities like *The Michigan Daily,* the student newspaper, *Mimes,* a theater group, several music and choral societies, religious debates, and an array of sports, but already the simple youth who merely wanted to play a game could not very likely make a varsity team; you needed a big high-school reputation to be considered. There were also University-sponsored lectures and concerts. A student could go somewhere free every night in the week if he wished, and to the detriment of his studies.

Dances were still given in fraternity houses in those days. Dinner jackets were de rigueur for the men but occasional dudes appeared in tails especially at the big annual dances like the Junior Hop. Women wore the sack-like, knee-length evening dresses depicted in the flapper cartoons of John Held Jr. The corset had virtually disappeared. The Charleston was given a lot of publicity, possibly because it was the first dance where the partners separated, but few danced it—there was seldom room. It was against the rules as well as the law to drink at any dance, but the restrictions were evaded by the hip flask and by midnight any dance floor was usually full of drunks, almost all of them male. Few girls drank then and no wonder. There was hardly anything to drink that wouldn't make you gag even when it was mixed with

ginger ale or soda water. Bootleggers from Detroit made the
rounds of the fraternity houses on Thursdays to make their sales
for the weekend. The whisky, a concoction of water, grain alcohol,
and caramel flavoring canted into bottles with the labels of lawful
prewar whiskies on them like *Old Crow* cost seven dollars a bottle;
if it claimed to be Scotch, eight. A poor youth was almost neces-
sarily abstemious but even he had resources—he could sit in the
kitchen of remote pelting farms and swill moonshine at fifty cents
a drink if he could find a way to get out in the country.

In 1925 students were still allowed to drive cars. They were
mostly delapidated parti-colored Model-Ts although there was one
glaring Stutz Bearcat, bright yellow, with wire wheels and a broad
calfskin strap to hold the hood down. The driving privilege was
revoked, however, before the end of the year. There was a freight
train that ran across the road to Detroit at one o'clock in the
morning. In the fall of this year three students, whose cars hit this
freight train on three successive weekends, were killed, and the
University forbade student automobiles. A few diehards hid them
in rented garages on the edge of town but after that it was not easy
for students to get around. A ride was a treat.

This lack of transport was an obstacle to the association of young
men and women. No rumble seat, no necking, and consequently
further explorations into sexual activity were curtailed because
there were few places to go where privacy was certain. Only grad-
uate students and those over twenty-five years of age could have
their own apartments. The males were restless—they wanted to go
to Europe or to find jobs as bond salesmen in Wall Street in the
honest hope of becoming millionaires before they were forty. They
did not want the responsibilities of the benedict. The girls prob-
ably felt otherwise. Their costume was resolutely feminine and
designedly attractive. They wore hats, gloves, and high heels to
classes, but there was little fear of the future then although it slyly
held the Depression. There was no urgent desire to found a home
and family and hardly any early marriages occurred. It was better
to go to parties.

The present subject of interest barely existed for students then,
national and international politics. There seemed to be a postwar
revulsion against European affairs. And the scandalous administra-
tion of Harding and the solemn idle dullness of Coolidge repelled

the attention of young people. Politicians were thought to be little better than crooks. The various disarmament treaties of the Twenties, when they were noticed at all, seemed to promise everlasting peace. While there were rumors that something was going on in Russia, Communism was unknown to the students of any college campus; Marx was an unreadable economist who, oddly enough, had once written articles for *The New York Herald*. Many of Ted's generation did not bother to vote in their twenty-first year or for many years afterward. Ted didn't. He said once in a lecture that he had never voted.

Going to college is always unsettling. It is the first thrust out of the warmth of the nest and often a chill is felt outside. A student is naturally proud of being accepted into this new society and often filled with hopes and misgivings about the talents he can exercise in it. The impact of new faces, new ideas, an apparent sophistication he feels he must live up to, and especially all these varied activities that are directed at him often trouble him. He finds it hard to study and, after his cozy high school, the difficulty of his studies alarms him. It is mere shock.

Ted does not seem to have done much traveling before he came to Ann Arbor, beyond a few trips to Bay City and the northern part of the state, possibly an excursion to Detroit, yet he was not confused by what he found. He knew what he wanted. He joined a fraternity, Chi Phi. By the upper-middle-class standards of the campus, it was not one of the best (the best were the Dekes, Psi U's, and Alpha Delts), but it offered a certain kind of companionship rather like the Canoe Club's, and the food was better than the local restaurants offered. The life of a freshman pledge in a fraternity was not easy then. He had to wake the upperclassmen every morning and see that they got at least a start toward their classes. If there were any errands to do, no matter how trivial or absurd, he could be sent on them. He had to conduct himself meekly before juniors and seniors or undergo idiotic punishments. Unless Ted needed the tiny pleasure of being so far singled out of the ruck as to be asked to join, he must have wanted the companionship. He knew there would be people to drink with and he may have nursed a shy and secret hope that one of his brothers would be someone he could talk to seriously about literature.

He also wanted to learn to write, not poetry yet, but his "chiseled" prose and he seems to have been naive enough to think there would be someone among all these learned professors who could teach him. It was a common fallacy. The teachers of writing or "Rhetoric" as it was then called, were protégés of Professor Fred N. Scott, who later achieved the left-handed dignity of a footnote making fun of him in Mencken's *American Language*. He was co-author of a textbook, *Scott & Denny's Paragraph Writing*, which was used in beginning Rhetoric classes. It was a dull, bad book and since Rhetoric was required of all freshmen, all had at least to own it. No courses were given in the short story or the novel as such; rather courses were given in Narration and Exposition as if the student, wishing to write fiction, and having learned how to narrate and expose, could hitch these together and come up with a short story or a novel. It was criticism played backward. The writing of poetry, not being susceptible to this facile analysis, was ignored altogether. Thus these men, though personally amiable, well-intentioned, and some of them quite learned, were thoroughly bad influences on any serious young writer who had come to them seething with murky, inconcluded intensities in the hope of being straightened out. Though they were aware from their reading that a work of art is a formal structure, they could not give any hints on how to achieve this since none of them had ever written anything he was willing to acknowledge except textbooks and learned articles. Later, when Ted became a teacher himself, he called his course in the writing of poetry, "Verse Form."

Ted dubbed the rhetoric teachers "soil guys." Some of them boasted they had come off farms but this was not the reason for Ted's epithet. One of them gave an account of the genesis and growth of a novel, comparing it to a tiny seedling, nourished by the soil, the sun, and the rain, which put forth little green shoots and roots and grew and grew and grew. While lovely and heart-felt, it was a bum analogy, Ted thought, because the task of the artist in all this burgeoning was by no means clear and that was what he wanted to learn. He was disappointed, of course, and since none of his contemporaries at Michigan ever heard him mention his ambitions, he seems not to have found the friend he could talk to.

Something of Ted's anxiety about the kind of instruction he was receiving is apparent in an autobiographical passage from one of his notebooks, written at least twenty years later:

> It was affectionately known as the ghost of Fred Newton Scott and his ploughboys. But let's be fair: I took freshman rhetoric from Carleton Wells: Why? He was a golf champion; and he wasn't taken in by the bums at the Saginaw Golf Club which happened to be behind the greenhouse. So there I was in my Johnston & Murphy shoes, me fur coat, a thug in hand-tailored suits, sprawled in the front row, writing themes in class, when I wasn't being shy to the girl on my right, name of Rankin she was, a professor's daughter and pulchritudinous in a non-fleshy way—but it wasn't, I insist to Mr. Wells an act: I really cared, cared about his judgment. I took notes on "The Genius of the Language" and got A minus, A, and A on the bluebooks— I can remember every grade I ever got (well, almost), and spent all Xmas vacation—so help me—reading all of Stevenson, read not one critical piece, wrote the paper: Grade, A plus. The comment, "Marked by a curious succinctness, rightness of phrase, etc." Naturally I thought I was in; and the final—my God, why finals in freshman rhetoric?—I *knew* I clobbered it. My grade, B or B plus. I claim that damned plus is as big as the solar system. I was crushed: I literally was: I thought I came down to learn to write prose—really to learn what a style is. Now I can't even get A in a freshman course. (There were plenty of As in other sections.) I quite literally decided then and there I would not try to be a writer. Fun was in order and the light reading in literature courses.
>
> True, there were some transgressions on my part. I handed in 12 themes—on the last day, as I remember—all in longhand. I couldn't type—still can't.
>
> And I was odious in a fairly literate way: a money-snob, a woman snob, a food snob. I looked rich—I really did, the bench-made suits, the soon-to-be-inevitable fur coat, the booze, the sexy dames, the rich heels, the roaring boys who were at least funny. I was fat, overfed, unhappy and looked 235 pounds.
>
> A conventional story? I daresay. But I *had* been translated into 26 languages—a mere fluke, of course. I was sent to a district Red Cross meeting in Flint . . .

Carleton Wells, his instructor, remembers him vividly. He says that Ted seemed "diffident, unhappy, uninterested. He took no part in class discussions and he seemed to have no friends nor to make any in the class. However, on the five or six impromptu papers assigned, he did brilliantly." He was somewhat heavier than the average student and Mr. Wells thought him just over six feet tall. He dressed inconspicuously, "rather slouchily." (This last would have been a serious affront, had Ted known about it.)

His program of study seems designed with a literary career as a goal. Literature and writing predominated: he took five courses in Rhetoric, twelve in English literature, two in Polish literature (in English), one course in Sanskrit literature (in English). Science he kept to the absolute minimum, the beginning course in Psychology, two in Geology. In what are now called Social Studies, he fulfilled the degree requirements but no more, two courses in History, two in Political Science. He took four courses in German, which should have been a respite from the continual reading he would have had to do in his literature courses, but after eight years of German at the John Moore School, he got only B's in the beginning courses. He took French I and II and was given A's but the language must have flowed over him like water, for when he got to Paris years later, he couldn't even order a taxi, and when Alain Bosquet in translating one of his poems, made a real howler and rendered "killdeer" as "l'assassin du cerf," he did not spot it although he was very meticulous with his translators.

He was a kind of pack rat and he preserved his college lecture notes and most of the letters he received as well. He seems to have wanted to keep a record of his past so as to be sure of it. (In the Suzallo Library at the University of Washington where his papers are deposited, there is a red metal locomotive and tender two feet long, boxes containing the birds' eggs and the flint arrowheads he had collected, a cloth bag that Dry Sack sherry comes in containing sixty-three pennies, none of them valuable, and a Commodore record of Panama played by Wild Bill Davison's band.) He was not responsible in any way he could yet perceive for his father's death and the sale of the greenhouse but they had demolished a continuity in his life he had always counted on. Now perhaps he was going to preserve a continuity of his own.

He did not know shorthand, so he did not reproduce everything the lecturers said. He wrote with a pen usually, sometimes a pencil on small-size notebook paper, occasionally on folded typing paper, and there are about fifteen pages on stationery pinched from the Detroit-Leland Hotel. Since he made selections from the lecturers' remarks, it is justifiable to assume that he was impressed by the ones he did set down and from them can be drawn some idea of his literary taste at the time.

April 15, 1929. On *Pamela:* ". . . Immensely absorbing. I wasn't overwhelmed by the sentiment for Pamela which the author tries to inspire. Most of the time I was cheering for Mr. B." On *Pride and Prejudice:* "This seems to have an unusual baldness of style. Miss Austen does not seem to get within her characters." On *The Vicar of Wakefield:* "It's a great thing for a man to arouse emotions and do it gracefully. "But so is life inconsistent and many an artistic representation of life in the form of a novel is inconsistent. Not all novels, of course. But some may be, at any rate." "This is why we acquire the feeling that *Jane Eyre* is such a true book. True to what? Not true to life—that's empty praise. It's true to the deepest connections of intelligent people." (These notes were taken for the course on The English Novel given by Dr. Louis Strauss, the head of the English Department. A learned and cultivated man, he was one of the teachers Ted liked and admired, and he was glad to recommend Ted when he was looking for an academic post. (He bore a striking resemblance to Groucho Marx.)

Notes on Whitman from a course in American Literature: "What are we to say of Whitman as poet? Selection? Defied rules. Can great art be formless NO!

1) An undying energy of life—a tang—vitalizing something.
2) A certain largeness—deals with deep things in life on a large scale.
3) Most great poetry is primal?"

On his entrance application to the University, Ted gave his height as six feet, two and a half inches, and his weight as a hundred and ninety-five pounds. There is a photograph taken of him at sixteen in the Arthur Hill annual, *Legenda,* that shows him no larger than the girls sitting beside him, and his cousin, Mrs. Mortensen, says he shot up quickly in less than a year. (His sister, June, says he was always tall and slender but she is five years younger and probably would remember him as tall.) Adolescent boys sometimes enlarge this way. Their new size gives them a new character, usually shy and making for taciturnity because they are taken for older than they are and do not quite know what is expected of them.

Rolfe Humphries said of Ted, "You know, he always wore a mask." This seems so plausible as to be beyond conjecture. It is not so much that Ted fabricated a mask deliberately; it is more that sometime in his eighteenth year he realized that he already had one he could use if he wished, this sudden, big, gross body. He was hardly in his teens when he became involved in the rigors of his own sensitivity through his responses to the natural life around him in the greenhouse, in the field, and in his rambles with his father in the woods. His responses were a moil of perplexed insights, unsorted, obscure, and he could not know how uniquely intense they were, only that there was no one he could mention them to, much less describe them. And since his father was the master of growing things, they were all tied up with him. His adolescence must have been a hell of bright awareness, frustrated because he did not yet know what to do with it, and it was constantly sandpapered by the incomprehension of those around him. And he had suffered deprivations greater and keener than he was going to suffer again.

In a paper written for a Rhetoric class about this time, he says, "I have a genuine love of nature. It is not the least bit affected but an integral and powerful part of my life. I know that Cooper is a fraud—that he doesn't give a true sense of the sublimity of American scenery. I know that Muir and Thoreau and Burroughs speak the truth.

"I can sense the moods of nature almost instinctively. Ever since I could walk, I have spent as much time as I could in the open. A perception of nature—no matter how delicate, how subtle, how evanescent—remains with me forever.

"I am influenced too much, perhaps, by natural objects. I seem bound by the very room I'm in. I've associated so long with prosaic people that I've dwarfed myself spiritually. When I get alone under an open sky where man isn't too evident—then I'm tremendously exalted and a thousand vivid ideas and sweet visions flood my consciousness."

This passage shows that he saw himself pretty clearly. His spirit is exalted by solitude in natural surroundings, "dwarfed" by association with people, a Wordsworthian idea that never left him. It is remarkable how few people beyond his family circle he admits to his poetry. If he was disappointed by the University, as he seems certain to have been, he would also have had the acuteness to see that in this prosaic environment his "sweet visions" would be taken as a sign of softness, the "sissiness" he had gone to such trouble to avoid in high school. Therefore they had better have some protection, a mask, a shield, a carapace to hide them.

Almost consciously then he adopted his mature stance, that of the tough guy. As big as he was, broad, thick, unhandsome, he looked tough. He began to wear what became his permanent costume, the double-breasted suit—he bought the coats a size too large to have room, he said, to carry books and papers in the pockets. It also added to the impression of great size and helped him loom over other people. He swung from side to side as he walked and his gait was often called "bear-like." His talk became profane, full of coarse vigorous, idiomatic phrases, often dirty, often very funny. If his drinking in high school had been experiment or to help him run with the pack, now there was more of a reason for it—tough guys drank. The public image of a poet, inherited from the Romantics, tended to be that of a willowy fellow in Latin-Quarter hat and velvet jacket, and Ted seemed to want to stamp this out. Some years later, when he was being interviewed at the Biltmore Hotel in New York by Lewis Jones, the president of Bennington College, for a job on the faculty, Ted lumbered in and said, "I may look like a beer salesman but I'm a poet."

It was at Michigan that his life-long fascination with gangsters began. The newspapers gave them a bad eminence as romantic figures of a kind. As criminals beyond the law, they seemed to live free of restraints or inhibitions and to many people immured in habit or frustration, this was attractive. Then, too, they were figures of immense power. When Al Capone went to the theater, he took five rows of seats for himself and his corps of bodyguards and it was said that no one could walk the streets of Cicero, Illinois, without his permission. Legends sprang up around the gangsters. They were heroes. As Jesse James, the bank and train robber, had been the typical, so to speak, the preferred criminal of an earlier generation, so the gangster was to Ted's.

It is impossible to prove that he ever met a real live gangster in snap-brim hat and double-breasted overcoat, all rodded up with a .45 in a shoulder holster. Although he talked of Chicago and Cicero with great familiarity, no one can recall that he ever was in Chicago except to wait between trains or to lecture at Northwestern University in Evanston. Bootleggers, yes, everybody met them but they were only delivery boys. In his senior year he did not have much money and he took on the job of steward at the Chi Phi house in return for his board and room. He was in charge of buying all the food and the liquor and this may have involved him more intimately with the house bootleggers than the ordinary purchaser would be, but hardly with their employers.

His roommate at the Chi Phi house, Robert Crouse, says that Ted sometimes went to Lefty Clark's at Ecorse. Ecorse was a wide-open suburb of Detroit lying on the Detroit River across from Canada. It was an import center for smuggled Canadian whisky. Smuggling implies secrecy but the bootleggers plied quite openly back and forth across the river. They used powerful Chris-craft or Hacker-craft launches. The U.S. revenue officers had been supplied with only a little steam tug that would go about eight knots. The bootleggers would dart across the river at forty miles an hour, take on a load of whisky, and dart back again and all the while a mile away the little tug would be going puff, puff, puff in pursuit. People used to come down to the riverbank to watch.

Lefty Clark's was a speakeasy but its prominence lay in its gambling hall which occupied the second floor of a big garage. You went up a stairway. Louring down from the top was a concrete pillbox with two Tommy guns poked through the slits. Before admission, you were asked to stand on one of those Pullman steps while the doorkeeper frisked you. If you had so much as a little gold penknife in your waistcoat pocket, he took it away and checked it. Lefty didn't want any trouble.

Inside there was plenty of action. No money whatever had been spent on the décor. The walls were bare concrete block and you found on inspection that the pillbox overlooked the gambling salon inside with two more Tommy guns for further intimidation. There were crap tables, a roulette layout, bird-cage, chuck-a-luck, tables for twenty-one, poker, and even faro out of the olden time. The place drew a mixed clientele of working and professional

men, farmers in bib overalls, students, tarts, and housewives. One
night a fight started, with fists. An automobile siren sounded
loudly and suddenly. The place grew quiet and out of the pillbox
came a bored voice, "Cut it out, cut it out or we turn on the
spray." Lefty's had an air about it, excitement, criminality, some-
thing, and it is no wonder Ted liked to go there but he never met
the proprietor.

The older he got, the more circumstantial his gangster "mem-
ories" became. When he was past fifty, Ted liked to say that he
had had friends in the Purple Gang in Detroit. ("I had such an in
with the Purples, they offered to bump my Aunt Margaret off for
me. As a favor, you understand.") It is extremely doubtful if he
did. The Purples were not a Twenties' gang; they were a Thirties'
gang. Their principal occupation was the rackets, not bootlegging.
They were not Irish or Italians like the Chicago gangs; they were
Jewish. They began in the late Twenties as a gang of young punks
throwing acid over clothes in dry-cleaning shops unless they were
paid protection. They expanded and became very powerful. Old
Henry Ford was rumored to have had Harry Bennett keep lines of
communication open with them for fear they would kidnap his
grandchildren. In the Thirties Ted was not near Detroit long
enough to ingratiate himself with the gang lords. He was at
Harvard, Lafayette, Michigan State, and Penn State. While his
claims of friendship with the Capone mob or the Purples are not
flatly impossible, they are so improbable as to be nearly so, for he
was basically what he was as a child, shy and timid. He may have
felt he owed his mask a certain bravado and while this undoubt-
edly gave it a spurious backing, his friendship with gangsters
seems to have been a fantasy of criminal power that had a source
of satisfaction deep within him.

In the second semester of his sophomore year and the first
semester of his junior year, he took French I and II. For one of
these courses he wrote a paper on *François Villon: His Character
and His Relation to His Age*. In it he says, "Some people there are
to whom a regular existence is anathema. Some spirits must escape
monotony or break under it. Villon was one of these. He loved the
luxeries (sic) of life in proportion far too great to be bought from
his slim purse. When the pangs of hunger gnawed at him, and he
lacking a sou to purchase viands, he stole. There is a certain

strength in the man for all his faults. He was not held in such a grip by fear that he would not risk life and freedom to get his comfort." Nowhere in the essay does Ted analyze Villon's poetry, discuss his metrics or his imagery. He takes him from a single point of view—the poet as criminal, and he admires him.

Some time during his undergraduate years it is likely that Ted began to write poetry seriously. He says he began in law school but there are scraps of poems among his undergraduate notes which he may have forgotten. It is impossible to fix a date with any accuracy because he was secretive about it. None of his friends from that time remember that he ever said a word about writing poetry. He was willing enough to talk about poetry if he could find anyone he thought sensitive and sharp enough to talk to, and he carried a well-thumbed book of Elinor Wylie around with him. (This is interesting because she was much less well-known than Edna St. Vincent Millay, who had the wild, bohemian aura of Greenwich Village about her.) He admired Wylie's precision and care for formal structure, but he was silent on any work he was doing himself.

If we consider the difficulties under which he was working and which he seems to have been fully aware of, a surprising conclusion may emerge. He was the first of his family to do anything in the arts. They did not oppose him openly but they could not give him any help or understanding. (Think of growing up in a family like Virginia Woolf's or Aldous Huxley's.) Except for a few lonely individuals, the people of the Saginaw Valley—both his immediate neighbors and the people to whose society he aspired—would have thought a serious poet a freak (at least until he had achieved national recognition), and he knew that, too. To write poetry as a career they would gloomily judge to be a waste of his schooling and all the money it took to send him to the University. And since from the first he saw poetry as a mode of expressing truth, they would have found his work, had they read it, unpleasant and unsettling because the kind of bone truth he wanted to tell was so rare, not something they were used to hearing. He must have come to Ann Arbor nursing hopes of a kind—most students do according to their tastes. When he found the writing teachers themselves men not worth talking to because they had nothing to say germane to his purpose, he may well, in his disappointment, have begun to suspect that poetry, having no voice in the community where he lived, was antisocial. It was even subversive because the poet tore down all kinds of carefully erected facades, went right into the house, and cut up rough. Poetry was akin to crime. Strange and unwelcome in middle-class America, the poet was a criminal. And since he was, he had better act like one.

Probably this was not so clear to him that he could have reduced it to syllogism, defended it in a court of law, or even explained it in a fraternity bull session. Hints, suspicions, inklings, the betrayals he felt he had suffered such as the blank injustice of his father's death, all these persuaded him to assume his tough mask. And from this time on, it is hard to penetrate, to catch any glimpse of the essential tenderness behind it.

For purposes of his artistic history the prime fact of his University years is that he began to write poetry but it is doubtful if he gave it the emphasis we give it. His wife once asked him, "Did you want to be a great poet then?" And he answered, "I wanted to be a great something." He was incapable of the cool, objective assessment of his situation that William Carlos Williams made of his own when at seventeen he decided to enter medical school and become a doctor in order to write poetry. He told me once, "I knew my fees would support me and a doctor is always in touch with people." People as sources were not so important to Ted as they were to Williams, and while he may have felt himself committed to writing poetry, he does not yet seem to have committed himself to poetry as a career. He had other lives to live, the life he owed his mask, for one, other than literary impulses to satisfy.

For instance, in the fall of his freshman year, he bought this splendid coonskin coat which cost him four hundred dollars. During the Christmas holiday he hung around a drugstore near his old high school, wearing the coat, the sign of his new estate. Only the rich and those who wished to be taken for rich wore coats like that. Others wore cloth overcoats or bushy affairs of black dogskin that shed hairs copiously. In 1927, his sophomore year, he won a little blue and gilt medal for playing tennis engraved, *Second Place, All-Campus Singles, 1927*. In 1928 he was elected to Phi Kappa Phi, the junior honorary scholastic society, as he was elected to Phi Beta Kappa his senior year. (He was graduated *magna cum laude*.) What is more interesting in explaining the many forces that drove him is his statement made years later when he was at the University of Washington and he said, "At Michigan I made Phi Beta Kappa Beta Phi. I hit both poles." Kappa Beta Phi is, of course, an illegal fraternity whose members are chosen for their ability to drink a lot and not show it. Since it is illegal, no records are available for inspection, but two men who were members during Ted's college years say flatly that he was never a member and this is plausible because membership was handed around among the "best fraternities" and Chi Phi was not one of these.

Why should he claim this? He was a large man furnished with more genuine desires and appetites than most people and publicly he seemed to want to make an impression of completeness as the master of many talents, poet, scholar, athlete, chef, lover, teacher. This was to be achieved through the management of ambiguities, the reconciliation of opposites, the apparent beer salesman who was nevertheless a poet, the Phi Beta Kappa who was also Kappa Beta Phi.

One of the ironies he never seems to have grasped is that all the little ambiguities that made up his public figure could be magnetized around one pole labeled The Others, while the sources of his poetry, the tenderness, the love, the terror, timidity, and guilt and the infrequent joy were drawn to another pole, The Self. Ambiguity, the perception of both inner and outer reality as a series of oppositions, seems to have been the very set of his mind. Fathers, the keepers of houses, did not keep; they died. Those who were to have taught him the right way misled him. In every bottle of whisky lurked exaltation and a hangover. Others can see life differently but this was Ted's private vision and one of the lines that gives a steady continuity to his long labor as a poet is the effort of reconciliation.

In the summers while he was at Michigan he worked in the Heinz pickle factory in Saginaw as laborer, weigh clerk, and finally inspector and buyer. He made $28 a week. In one of his notes he says, "When I was eighteen I wrote two advertisements for Mitchell, Faust & Co, of Chicago which were used in a national campaign."

VI

The Beginnings of Poetry

If Ted had a vocation to poetry it was a long time coming. It did not seem to him to be the only possible career. He was not driven to it early and inescapably. It is an interesting conjecture whether, had his father lived, he would have been a poet at all. His decision seems to have come as a deliberate choice, not necessarily the most prudential, between alternatives.

In a letter to Kenneth Burke, he says, "I became a teacher against the wishes of a family who wanted me to enter the law. Where a very comfortable income awaited me if I chose that career. I did enter law school but gave it up in disgust. I did not wish to become a defender of property or a corporation lawyer as all my first cousins on one side of the family have done."

A greenhousekeeper is not customarily regarded as a professional man and Ted's father undoubtedly wanted his son in one of the professions because it would have been a step upward. His mother, surviving, would have preserved her husband's wishes. Quite illogically Ted felt that his father, by dying, had betrayed him, left him far too soon without his love and guidance, and intermittently in those moments when he remembered his father as flawless, Ted was tormented by guilt for even having entertained the notion that a great man like his father could have done anything so base as to betray his son. Going to law school may have been a small act of propitiation.

Yet he did not enroll for the full program as if he were sure of a legal career. He took one course in Criminal Law because he was, I think, personally fascinated by the nature of the criminal, and he did not do very well. Judge Eugene Huff, a schoolmate of Ted's from his days at the John Moore School, was in law school at the same time and he said that Ted used to come to his room at night cursing Professor Waite's assignments. "It was very hard for him," Judge Huff said. "He had no head whatever for the law. His mind didn't work that way." This is very likely true. Although he said later he had gotten a C as a grade, the record shows he got a D. After finishing one semester's work, he withdrew in February, 1930.

"During the struggle and unhappiness involving this decision, I wrote my first verse," the letter to Burke continues. "It was printed in magazines like *The Harp, The Commonweal,* and *The New Republic.*" Many writers honestly do remember their first work as the first work they were able to publish. It seems fairly certain that Ted had written some poems as an undergraduate but, since nothing came of them, it is quite likely he forgot them.

It must be remembered that the stock-market crash occurred in October, 1929, while Ted was wrestling with the law. Its immediate effects were certainly apparent in Wall Street but not to everyone in the country and its lamentable long-range consequences, the complex of lacks that made the Depression, took time to emerge. Ted's mother was living and supporting her son and daughter on the money her husband had left her and she seems not to have felt any panic, financially, for she allowed Ted to enter the University of Michigan Graduate School to begin his studies for a master's degree in the second semester of the 1929–1930 academic year.

Here he was back on familiar ground and he did well. In the spring of 1930 he took courses in Victorian Literature, the Age of Milton, Literature from the Restoration until 1730, a Pro-Seminar in English Drama, and he did some special research in the works of D. H. Lawrence.

He took a large apartment at 1087½ Willard Street, almost the whole upper floor of a house. He made batches of home-brewed beer, not always successfully for—a common mishap with amateur brewers—the bottles exploded and blew foam all over the place. His friends, Otto Graf and O. M. Pearl, recall that he often threw parties on Saturday nights when he would drink heavily and, drunk, he grew wild, broke furniture, and beat out windows with his fist. It was part of the general defiance of the period to bring girls illicitly to student parties but Ted never brought any and neither Professor Graf or Professor Pearl remember seeing him with any.

He was not happy. He said he was committed to a future as a writer (not yet a poet) but he made no friends with other writers and he did not belong to the literary cliques in the university. He wanted to be taken as an eccentric, a nonconformist who relied solely on his own judgment. Wary of any emotional claims on himself, he seemed always ready to lapse into gloom and he kept saying, "God, I'm depressed." He repeatedly badgered Otto Graf with the question, "Do you like me?" and then answered it himself, "No, you don't really like me." He had a sharp wit, both malicious and benign, and when he let it out, he could be very funny but he rarely did, rarely seemed cheerful.

A literary education gotten in public institutions is largely an exercise in the critical faculties and criticism is impossible without analysis. Ted had read more widely than most and, aside from the knowledge accumulated about the works, he had written dozens of papers analyzing them. But the writing of poetry is an act of synthesis. A beginner in any of the arts, while he may be sensitive, knowledgeable, and critically intelligent, begins as a child begins, awkwardly, imitatively, totally unable at first to use his knowledge, intelligence—and often his taste—at all. His studies seem to be useless lumber in his head. Ted went at anything he decided was worth doing in the same way he went at tennis, eager to be the best, throwing all his energies into it, enraged at himself for his failures.

He had already tried his hand at serious poetry and this spring in the Graduate School, he seemed to have been secretly and painfully approaching his decision to make a career of it. It was the decision of an idiot in the strictest sense of the word, a purely private person. There is never any public demand for new poetry; in fact, the society in which Ted had grown up seemed to conspire subtly to discourage it. It is the task of a new poet to impose his work on the public. To make any impression on the expected apathy, the work must be original in order to be striking; it must be moving and profound. Could he look at his apprentice pieces and conscientiously judge them to be all these? It is not likely.

And he knew it was no way to make a living. Editors paid little for poetry. In the face of the growing economic paralysis of 1930, it was possible that many magazines would fail, the small market for poetry would shrink, and there might not be any money in it at all.

It would be flattering to call it courage; more accurately it seems to have been an angry, defiant, Prussian pigheadedness that was leading him to his decision. It is no wonder that he drank, that he seemed distraught. The windowpanes he beat out with his fist were very likely the obtuse foreheads of all those who opposed him, his family, the crass fraternity types around him, the stupid teachers, inimical editors and readers who had not yet had the chance to read him but whose enmity he counted on nonetheless. And when he looked at his own first pieces and saw how bad they were, knowing simultaneously that they were the best he could then do, all the basic fear, timidity, and shyness of his character must have overwhelmed him and made the future seem hopeless.

In May, 1930, Ted sent letters to a number of private schools and small colleges asking for a teaching job but none accepted him. It is impossible to gauge his discouragement but it was the kind of disappointment he would suffer often. No job satisfied him. No matter where he was, what the pay, what the rank, he wrote letters like them all his life.

He entered the summer session and continued his work toward a master's degree. He took courses in Chaucer, Shakespeare, American Literature up to the Revolution, Aesthetics, and Russian Literature (in English). He was not approved for the degree at the end of the summer because he was short several papers. It was not until 1935 that he completed his work. The degree was approved in October and he received his M.A. in 1936.

Some fraternities augment their income by renting rooms during the summer and Ted took a room at the Trigon House. He was seeing Otto Graf often and he liked to hear him play the piano. [Graf has great abilities and might have been a concert pianist.] He said Ted's tastes ran to the Beethoven sonatas and "anything fast and loud." But Ted never mentioned that he himself had ever played. Indeed, Graf was surprised to hear it.

An eccentric himself, Ted seemed to attract eccentrics and he took a man named Thornton as a roommate. He was an academic floater who had gone to a number of colleges and when he moved in, his only luggage was six packing cases full of books, shirts, and Brooks Brothers suits. His travels had given him a certain sophistication. Ted thought him intelligent and he made a good drinking companion. Thornton entered the University and the Ypsilanti State Normal College, seven miles away, simultaneously, and went to classes at each on alternate days. This clever plan did not last—fatigue overcame him. Since he had already accumulated one hundred fifty-seven hours of class work at the various institutions he had patronized, he despairingly petitioned Dean Effinger of the University of Michigan College of Literature, Science, and the Arts for an A.B. degree but it was not granted him.

His association with Thornton seems to have relaxed Ted a little, for his friends remember he was talking a lot about poetry quite openly, other people's, as if it were a perfectly legitimate occupation. Elinor Wylie still got most of his praise. He admired E. E. Cummings for his "daring" but said he preferred stricter forms. He was a good friend of Professor Peter Monro Jack (Aberdeen and Cambridge) who had been imported by President Little to shake up the Rhetoric Department and Jack was the local proprietor, so to speak, of T. S. Eliot but Ted rarely acknowledged Eliot's abilities.

In the May–June, 1930, issue of *The Harp*, a long-dead little magazine, three poems of Ted's appeared. He said much later, "My first verses, and dreadful they were, I sold for $1." It was a just estimate of their worth, both the adjective and the pay. "Method" (originally entitled "Advice to a Young Man") and "To Darkness" are reprinted here:

METHOD

Sweep up the broken dreams of youth!
(The broom to use is utter truth.)

TO DARKNESS

Thou are not light's negation;
Thou art another light
That lives in sweet relation
With souls that have no sight.

Ted must have thought these poems good enough to submit, and since there is no pride like that in one's first published work,

he must have felt proud. *The Harp* was a very small little maga-
zine with hardly any national circulation. People in Ann Arbor
were not likely to see it and no one remembers that Ted ever told
anyone he had achieved publication. His pride seems to have been
muffled by his characteristic rage that these poems expressed so
little of his capabilities, an aphorism and a petty "metaphysical"
conceit. If anyone had made the snide remark to him, "Such little
poems for such a big man," he would have exploded in anger, yet
these poems, small as they are, point to certain permanent features
of his later work.

"Method" does not reveal, it shouts his personal sincerity, comi-
cally perhaps but honestly. If the essence of lyric poetry may be
defined as a profound concern for the successive states of the
poet's emotions, Ted was a lyric poet. Until the very end of his
career when he began to look outward, the only world was *his*
world, and he towered over any other figures he admitted into it,
and it was what he felt, not they, that was paramount. While five
years later he would not have been found dead with a phrase like
"broken dreams," he obviously felt that his dreams *were* broken,
some hope extinguished, some promise killed. And he was strug-
gling to do without them. The poem does not work at all unless it
be taken as the outcry of the poet.

Aside from himself, his chief concerns in poetry were with the
permanencies of life, the filial bond, natural growth and decay,
love between man and woman, and the nature of God. To them
he brought all his passion, but this passion had to be balanced in
an image with a surface of simplicity yet with many levels of
meaning so that any reader could respond according to what he
brought to the poem, and this image was to be disposed in words
of a proper rhythm, subtle, intricate, yet easy to read aloud. He
wanted everyone to read his poetry and to achieve this loaded
simplicity he devoted his technical struggles. He wrote only about
things he could feel deeply and he had acquired most of his stock,
like many poets, before he was fifteen. W. H. Auden said, "Ted
had hardly any general *ideas* at all."

It was not a modish poetry, not topical. It did not express, nor
try to, the timbre of a civilization as "The Waste Land" did. He
worked within the circle of his own emotions, and judging himself
to be a sample of humanity, he conceived that his emotions would

be common to all. This was interpreted by some critics as a purely private outpouring and it delayed his recognition as a serious poet.

In "To Darkness" he takes one of the eternal phases of life, cleverly somersaults it to its opposite, and ties it gloomily to "the blind," a condition capable of a wide latitude of interpretations. Crude though it is, it shows indications of the future.

Sometime during his work on his Master's, his decision to be a poet crystallized, and between interludes of study and drinking, he must have worked steadily. In the fall of 1931 he entered the Harvard Graduate School. It was while he was in Cambridge that he got the first encouragement he could respect.

It was a big thing in those days for a Middle-Westerner to brave an Eastern college, especially Harvard, but Ted left no record of his impressions except to say later, lumping it with his high school and his years at Michigan, that he hated it. He lived at 48 Parkin Hall. A letter from John Warriner, whose friendship he valued, suggests that he was lonely, busy but lonely:

> I had a typewriter and Ted used to appear in my dorm room at any hour of the day or night bearing a poem that he had finally wrestled into shape. He would hover over me, watching me type a copy, asking, flatteringly, for my opinion of it or of a troublesome word or phrase. Criticism always seemed to depress him, and so I learned to accept my role as amanuensis without trying to act as critic. I would address a letter to Cowley or Benét and we'd mail the letter. I was excited by all this and as excited as Ted in the outcome. As far as I can remember, he didn't succeed that winter in getting anything accepted, but he certainly softened up the editors for future conquest.
>
> We had a lot of good times together that year. I suppose we were a pretty strange combination—opposites in so many ways— but graduate school can be a pretty lonely place and together we were not lonely. He was a strenuous companion. I remember vividly those spring mornings when, after having kept me up to 3 AM, he would be shouting beneath my window at 8 o'clock, impatiently insisting that I get up and out to the tennis courts with him so he could lick the socks off me . . .

The encouragement came out of a desperate brashness that often seized him later. He says in the sketch of himself in *Twentieth Century Authors:*

I was moping through the Harvard Yard one night. I saw a man I thought might be Robert Hillyer. I said boldly, "Pardon me, sir. I think I have some poems you might like." A look of pain came over his face. "Come to my office about eleven," he said. I did, complete with fur coat and fancy suit. (Those Harvards weren't going to have it over me!) Ushered in by his secretary, he took the verse, started reading. Suddenly he wheeled in his chair. "Any editor who wouldn't buy these is a fool!" he said. I was overwhelmed (though I had thought so too!). There were only three poems but Ridgely Torrence of the *New Republic* and George Schuster, then of *Commonweal*, did buy two of them.

I felt I had come to the end (really the beginning) of a trail. I had learned how to get high grades but that seemed meaningless. Now I didn't have to go into advertising (I had written, at eighteen, copy which had been used in national campaigns), or the law. I wasn't just a spoiled sad snob. I could write and people I respected printed the stuff.

The poem printed in *Commonweal* was "The Conqueror," in October, 1931, and the *New Republic* poem was "Silence," in January, 1932. Ted thought "Silence" was good enough to be reprinted in his first book, *Open House.*

Ted always wrote much more poetry than he published. Some went unbought. Some he suppressed utterly and finally—he threw it away in disgust. His progress, then, cannot be traced smoothly through the papers he has left, and, as a result, his published work seems to improve in big jumps. Since it was published in January, 1932, Ted would have worked on "The Silence" either at Michigan or at Harvard and it is obviously a much better poem than his two maiden attempts. He seems to have been reading or been impressed by Poe's "The City in the Sea." It has Poe's nouns and his smoothness of diction. For many high-school students, the first serious poet they encounter is Poe. His rhythms are beguiling and many of the sensitive readers may remember him as great because he was the first. There is also an echo of Blake. But the grief comes through as a real grief; it is not wholly smothered by literary convention. It rises probably from the desolation he felt at the loss of his father, which was to endure until his own death.

In the letter to Kenneth Burke, Ted says, "In 1930–31, I went to Harvard, principally to work with I. A. Richards, the English critic." In the knowledgeable literary coteries of the time, I. A. Richards was chic. His *Principles of Literary Criticism* had come out in 1924 and his *Practical Criticism* in 1929, both of them issued as part of the International Library of Psychology, Philosophy, and Scientific Method. Richards had, of course, been trained as a psychologist, and however quaint it may seem now, his application of psychological principles to the interpretation of literature was a ground breaker in the field of criticism. Since Ted says he went to Harvard chiefly to work with Richards, Richards' chapter on The Normality of the Artist in *Principles* which begins, "If the availability of his past experience is the first characteristic of the poet, the second is what we may provisionally call his normality." may have spoken to Ted directly. His past experience seems to have been emotionally available to him every minute of the day but not poetically so. This was to take a continuing effort of technique. And his sense of the poet as an antisocial being may have been alleviated by Richards' insistence that a high degree of impulsive conformity was necessary for communication to take place at all. However, the question of the poet's normality did not die in Ted's mind.

He seems to have intended to proceed to the Doctor's degree at Harvard but he was stopped by the Depression which by the summer of 1931 had showed its full face and frightened everyone. It would have cost his mother too much then, especially since she wanted his sister, June, to go to college. Ted applied to several colleges and universities for jobs and he was given one by Professor J. W. Tupper, the head of the English Department at Lafayette College in Easton, Pennsylvania. Lafayette has Presbyterian affiliations and the fact that Ted's application said he was Presbyterian may have given it the crucial weight.

He spent the summer at home in Saginaw, writing, playing tennis and, as he complained, helping his mother with the washing to save money. For amusement he would go to the movies or hang around with Buzz Morley, drinking a little and listening to jazz. Not much good Negro jazz was available then and Ted's taste ran to the music of Beiderbecke, Red Nichols, and the Chicago School of Sullivan, Freeman, and Teschmaker. Morley says that occasionally Ted would make a Welsh rabbit in the Morley kitchen and talk of becoming a great cook some day.

When Ted went to Easton in the fall of 1931 to begin his work at Lafayette, it is doubtful if he realized that he had begun a second career that would be permanent. Work of any kind was very scarce then, and he took the job he was best fitted for, college teaching; but this is not necessarily what he would have chosen. However, the pay was $1200 a year and since hogs were selling for 3 cents a pound in Chicago and many married couples were subsisting on $15 a week, this was larger than it seems to be now. He was independent of his mother and he seems to have approached his new post with the burst of energy a change of scene sometimes gives.

Easton, at the joining of the Lehigh and Delaware rivers, was an old town with a history going back to Revolutionary times. There was money there, both inherited and made. A kind of armed truce existed between town and gown, although the Country Club admitted college faculty members for half price and this helped to break down barriers; and a few townspeople turned up for college lectures and little theater performances. It was a good deal smaller than Ann Arbor or Cambridge, and a pleasant place to live.

Lafayette had about eight hundred students then and the English Department was small, only Professor Tupper as head, two Associate Professors, no Assistant Professors, and four instructors of whom Ted was one. He taught four classes, three of English I, and one of English VII (Writing from Models), a required sophomore course. He approached teaching with élan and without any academic clichés. As a working poet he had a profound interest in literature. He was excited about it. He was making discoveries. Because he was candid and colloquial he made a knowledge of literature and writing seem not a mere intellectual ornament but something that any student would eventually come to, something to be taken for granted because it was so important. Deeply absorbed, interested, and fascinated by his subject, he awoke interest and fascination in his students. It was Professor Tupper's habit to keep his young instructors two years only. He kept Ted four and the students petitioned to have him kept longer. Professor Donald McCluskey, now a teacher at Lafayette, says that in the summer of 1965, the class of '35 was having its thirtieth reunion and Ted was the only teacher they remembered clearly and as a teacher, not a poet, but many recalled the note-book he kept.

Most poets keep a notebook of one kind or another. Ted's was a large loose-leaf affair he carried with him most of the time. He lived his first year at the Faculty Club and, with a certain bravado, he would throw it on the table in the lobby where anyone might look at it.

During his other years at Lafayette Ted lived in Easton Hall, a dormitory where he acted as a proctor in return from his room rent. He was very popular with the students and they delighted in his eccentricities. When he lived in 100 Easton Hall, it was in a ground-floor room. He had a class at eight o'clock in the morning in the building next to it. Nobody likes eight o'clock classes. The group would gather and send a spy to see whether the window of Ted's room were open or shut. If it were shut, it meant that he was sleeping in and the class could dismiss themselves. If it were open, it meant that he was awake, taking the first fresh air of the day, and he would soon be ready to teach. Ted had slept on a sleeping porch in his early years in Saginaw, and he believed, probably rightly, that he had contracted sinus trouble and asthma from doing it. After he left home he always slept with his head wrapped in a blanket in cold weather or in a pillowcase in hot to guard against chills.

Another bond with his students was his drinking, which he did openly. He was often seen in a bar called the Press Club off the Square in downtown Easton, and in another, now demolished, at the corner of 4th Street and Spring Garden. He does not seem to have drunk more than other members of the faculty but they tended to do it privately. Professor Eric Rhodin, now of the Lafayette English Department, says Ted was very intense about drinking, that he seemed to be seeking a kind of oblivion.

In the springs he played tennis with his usual ferocity and in 1934 he became the college tennis coach. How anxious he was to do well and his honest interest in the sport can be seen in a letter dated June 29, 1935 to D. L. Reeves, the graduate manager of athletics at Lafayette:

> Dear Mr. Reeves:
>   This is a letter regarding my coaching of the tennis team dur-ing the past three years.
>   You will recall that I received $20.00 for equipment as coach

of the team in the spring of 1933. This money plus another $5.00 of my own was used for purchasing two rackets. One of these rackets was used as a spare by various members of the squad during that season and the next. During the season we were forced to practice for about six weeks on cement, this necessitated the purchasing of extra balls out of our own pockets by me and some of the squad members.

The team that year was very green, and, despite intensive practice, most unsuccessful.

During the season of 1934, we were able to play more on clay, but I bought several boxes of balls myself. That year we won two matches and came close to winning others. But again we were greatly handicapped by bad weather. "The Lafayette" carried two editorials that year praising the efforts of the squad and myself.

This spring the team won two matches but actually the squad at the close of the season was superior to six of the teams on our schedule. For instance, Stevens, whom we defeated, won about two-thirds of its matches against good opponents.

During practice period, it was my custom usually to play two men on the squad each day. This was necessary because the men were green and had to become accustomed to a steady and varied game.

I do not claim to be a master-mind as a tennis coach, but I do know a good bit about the game, have had much tournament experience, have beaten many professional coaches.

There is a very definite limit to what can be done with green men in college tennis. The better college players have usually played since childhood, frequently have had sound coaching and considerable tournament experience. Only one or two Lafayette players have had any sound coaching or the benefits of more than one or two tournaments a summer.

Next year, however, the team should be the strongest in several years. Captain Frank Fine is a good natural leader and has a sound game that is improving. He won nearly all his matches this year, playing at Nos. 3, 2, and 1. Other players and freshmen should also be better.

I am aware that the money I spent was entirely on my own responsibility. I am also aware that your budgetary problems are indeed difficult. But I feel that a reimbursement to the extent of $30.00 would be most reasonable. Actually, I spent more than twice that amount for rackets, balls, and re-stringings.

A word about the tennis courts at Lafayette. There is a very

serious need for at least two well-drained courts with special
surfacing, such as red brick-dust, "har-tru," or similar special
composition. The present courts dry very slowly and, once dry,
begin immediately to break up. However, this year the present
courts were kept in better shape than previously by rolling with
the heavy roller and applying chloride. As Mr. Miller realized,
there wasn't a sufficient supply of the chloride compound. It
takes at least a full drum per court to do anything very effective.

No doubt this rather lengthy account includes many things you
already know. But my chief reason for writing at such length is
that I would like to see the game continued and encouraged at
Lafayette. Your office has furnished interesting schedules. The
boys haven't been stars, but they have been a real credit to the
College. A good many times I've had compliments from out-
siders on their conduct. It is important, it seems to me, to have
such a tradition continued.

When Ted was writing to get something from someone he
didn't know very well personally, he tended to be rather stately
and to lard his sentences with hackneyed epistolary phrases. This
was, however, an altruistic letter. From the date it can be seen
that it was written at the end of the spring term of 1935 and Ted
knew he was leaving Lafayette for good; but he liked the place
and he wanted to do his best for it. At Commencement that year,
as he talked to the graduating seniors and shook their hands, he
said, "I nearly broke down for some reason. I went over to the
Faculty Club and bawled."

He also acted as Director of Public Relations for the college and
as the editor of the college catalogue. In a rather heated letter
written later to a friend, he describes his public-relations activi-
ties:

Why, during the very late spring of 1935 and the fall of 1936,
I got the college more really good breaks in space in the metro-
politan rags and in the smaller papers around, than they'd had
in four or five years. In the fall of 1935 young Clayton Cook and
I rolled out more football stuff that really clicked, and with a
lousy team at that, than they'd had since their thug team was in
the national spotlight." *

* This letter is almost certainly misdated. Ted was at Michigan State in 1935 and
at Penn State in 1936. He must mean the spring of 1933 and the fall of 1934.

As if his energies needed still more outlets, he began the first of many love affairs. One day he had a tooth pulled. In the Circle in downtown Easton (actually a public square) he met Mary Kunkel, the daughter of Professor Beverley Kunkel of the Biology Department. She also had just had a tooth pulled. Their plight brought them together and they began dating. She had finished her work at Sarah Lawrence College and she was working at painting in a studio in Easton.

She was attracted by Ted's vitality and the wit and brilliance of his conversation. And in turn he was impressed by her: he went to the trouble to improve his past—he told her he had owned a Stutz Bearcat at the University of Michigan. She said he was a good dancer, and one night at a dance she slapped a man named Willis Hunt because he had disparaged Ted in front of her. Ted was nearby. He saw her do it but he did not intervene. He was willing enough while he was drinking to talk about the gangsters he had known but he was not a violent man in spite of his surface toughness.

It is clear from his summer letters to her from Saginaw that he believed he was in love with Mary. Marriage was frequently mentioned, and the happy prospect of a life together. However, Professor Kunkel and his wife, while they liked Ted and often asked him to dinner in Easton and to visit them at their summer places on Cape Cod and in Connecticut, had misgivings about him as a husband for their daughter. "They were far too shrewd to oppose it openly," Mary says. "They were quite subtle." (And when Mary married Jeremy Bagster-Collins, Mrs. Kunkel said, "Now we can relax and enjoy Ted." Mrs. Kunkel wrote verse herself and Ted was always willing to read and criticize it, and do it politely.)

Mary and Ted often drove down the Delaware River to New Hope, and they found a small valley watered by a stream called Mud Run where the spring came earliest, the skunk cabbage and the first green.

It was a busy life quite aside from writing poetry, yet in 1932 he published five poems, the fruit of his year at Harvard, in such magazines as *Poetry,* the *New Republic,* the *Saturday Review,* and the *Sewanee Review;* in 1933, only one but it was an appearance he was proud of, a poem untitled then but later called "The Buds Now Stretch" in the *Adelphi* in London, his first foreign publication. In 1934, however, a sign that he found his situation congenial to his work, he published thirteen poems.

To his career as a poet, the most important event of his Lafayette years was his meeting three poets who were to become friends, acute critics of his work, and helpful advisers, Rolfe Humphries, Stanley Kunitz, and Louise Bogan.

Humphries had a summer place at Belvidere, New Jersey, a few miles from Easton. One of Ted's students, Cy Greenberg, knew Humphries and Ted asked Greenberg if he would introduce him. One night at the University Club Greenberg found the opportunity and Ted was able to show Humphries some of his poetry. Shortly afterward Humphries gave a party. Greenberg borrowed a car and drove Ted to Belvidere. Humphries' little house was full of convivial guests, but he said he talked to Ted and Greenberg a long time nevertheless, and this meeting was the beginning of a long friendship. Greenberg said he did not remember how they got home but the next morning he found he had driven back on a flat—the tire was all chewed up. (The current legend at Lafayette is now that Ted drove and one whole wheel was off.)

Humphries was an established poet and a classical scholar, enough older than Ted for him to respect the man and his work without reservation. Humphries, recognizing Ted's intense concern with a purity of diction, tried to interest him in the Greek and Roman poets of whom Ted knew little, and in Pope. "But it was no good. He always liked the wild ones." Humphries said, "He knew modern poetry—that is, since 1900—really well, especially the English."

Humphries was the first poet of ability with whom Ted could have a continuing association. After the years of drought, merely to meet a live working poet was a revelation to him and he began to show his work to Humphries and ask for criticism, a practice he was to expand as his acquaintance with poets widened. In this he was genuinely humble and genuinely hard-boiled. He was eager to learn and he did learn from mistakes, lapses in taste, flawed imagery that were pointed out to him. Simultaneously, and from a practical standpoint, he knew that the oftener a poem was gone over by critics he could trust, the better chance it had of being accepted when he submitted it to a magazine. This ambiguity of motive was characteristic.

Humphries' kindness, patience, and critical acuity are clear in this excerpt from a letter he wrote Ted, October 13, 1934:

About the poem you enclosed: possibly all I have to say is wide of the mark and not really about the poem at all. But I think of one or two sermonish remarks about technique, and will blame you for sending me the text and the impulse. The questions you wrote in hint your own doubts, the first two you can dismiss, and I'll try to meet the query of your 3rd question—"fair traditional piece?" It is certainly in the historical and traditional manner but you could make more use of the manner and exploit it to better advantage than you do here. If the editors have any intelligent reason for rejecting the poem, it may be that they are fighting shy of it on the ground of its conventional rhymes: desire-fire; shock-rock; mirth-birth; sky-die. It just misses breath-death, as it were! and brute-fruit and sun-bone are not enough to carry it. And "agony of birth" is pretty trite, at least it must seem so to the conventional mind, almost regardless of where it is set. And personally I am a little bothered by your monotonous adjective-noun combinations: 6 such combinations in the first 6 lines, while each may be used advisedly, is a good deal to ask the reader to endure: or, if he can achieve such endurance, you condition him to a frame of mind which he has to throw off with a most violent wrench when he comes to "strange impalpable fruit." About that last phrase I do not know what to think, and wonder what you think yourself; my guess is either you think it is a mess or else consider it the central technical triumph of the poem. I am uncertain of its strength either as to sound or as to metaphor. I know, for sound, you need something to lead up to it, but the adjective "strange" by over-declaring, weakens the paradox of saying "impalpable" in connection with "fruit." If it is impalpable, that is strange enough. I think there is some other word, beginning with "un-," a quadrisyllabic word that would eliminate "strange," or a trisyllabic one that would follow it. You have to go, metrically, too fast and bumpily with "impalpable" to get either the feeling of "impalpable" or "strange." Is all this laboring the obvious? What I think could be done with this kind of poem is deliberately advertise the conventional by calling it "Poem with Old Rhymes" or something like that, and then work in the idea by way of counterpoint to the simplicity, and have it come out in the end, the emotion breaking the pattern as the faith the rock. Or another thing to do would be, in each of

the first three stanzas, hold a rhyme in suspense and precipitate
them all in the last stanza, viz.

> "This elemental force
> Descended from the sun
> Is locked in narrow bone."

> "This something or other else"

—and so on, and keep the reader wondering what has happened
to those rhymes until they clinch the poem at the end. Auden has
something along those lines in one of his poems called Epilogue,
or something like that. Is this all too tricky or am I being a dull
and witless oaf deluded by my own conceit and failing to see at
all what you're driving at? I always distrust myself when I start
thinking I am Father Superior among the novitiates. Enough
preaching.

The poem under discussion is "Genesis," which was first pub-
lished in *The Nation*, June 24, 1936, and in its final form in Ted's
first book, *Open House*. The drafts of the poem have not been
preserved.

They saw each other oftenest during early summer. Ted would
get someone to drive him over to Belvidere from Easton and they
would sit in the kitchen drinking and talking. Humphries had a
much wider range of knowledge about literature than Ted and, as
the elder, he knew more about things in general. It was good talk
and Ted learned much from it as he later and vehemently ac-
knowledged, yet in the course of these evenings it came out that
Ted not only feared that he might lack talent as a poet, talent
enough to be the best one writing, but also kept touching up his
image as a man. (Man and poet were still separate in his mind
then.) He claimed to know the Purple Gang well, said they had
offered him a job driving a truck for them. "The kid's good," he
said they said. Humphries shrewdly discerned that this was fan-
tasy, part of the mask Ted always wore. Similar was Ted's in-
sistence that women were always falling in love with him. "But I
just let 'em adore me," he said.

Humphries, however, penetrated the mask. "There was a lot of
self-hatred in Ted, you know," he said. Everyone who knew Ted
well recognized this eventually, that he was host to a mass of
free-floating guilt that made him loathe himself. Nothing shows

the power and depth of his interior life more than this, for what had he ever *done* so wrong that guilt for its commission should ride him incessantly? Very little. He had had a "normal" youth and had acted like dozens of his peers. It was thinking and the reservoir of emotion that saturated his thoughts which tormented him. Thoughts were like deeds to him and, once entertained, they seemed to crystallize and remain in his mind to oppress him. And as he plunged into fantasy in the concoction of his mask, so his thoughts and even the memory of his thoughts swelled in his mind to shame and terror, and it was this excess that was to become the source of his best work. Having discerned this, there was nothing Humphries could do to alleviate it except to encourage his writing. He did this through a long correspondence and by introducing Ted to Louise Bogan who became even more a guide and mentor than Humphries himself.

As John Warriner has indicated, Ted had already discovered Stanley Kunitz's *Intellectual Things* and felt more of an intellectual and emotional rapport with him than any other contemporary poet. In the early 1930s, Kunitz was living on and working a one-hundred-and-fifty acre farm in Bucks County, Pennsylvania. One cold day there was a knock at his door and there stood Ted in his fur coat, shy and frightened. Kunitz asked him in and talk began. After Ted had paid Kunitz many compliments on his poetry, he brought out some of his own. Kunitz recognized his abilities and out of this mutual respect friendship sprang up. Kunitz thinks Ted liked him and his work because he was, like Ted, a lonely poet, out of the main stream of the time. Also, Kunitz's father had died before he was born and the deaths of fathers made another bond between them. Kunitz saw almost immediately how important Otto Roethke's death was to Ted, what a gap it had made in his life, and without any cynicism, its possibilities as a source of poetry.

Kunitz thought Ted's early poems were too tightly constructed, too mannered, and he warned him that they had a feminine cast to them in certain softness of phrase that seemed to derive from Ted's close study of the works of Elinor Wylie, Louise Bogan, and Léonie Adams. When he mentioned Yeats to Ted, Ted said he was "too soft, too full of that Celtic twilight" and it was obvious that Ted had read only Yeats's early poems at that time. Later,

Kunitz says, Ted learned from Yeats's later work a line with a
heavy beat, self-contained but still related to a dramatic action,
and, a minor point, not to use an indefinite article when he could
use a demonstrative pronoun.

As they met more often, they used to play tennis. Kunitz was a
good player and once when he won, Ted broke his own racket in
a fury at what he took to be his own bad play. They used to play
for what they called The World's Championship for Poets. They
also made up a game to play while drinking. First one, then the
other would name an obscure English poem and ask, "Who wrote
it?" and, getting a right answer, ask "When?" Eventually they
reached a level of expertise when they could spot the poet and
the date within ten years.

In the Thirties most intellectuals were anti-Fascist and many
were pro-Communist. (Few were actually Communist Party
members. The party demanded hard work from its membership
and laid them under heavy contributions of cash, which was hard
to come by.) Humphries, who translated the New York poems of
Federico Garcia Lorca, said that Ted gave money to the Spanish
Republican cause. Kunitz, however, said that Ted's sympathies
were pro-Fascist in the late Thirties but qualified this by saying
that Ted did not seem to be politically minded and seldom had
any information about political situations, domestic or interna-
tional.

Like Humphries and Miss Bogan, Kunitz came to be a friend on
whom Ted leaned heavily for encouragement and criticism. They
became an ideal audience for his work.

In the summers of 1934, 1935, and 1936, Ted worked for
J. Robert Crouse, a wealthy Cleveland man who had interests in
the National Lamp Company, the Arctic Ice Cream Company, and
other corporations. Crouse had founded a community at Hartland,
Michigan, about twenty-five miles north of Ann Arbor, using his
father's farm as a nucleus. Among Ted's papers there is an outline
describing the Hartland Area Project.

I. OBJECTIVES as defined by J. Robert Crouse, Sr.
    1. To lay out a typical rural community with a village center.
       a. school population of about 1000
       b. total population of about 4000
       c. size of area and limiting factors.

II. GENERAL PLAN

1. To bring to bear on this group creative, constructive, social, and educational influences
   a. to the end of more rapidly and effectively evolving a richer and more abundant individual and community life.
2. To create a series of financial Foundations.
   a. to give force and effect to activities and to the specially qualified persons selected to carry them out.
3. To set up and put into operation from time to time a specified group of activities and others that may seem desireable.
   a. to have a qualified director for each activity or group of activities.
   b. to develop each activity with reference to needs and conditions in this particular area.
4. to continue the support of an activity until it becomes an accepted social and educational practice after which time it would be carried on as a regular public function.
5. to avoid relieving the community of responsibilities or tax burdens that should be accepted by it.

III. ADMINISTRATION

1. Give to each director the utmost freedom in the use of his initiative, creative and visionary powers.
2. Require for each year a new or revised five-point program which will include the objectives, the plan for carrying out the objectives, the administration, the cost, and the expected results.
3. Local and other advisory associated committees for each directed activity.

IV. COST OR FINANCIAL SUPPORT

1. A specially prepared annual budget for each activity, which is subject to approval.
2. Source of support, list, and original amounts of Foundations.
   a. Eighty per cent of the income from the Foundation to be used for specified activities and twenty per cent of the income to be added to the principal amount until the latter reaches a predetermined amount.

V. RESULTS

1. of a material nature
   a. Library

    b. Music Hall
    c. Waldenwoods
    d. Enlarged and more effective church facilities
    e. Arts and Crafts department
    f. The Farm Laboratory
    g. Pure bred sheep and other animals
  2. of a human service nature
    a. helping teacher
    b. Ministry of Music
    c. Health & Physical Education
    d. Social Service and Welfare
    e. Dramatics
    f. Library
    g. Agriculture
    h. Continuing Education
  3. the long look
    a. in terms of generations
    b. in regard to its state and nation-wide influence

No plan could be more American than this. The assumptions on which it rests go deep into the history of the country, probably far deeper than J. R. Crouse was aware. That a community could be started by fiat, that it would be Utopian in the style of Phalanx, New Jersey, the Oneida Community, New Harmony, Indiana, and the Mormons, that it would be dreamed up and financed by a wealthy man, these assumptions show how inescapably even our dreams of the future rise out of the past.

J. R. Crouse was the father of Ted's roommate, Robert Crouse, at the Chi Phi House in Ann Arbor and it was the son who introduced them. J. R. Crouse was a man as big as Ted with the same kind of explosive vitality. Ted's own father was never dead to him emotionally; he remained a presence in Ted's mind, the ideal source of love and authority, but no longer operative, and so J. R. Crouse became one of a series of surrogate fathers. One's own father is powerful from the very nature of his position—he is bigger and he slaps you with his hand when you do wrong—but another source of power is wealth and it may be that Ted's fascination with money and his somewhat ambivalent admiration for the rich was a try at imitating Otto Roethke, an attempt to gain a like authority. It was not long before Ted was referring to Crouse as "Pop" in letters. He became almost a member of the family. He lived with them at their house in Hartland, and when they went to their summer place at Stony Lake, near Peterborough, Ontario, he went with them. He got such a bad case of sunburn one summer from lying on a raft in the lake that he had to wear pajama trousers for days because he could not bear the weight of his ordinary clothes.

Ted was hired to write a history of the Hartland Area Project, or, rather, three histories, as Crouse explained in a letter to Ted, "I would like the whole thing prepared along three lines: one account being adapted for the use of the intelligentsia; one account written up in homely fashion for the people in that area; the third account on the order of the Russian Primer for use in the schools." As Robert Crouse remembers, Ted received about three hundred dollars for the three summers. If this seems little, it must be remembered that a job paying a dollar a day and room and board was a good one. Ted complained about the work in letters to Mary Kunkel. An excerpt: "I'm far from finished with Pa Crouse's work and I do want to get it finished. . . . the reason I haven't gone as fast with Pa Crouse's work—the real reason—is that it is a compromise with my integrity (my integrity as a writer which is practically all I have left). Yet I can't chuck the thing because I'm fond of Pop C. and he thinks I'm just a genius on wheels." The history was never finished and the portion Ted did write has been lost.

He did not seem to feel that the title "Historian" had the weight he wanted to attribute to himself and, on every job application and *Curriculum Vitae* he wrote from this time forth, he described himself as "Public Relations Counsel for J. Robert Crouse," or "Public Relations Counsel, Hartland Area Project." Ted rarely told outright lies to make himself look good; rather he confected versions of likelihood that sprang from wishes and hopes. When he tells Mary Kunkel that he drove a Stutz Bearcat as an undergraduate, he seems to mean that she is to take him as the kind of student who would or at least should have had such a car. And when, in the spring of 1935, he is filling out an application form for the Albert Teachers Agency in Chicago and he comes to the question *Foreign Travel?* and blandly writes in "Germany, Russia," the fact that he had never left the United States does not trouble him in his eagerness to convey the impression that he is the kind of man who is naturally well-traveled. There is a letter from J. R. Crouse to Ted in which he says, "About using outside the Area the term 'Public Relations Counsel' I see no objection if it will be helpful to you," and Robert Crouse says, "There weren't any *public* relations to keep up. Ted just worked on that history." Ted was like a turtle who worked at ornamenting his own shell.

The years of his work in law school, on his master's degree, at Harvard and of his employment at Lafayette are a lustrum of the highest importance to his career. During them he accumulated a much greater knowledge of literature; he wrote his first poems and out of the confidence the act of writing gave him and the encouragement he received from Robert Hillyer, he decided to become a poet. Almost inadvertently, spurred mainly by the money fears rising out of the Depression, he assumed a teaching post which offered present financial support and later was to become a second career. He met and made friends with three poets who entered, with mutual generosity, into friendships with him that gave him sound criticism, guidance, and, what was most necessary, praise. On the face of it, the period seems to have had the greatest possible value for him.

Perhaps not, however. He was working himself very hard. In his last year at Lafayette he was able to teach a writing course for seniors the way he wanted to. It was the kind of teaching that was to distinguish him. Each hour was an emotional performance, totally sincere but exhausting. He liked tennis and he threw himself into coaching. As titular Public Relations man for the college, he had an entrée into the city rooms of newspapers and a comradeship with reporters that pleased him and he worked hard at that. His affair with Mary Kunkel had progressed to the point where he and other people believed he was going to marry her. A letter from Professor Henry Hutchins, formerly a tennis-playing teacher at Michigan and then at Yale, says, "You were a sly rogue not to mention your engagement and your very lovely future wife." Although he liked to pose as one, Ted was not a Don Juan, and when he was involved with women, he was passionately involved.

He watched his own emotional states as if they were a barometer of his well-being. When he was depressed, it made him slothful and he could not work at anything. If a task or a relationship was emotionally rewarding, he could throw himself into it. He was not the kind who could take himself in hand and do a given job out of an act of will no matter how he was feeling. In a way his whole career as poet was an act of will and it was on this he concentrated. The other occupations however germane, however pleasant perhaps, made certain abrasions of fatigue. His years at Lafayette were pleasant, his friends say, and he seemed to stay on an even keel.

As he learned more about the technique of poetry, although the technique was always important to him, it came to matter less than the *kind* of poetry he wanted to write. By the end of 1934, he had published twenty-three poems. If he were not as accomplished as he wished to be, at least his school pieces were over and he was constantly assessing what he had to write *from*. This demanded a persistent attention to his own past. Idiosyncratically he was its central figure and he did not think he had lived an easy life. His history, as he saw it, was one of losses, betrayals, shame, many fears, and guilt. To immerse himself in these, to force them into images or to contemplate them until they became images that he, hence others, could accept, and to find a suitable diction for them was not only taxing but may have been dangerous.

VII

Trouble

It was at his next post at Michigan State College that Ted endured a bout of mental illness, the first of a series that disturbed, even terrified him. Since it was the first, it may be illuminating to describe it in some detail.

After his successful four years as a teacher at Lafayette, Ted hoped to be taken on at his alma mater, the University of Michigan, but he was very late in arranging for the necessary letters of recommendation. A letter from Professor J. W. Tupper, the head of the Lafayette English Department, to Professor Louis Strauss, the head of the department at Michigan is dated September 19, 1935, almost the beginning of the fall semester. It is, however, highly laudatory:

> Dear Professor Strauss,
>
> Mr. Roethke completed last June four years in my department and in that time conducted courses in Freshman English and gave a course in advanced composition for juniors and seniors ... Mr. Roethke has exceptional ability, indeed a touch of genius as shown by his poetry which has been accepted by the best magazines. He has been an inspiration to his students who admired and worked for him and who on the eve of his departure presented a petition to the President that he be retained on the faculty. He did well the humdrum work of correcting themes and conferring with students of all varieties of intellect and background, and his classroom was neither a dull recital of lessons nor mere entertainment.

Although many such letters are, this one is not perfunctory. Professor Tupper seems to have taken time and thought with it but, as he says Ted has "a touch of genius," so he shows a touch of frightening academic naïveté in believing that publication in the best magazines guarantees any portion of genius whatsoever. While Ted was a green undergraduate he trusted academics, but he viewed them with increasing contempt and suspicion as his career went on, wrongly in many instances, all too rightly in others. Tupper's letter came too late, Strauss had a full department and Ted looked to Michigan State College in Lansing.

He worked fast and deluged Professor W. W. Johnston, head of the Michigan State English Department, with commendatory telegrams, one from Tupper:

> Recommend very highly Theodore Roethke . . . sound scholarship, attractive personality, inspiring teacher in classroom and conference, high quality of creative work in poetry and prose.

One from Professor R. D. Noyes, Cambridge, Massachusetts:

> Recommend Theodore Roethke enthusiastically. Only illness prevented the highest grade in my drama course at Harvard.

One from Arthur A. Hauck, President, University of Maine, (formerly Dean at Lafayette):

> Enthusiastically recommend Theodore Roethke for position in English. He is able, industrious, co-operative.

One from Robert Hillyer, Harvard University:

> I understand that Theodore Roethke is applying for a position in your department. He is an interesting poet and reports of his teaching are highly favorable.

One from Professor Harold Chidsey, Department of Philosophy, Lafayette:

> Glad to recommend Theodore Roethke applying for position with you. Stimulating teacher with good future in creative work. Always found him a very pleasant colleague.

The telegrams were effective and Professor Johnston gave Ted a job teaching freshmen.

Michigan State had only recently changed its name from "Michigan Agricultural College," and while its students were not so resolutely dull and bucolic as the types Thurber found at Ohio

State, it is safe to say that the arts were not as much the focus of
the college's attention as, say, chicken husbandry. (It was a sign
of the growing urbanization of the country that, even in 1935,
institutions that had frankly and proudly called themselves "Agri-
cultural Colleges" were now changing their names to "State"
colleges. It coincides with the dwindling and eventual disappear-
ance of the "hick" joke where the farmer is the butt.) Lansing is
the capital of Michigan. The Oldsmobile factories are there, and
the business of the town is split between politics, industry, and the
College, now the University.

Ted took a room at the Campus Hotel and quickly turned it into
the sty he made of all his habitations. He could seldom remember
to send his laundry out and the room was a chaos of dirty clothes,
piles of books, scattered notes and manuscripts, loose papers,
empty liquor and aspirin bottles. It would be pleasant to say that
despite the mess he always knew where everything was, but as a
matter of fact he never did. Books, papers, student themes, poems,
even checks would be buried for months, sometimes mislaid for-
ever. In the face of this helpless carelessness, he was personally
very clean. He bathed every day and was, at least at the beginning
of the day, fastidious about his appearance.

He became friends with three other young English instructors,
John Clark, Peter De Vries (not the later well-known novelist),
and A. J. M. Smith. Smith was a Canadian and an extremely able
poet himself. Ted's social life at Lansing was chiefly in the com-
pany of these men and their wives. They were people of varied
interests and the talk was not always about literature. Ted par-
ticularly liked to talk sports. He followed the big tennis matches
closely. Wherever he was, he was always a fan of the Detroit
Tigers, and while he had not yet learned to box, he took a knowl-
edgeable interest in the big fights.

As he had at Lafayette he captured his classes at once by his
rampant sincerity. Although he prepared the subject of his class
hour, he did not prepare his presentation. He spoke off the cuff,
freshly, candidly, with a flamboyance of manner that commanded
attention and no cow was sacred to him. There is a story that has
become part of the college legend. Ted had a class in a building
with windows on three sides of the room. He said he was going to
give them an assignment in the description of a physical action.

"Now you watch what I do for the next five minutes and describe it," he said. He opened one of the windows and climbed out on a narrow ledge that ran around the building. He edged around the three sides of the building, making faces through each window, and climbed in again. Teachers do not usually do this.

To most of the freshmen the study of English had been mainly grammar drill. To meet a man who talked to them seriously and without condescension about their growth and the problems of their lives, who showed them how poetry could help them define their own emotions, was a new experience. A set of Ted's students' papers have fortunately been preserved and something of what he was doing as a teacher and the impact it was making can be gauged from the following little essay. (Ted had begun by reading a poem of Louise Bogan's.)

WHAT I REMEMBER FROM LAST HOUR

The majority of people do not realize today what they really are, who they are, or what they want to be. They do not try to discover these points either but instead try more to cover it up or pretend such things are not important. When people have truthfully and completely analyzed themselves, only then do they realize what they really are living for and what they can do. They discover and notice the filth and uncleanliness of the world and its inhabitants and almost get to the verge of insanity thinking about it and wondering where it will all lead to. Be yourself and quit acting; try to find out where you stand, how much you know, who you are.

I really think, if I may have the privilege to say, that the ideas you have "put across" to us are excellent ideas and actually put us to thinking over what you have said to us and knowing in our hearts that is the truth and the bare facts. Your method in telling us these points and your talk is not always the best way. Sometimes when you begin to tell us something and get us prepared to listen, you say, "Oh, well, never mind," and start something else. This rather discourages us and makes us feel as if we have missed something you could have told us. We know that if you had finished telling us what you started, more would have been accomplished in the end than the exercise we did.

This class is altogether different from any class I have at the present time or ever have had. I really think it is very interesting, especially when you begin to talk to us, and each day I come to class wondering what we will have today.

Since young people in the United States can still grow up to voting age, in college or not, without having anyone talk to them this way, his students must have been charmed and startled.

Now a curious train of action begins. John Clark and Peter De Vries said that Ted was drinking a great deal. He had started almost as soon as the semester began, not only whisky and beer—he hardly ever drank gin—but dozens of cups of coffee and cokes every day. He also was taking aspirin tablets by the handful. He seemed to reach that happy drunkard's state where it took only a few drinks every day to keep him affable. He did not miss any classes. He kept himself well in hand most of the time but both Clark and De Vries thought his behavior unusual for a man in a new position, especially when the students circulated a story that Ted had climbed up on top of a desk, crouched, and went, "Ah-ah-ah-ah-ah!" as if he were mowing them down with a Tommy gun. Catherine De Vries went walking with Ted in the country once or twice. He said to her, "I could throttle you and stick you under a culvert and they wouldn't find you for weeks." Mrs. De Vries is not a large woman and she says she had sense enough not to act scared. His friends could feel something preparing, rushing to a crisis, but what it was, they didn't know.

Some time during the night of November 11, 1935, Ted left his room at the Campus Hotel and walked out to a stretch of woods on Hagedorn Road, then owned by the College. While he was in these woods, as he told Peter De Vries later, he had a mystical experience with a tree and he learned there the "secret of Nijinsky."*

---

* It is very hard to tell what Ted had in mind here. However, on pp. 32–33 of *The Diary of Vaslav Nijinsky* (Simon and Schuster, New York, 1936) occur the following passages which may be relevant: "I sat, I sat a long time, then I pretended to fall asleep. I pretended because I felt that way. Whenever I have a feeling, I carry it out. I never fight against a feeling. An order of God tells me how to act. I am not a fakir and a magician. I am God in a body. Everyone has that feeling, but no one uses it. I do make use of it and know its results. People think that this feeling is a spiritual trance, but I am not in a trance. I am love. I am in a trance, the trance of love. I want to say so much and cannot find the words. I want to write and cannot. I can write in a trance and this trance is called *wisdom*. Every man is a reasonable being. I do not want unreasonable beings and therefore I want everyone to be in a trance of feelings." . . . "I went on and came to a tree. The tree

It was a cold night, and as he left the woods and went on down Hagedorn Road, he thought one of his feet was freezing. To stimulate circulation he took off his shoe and left it beside a telephone pole. After walking several miles he found himself on the road to Owosso. He hitched a ride at a gas station with a young man who brought him back to Lansing.

He went back to his room and, as he told Mary Kunkel in a letter a few weeks later,

> I took a long hot bath to take the chill out. Then the next morning I decided to cut my eight o'clock class deliberately just to see how long they would stick around, then go to see the Dean to explain one or two things about this experiment. (He hadn't asked to see me.) Well, I decided to take a little walk in the country again without a coat before doing so. It was damp and quite cold, and I got so chilled and so frightened that when I finally reached the Dean's office, I was a mess. I was so cold and chilled and frightened that I was delirious, I suppose, although they didn't have sense enough to realize it. They finally called the ambulance and a doctor who led me to the damned car, just groggy as hell. Well, about two hours later, I woke up in the hospital, very conscious and lively, determined to get out *immediately*. I wasn't sure just what the hell I'd done or said in the Dean's office but I didn't care. I wanted to quit anyway, finish Pa Crouse's work, and get a better job. Well, finally the hospital got in Pete De Vries from the Department, whom I trusted, who convinced me that the thing to do was to stay in the hospital a while and take orders from him and the doctors.

The Dean was Lloyd Emmons who had been trained as a mathematician. He had done one summer's work at Harvard and, during the interview with him, Ted had called him a "Harvard son-of-a-bitch," and thought Emmons so pleased that Ted knew he had spent a summer session at Harvard that he overlooked the "son-of-a-bitch." The hospital he was taken to was Lansing Spar-

---

told me that one could not talk here, because human beings do not understand feelings. I went on. I was sorry to part with the tree because the tree understood me." Nijinsky was in an asylum at St. Moritz when he wrote his *Diary* yet the first passages make a formulation of sorts, and for Ted perhaps it was the first time he had seen one, of something he believed in, the primacy of emotion over reason. These two sentences seem important also: "I want to write and cannot. I can write in a trance and this trance is called *wisdom*." Perhaps Ted was seeking this trance.

row Hospital and he was first attended by a Dr. Albers, who seems
to have diagnosed Ted provisionally as a patient with delirium
tremens.

Peter and Catherine De Vries reached the hospital about noon.
They found Ted highly agitated and, although De Vries's memory
is hazy on this point, he thinks he was in a straitjacket. The doctor
said Ted had refused to be given a sedative of any kind and had
barricaded himself naked behind a mattress in the corner of the
room to prevent it. Ted wanted some beer and Catherine De Vries
went out for some. The doctor opened one bottle, put a sedative
pill in it, and put the cap back on. When they offered the bottle to
Ted, he spotted the replaced cap and refused the beer. "Don't try
to pull that stuff on me," he said.

He was discharged from Sparrow on Thursday, November 21,
and he stayed a few days with Robert Crouse's brother, "Heinie,"
and his wife. Then he called the De Vries and asked if they would
take him in and they agreed to. He stayed with them until the
next Thursday.

He seemed very tired. His doctor had ordered rest and long
walks. Ted did not get dressed until sundown and then he wanted
someone to walk with him until late at night. It was on one of these
walks that he pointed out the tree to Peter De Vries, and on an-
other with Catherine he retrieved his shoe from beside the tele-
phone pole. On Thanksgiving Day, November 28, the De Vries
drove him to Saginaw.

Ted's sister, June, was in her freshman year at the University of
Michigan, and among her teachers was Ted's friend, Otto Graf.
When she heard that her brother was in Sparrow Hospital, she was
frantic with worry. Her mother was not well and she was anxious
to spare her as many of the details of Ted's illness as possible, es-
pecially the drinking which seemed to be a contributory cause of
it. After Ted had come home, she was eager to join him there but
her mother told her to stay in Ann Arbor. It was very hard on her,
not to know first-hand what was happening to the family and quite
naturally she worried about Ted, about money, about what people
would say.

While he was at home, he seems to have been quiet enough and
he continued his regimen of rest and long walks, but after a couple
of weeks in Saginaw he was seriously worried about his job. He
wrote the De Vries and asked if they could put him up so that he

could talk to Professor Johnston and Dr. Albers about the possibility of resuming teaching after New Year's. He arrived in Lansing on December 14 or 15 and talked to Johnston and apparently to Albers but the talks confirmed his fears—he would not be able to teach. Johnston gave him an unpaid leave of absence for the term beginning in January.

Ted did not feel he could impose on the De Vries by staying with them any longer because he did not think he knew them well enough—they had met for the first time only in September. Since his mother was ailing, he did not want to live at home. As Robert Crouse remembers it, Ted called him at Hartland. Crouse agreed to pick him up in Lansing and drive him to Hartland for a visit. On the way Ted talked too much, too loudly and fancifully, and it was clear to Crouse that he still was not recovered. Crouse stopped in Howell, Michigan, and persuaded Ted to visit a Dr. Hill, whom the Crouses knew. Dr. Hill recommended that Ted put himself into Mercywood Sanitarium on the outskirts of Ann Arbor. With surprising docility, Ted agreed. Crouse drove him to Mercywood and he was admitted.

Otto Graf says that he and June Roethke in company with Robert Crouse were present when Ted was admitted. He says that he and June discussed whether Ted should be admitted to Mercywood or taken to the Ypsilanti State Hospital. June was very definitely against the State Hospital because her mother would have had to commit him, and, with her mother sick, June wanted to minimize the whole affair as much as possible. Mercywood was decided upon.

Mercywood is a well-appointed even luxurious place and Ted was very comfortable there. He spent, at least during the early part of his stay, six hours a day in the hydrotherapy tubs, eating, reading, even writing there. (He carried on a voluminous correspondence with Catherine and Peter De Vries, Rolfe Humphries, and Mary Kunkel.) When he emerged from the bath, he said that he was full of energy and he worked it off playing ping-pong. All his visitors remarked how calm and rational he seemed.

On December 18, 1935, he wrote out a long examination of himself, apparently for the head of the sanitarium, Dr. Theophil Klingman. It seems to answer questions he had perhaps been asked and also to volunteer information on other aspects of his character as he saw it then:

1. Concomitants of civilization without having my inferiors? Without the concomitants of insanity.
2. Light complex—fear of dark is very primitive—also in father. Probably a father fixation?
3. The ultimate death is the death of the will.
4. Use of associational thinking. (This is always misunderstood by the stupid.) It is a means of mental play, mental relaxation. My chief interest as a teacher and writer is keeping in what I call the foreground of contemporary consciousness. Now this is not confined only to poetry or prose but it is related to all the sciences, the arts, etc.—obviously, but it is *especially* the concern of the poet and the poetic sensibility. The poet is nothing if not aware. He has always had a toughness of spirit—the real poets, that is—Rimbaud, running to tropics, Corbière and pig—spiritual toughness.
5. If I have a complex, it's a full-life complex.
(There is no Number 6.)
7. Worked always in streaks. College routine—sleep in afternoon, always sleepy, now hardly ever sleepy—which is exactly what I wanted at last. A delayed physical development?
8. In the Crouse work, there is really a great social idea. Ex.: Hadfield and Cambridgeshire. As set up, can do the University and Michigan State a great deal of good.
9. Seeds of breakdown lay in question about a line of poetry.
10. What about letters received, use of telephone for personal calls, sun lamp?
11. Do you want evidence of teaching ability, etc.etc. can be procured very easily by writing to——
12. Find out about decision of Dean and others. Horror of being kept in suspense.
13. Gland hurts.
14. Cut on leg.
15. Routine in summer, life as a kid.
16. Riding on bus, always watching.
17. Reckless with destiny but now very careful of it.
18. Belly laughing a great deal.
19. My own self-analysis: Chidsey, Norton, and—
20. Mimetic.
21. Not an exhibitionist—really very shy. Only want to speak when paid or for a *real* reason.
22. Horror of random noise.

23. Almost complete reliance on intuitive judgment. Power in sister to detect frauds much higher.
24. Afraid of the city yet must be there.
25. Expressing aesthetically in words and sounds the problem of modern sensibility.
26. Can learn only obliquely. Hate classes with discussion and want only lectures or analysis of material. Love competition always.
27. Forget languages easily. Hate grammar.
28. Probably the happiest in this room in years.
29. Afraid of marriage, of what it will do to the girl, etc.etc.
30 and 31. (Illegible, blank.)
32. Room at Laf. (illegible) in relation to present habits.
(There are no Numbers 33, 34, 35, or 36.)
37. Frances Fox Institute. Care of hair also imprinted with relation to drinking. (?)
38. I resent anybody lying to me if I think they're lying to protect me for their good. (Two words more but illegible.)
39. (Two words illegible.) A poetic theme.
40. I have personal reasons to resume my contract at Mich. State, from standpoint of my previous record, etc. I will *not* return to Ann Arbor.
41. The woman in charge of freshman English (two words illegible) is responsible to my present condition and increases my desire to return home for a rest from these people.
42. I do not wish to go home for Christmas but wish to stay here. This is a very important decision.
Another No. 42 is crossed out but legible: Ask Mrs. Cannon to get Nijinsky's life.
43. Afraid of being localized in space, i.e. a particular place like W. E. Leonard in Madison. Question: What is the *name* of this? Hate some rooms in that sense, a victim of claustrophobia (sp)? Wasn't Dillinger a victim of this? Aren't many of the criminal leader types of this sort
44. Editing college catalogue—most nerve-wracking.

Then follow a few random notes:

Inextinguishable song
Compact of faith

We all fail
It depends on the scale

Rage cut the circle bare
Defines my proper sphere.

On January 17, 1936, Dr. Klingman wrote Professor W. W.
Johnston as follows:

My dear Prof. Johnston,
I am writing at the request of Mr. Theodore Roethke, with
reference to his recent illness, and I can frankly state that the
unfortunate excessive drinking was not the basis of his illness
but there was a basic nervous condition which eventually led to
a hypomania, which he attempted to control by stimulants such
as he took but failed. He is leaving the hospital today, apparently
completely recovered from the nervous condition.

Yours truly,

Theophil Klingman

Meanwhile, the problem of paying the bill struck June Roethke
with greater force than it did Ted. In the interval between Sparrow
and Mercywood, he told his mother not to worry, that he would
take care of any bills out of his pay because he expected to be
teaching when the term began after New Year's. This expectation
was disappointed in his interview with Professor Johnston. When
he entered Mercywood and found that the charges would run
between $125 and $150 a week, he still was not greatly alarmed—
he counted on "Pa" Crouse, who once had suffered a mental epi-
sode similar to Ted's and had himself committed to a state hospital.
At first J. R. Crouse indicated that he might pay all the charges.
Later, however, after thinking it over, he decided to pay only a
part of them because he thought Ted's family should come for-
ward. These matters were settled between June Roethke and
Robert Crouse and his wife. J. R. Crouse did not want his name
mentioned at all in this connection because he feared that Mercy-
wood would triple the rates if they knew Ted had a rich man
backing him. In the end, J. R. Crouse gave Ted $375, which Ted
accepted as payment for the work he had done on the history of
the Hartland Area Project.

In answer to Dr. Klingman's letter of January 17, 1936, Professor
Johnston wrote him on January 20:

My dear Dr. Klingman:
I have just received your letter of January 17, and wish to

thank you for writing me in regard to Mr. Theodore Roethke. I am glad to know that Mr. Roethke has apparently recovered from the nervous condition.

Doubtless by this time he has been permitted to see the letter written him by Dean Emmons in which he was told that he had been granted leave of absence without pay for the winter and spring term. Toward the close of the fall term the administration reached the conclusion that it would be impossible for Mr. Roethke to take up his teaching at the beginning of the winter term, and as it was necessary that the classes be met, the decision was to employ someone in his place but to make it possible for him to return to his work at the beginning of next fall if by that time he had fully recovered.

Very sincerely yours,

W. W. Johnston
Head of Department

When the ineffable falsity of the sentence "he had been granted leave of absence" be considered, it is easy to see how the combination of Johnston and Emmons would be too much for Ted. No one ever petitions to be given a leave of absence without pay, especially in the midst of the worst depression the republic has ever known; hence it is incorrect to say one was "granted." It is a fumbling attempt to preserve the academic amenities, that is all. Johnston was a nice man by all accounts, a vegetarian, a respecter of all life like a Jain in India, who would not step on an angleworm, who would terrify his passengers by nearly throwing his car into a ditch to avoid a sitting squirrel. But his respect for life seems to have shown itself only in not killing it.

While Ted was in the hospital, Johnston pried into Ted's past with an electric energy. He wrote letters to Tupper, Noyes, Strauss, in fact all the men who had recommended Ted, asking about insanity in the family, other mental attacks Ted might have had, and his drinking. (This was faintly insulting since it insinuated that their earlier enthusiastic recommendations had been mendacious.) Professor Tupper's reply contains one paragraph of great interest:

Since my last letter to you I have learned that during my absence on sabbatical he had an attack not very unlike the one you describe but not so violent. It occurred at the house of one of his colleagues and was kept so quiet that very few knew about it and I learned about it only by questioning one of my friends who was Roethke's host.

Since Professor Tupper is dead and no one still at Lafayette knows who Ted's host was, I have been unable to learn anything more.

As an example of the kind of mind Ted had to cope with, the kind that made him bristle with suspicion of all academics, I quote in full a letter which he never saw, written November 22, 1935, to Professor Johnston from the University of Michigan. Since the writer hides behind the Shakespearean pseudonum of "Nym," I don't know who he was.

Dear Pistol,
    First I shall set down for you such data as I have gathered regarding R.
    A. As far as I have been able to ascertain, there is no insanity in his family.
    B. There seems to have been a struggle on the part of the mother to rule the boy's destiny. He resented this. How far the experience bit into his nature, I don't know. It may have something to do with the Byronic glower which he often carried on his face. This expression, I understand, could quickly turn to one of sunny sweetness.
    C. His heart's desire seemed to be first to write and second to teach. He thinks of himself as a writer.
    D. He could never take discipline gracefully here, and left a record full of holes. He was granted his degree, I understand, not because of his having done his academic work successfully, but because it seemed a shame to hold him back, a shame in view of his other unusual abilities.
    E. At Lafayette College he seemed to have an unusual success with students. He has the power of magnetizing them, of drawing them to worship him. But his work there was conditioned by his tendency to use drink.
    F. Drink he does. The report is that he drinks heavily, and that the habit has tended to make him rapidly gross. I mean gross in appearance. At Philadelphia last year, he was badly drunk.
    These are the things I have gathered. My regret is that I do not myself know the man. I feel helpless to give you the information that might be of most use to you.
    Needless to say I am dreadfully sorry about this thing's having happened. I am sorry because R. is a Michigan man, and because

he was recommended to you by a Michigan man. I am sorry, too, to think of the concern you must feel in dealing with the case. Too bad! Too bad!

Lloyd Emmons dropt in to see me the other day—just after I had left my office. I trust that he had not come to see me on this case.

Pistol, the more I see of this little world, the more I value the plain virtues. I get sick to death of brilliance, sophistication, dramatic show, egotism, envy, and selfishness. Those qualities play all about; but a little wholesome honesty seems to me to be worth them all, and more. Kindness is, of course, the great thing. But what need does it have outside itself? Then, too, doesn't a little home-made self-respect feel good in a man's gizzard? . . .

Kindness is the great thing, sure enough. The writer could hardly have been unaware of the damage a letter like this would do to any man's professional reputation. The record, for instance, shows that Ted did not fail to do his academic work successfully but that he was elected to Phi Beta Kappa and was graduated with honors. It would have been a kindness tinged with a little wholesome honesty to have looked up the record instead of depending on hearsay or imagination.

Professor Johnston also ordered his instructors to question the members of Ted's classes as the following memorandum shows:

INTER-DEPARTMENTAL CORRESPONDENCE

MEMORANDUM   DATE Nov. 21
TO Professor Johnston
FROM W. B. Moffett

At your suggestion I questioned a number of boys in Mr. Roethke's ten o'clock class. Three different groups assured me that they had observed no sign of his "nervousness" before the Monday class—his last one. I also asked if they felt that any of the girls had been frightened by his strangeness; they agreed that no such alarm had been evident. All Student inquiries about his condition seemed to me to be kindly and sympathetic.

SIGNED W. B. Moffett

After he was discharged from Mercywood, Ted went home to Saginaw. He nearly, through Professor Strauss's good offices, got a part-time job at the University of Michigan, but this fell through

and Ted thought that he was waiting out the academic year until
the fall of 1936 when he could resume teaching at Michigan State.
However, Michigan State had other plans and they waited until
well into the spring to reveal them. Some time after the middle of
April Ted received this letter from Dean Emmons, dated April 14:

> Dear Mr. Roethke,
>
> We are trying to complete our budget arrangements for the
> coming year at this time and are, therefore, making several
> readjustments in the personnel of the various departments.
>
> After giving mature consideration to the question of your re-
> turning to the staff of the English Department, we have decided
> that it will be better both for you and the College if your ap-
> pointment for the coming year is not renewed.
>
> I hope that you have completely recovered in health and that
> you may succeed in securing a satisfactory position.
>
>   Very truly yours,
>   L.C.E. (signed)
>   Lloyd C. Emmons
>   Dean of Liberal Arts

Quite aside from the endemic fear of poverty then and that the
blot on his copybook might keep him permanently out of an
academic position, the bland, inhumane, euphemistic indirection
of this letter must have made him grind his teeth. There was
nothing for him to do but to begin the weary business of applying
for another job.

The reasons Ted circulated as the causes of his stay at Sparrow
and Mercywood are many and various. He seems to have con-
sidered himself still engaged to Mary Kunkel for he wrote her that
he was at Mercywood taking a "real rest" over the holidays so as to
get himself into the best physical and mental condition for her pro-
tection and for their families' protection. (He does not seem to
have realized how ominous this last phrase was.) He said there
was no great mystery about his going to the hospital—he had
nearly ruined himself in a mad attempt to go without sleep, work
hard on everything, eat only one or two meals because he was so
intent on "this experiment" he was making in his classes. To Rolfe
Humphries he wrote that the reason for his stay was his own
stupidity in suddenly trying to live "a pure and industrious life all
of a sudden." He had over a hundred students in his classes and he

said that the teaching, the student conferences, reading, running in the country to build up wind, and trying to go without sleep landed him in the hospital. It will be noticed that the causes he gives to both his friends are perfectly rational.

Nine years later, when the perspective of time had made the episode manageable in his mind, he told me this story:

> For no reason I started to feel very good. Suddenly I knew how to enter into the life of everything around me. I knew how it felt to be a tree, a blade of grass, even a rabbit. I didn't sleep much. I just walked around with this wonderful feeling. One day I was passing a diner and all of a sudden I knew what it felt like to be a lion. I went into the diner and said to the counter-man, "Bring me a steak. Don't cook it. Just bring it." So he brought me this raw steak and I started eating it. The other customers made like they were revolted, watching me. And I began to see that maybe it *was* a little strange. So I went to the Dean and said, "I feel too good. Get me down off this." So they put me into the tubs.

This was a version he felt he could tell but whether it actually happened, I have no way of knowing.

After he had married he told his wife that this first episode had been self-induced "to reach a new level of reality." Both Peter De Vries and John Clark, as they looked back on it, felt the same thing. There seemed to have been a deliberateness in his behavior that autumn, and his drinking and pill taking seemed to have a purpose. Perhaps he was trying an experiment in his classes but he did not say what it was or why he needed a new emotional thrust to make it. Later, at Penn State, in conversation with William Haag, he mentioned Rimbaud's *"derèglement de tous les sens"* approvingly, saying it was one way of breaking out of one's self, but at this time, at Michigan State, it is doubtful if he had read Rimbaud.

He had many later episodes and under treatment, he was diagnosed by his psychiatrists as a "manic-depressive neurotic, but not typical," as a "manic-depressive psychotic, but not typical," and as a "paranoid schizophrenic." Each of the psychiatrists told me that one of the characteristics of manic-depressive patients was their insistence that they brought their attacks on themselves.

The actual causes of these states are unknown. A few years ago psychiatrists attributed them to purely psychic traumata, often occurring very early in life. Now there is a tendency to view them as biological, possibly enzyme changes in the nervous system, but nothing is definitely known. It is also possible that a patient's environment, if it seems unfavorable, may exert a pressure on him and that this pressure may institute biological changes that cause an episode.

If this is so, it is not clear just what particular stresses Ted was suffering from in the fall of 1935. He had taken a new job, true, but he had undergone much the same situation at Lafayette without mishap. While he missed seeing Mary Kunkel, the tone of his letters to her does not suggest a man driven to the edges of sanity by her absence. He published two poems, "Feud" and "Prayer," in *The New Republic* in 1935 but both appeared before he came to work at Michigan State. In 1936 he published three poems in May, June, and July, "Genesis," "Long Live the Weeds," and "Open House." The standard he set himself made his poems come very hard and composition was an emotional drain on him but he does not seem to have been writing much poetry during the fall of 1935. The 1936 poems seem to be products of that year, done after he had been discharged from Mercywood and was living at home in Saginaw.

There is another possibility, remote but perhaps operative: in the early fall of 1935, Ted received a public and favorable criticism of his poetry. (It was not the first critical notice he had been given. That came in the November, 1934, issue of *The American Poetry Journal*, which printed eight poems of Ted's, followed by a commentary written by John Holmes, a fine poet, then an instructor at Tufts College, who had been a great friend of Ted's at Harvard.) The 1935 essay, however, was much more laudatory and it was written by a poet whom Ted looked up to, Louise Bogan. It came about in this way: in March, 1934, there had been an exchange of letters between Ted and Ann Winslow, the Executive Secretary of the College Poetry Society of America at Berkeley, California. She was planning an anthology of the verse of thirty young poets with an essay appended to each poet's work written by a reputable critic, men of the stature of Malcolm Cowley, Allen Tate, Horace Gregory, and R. P. Blackmur. She had asked Archibald MacLeish to do the one on Ted's work, but she seemed to be unsure of his acceptance and, without knowing that Ted already knew Rolfe Humphries, she wondered if Humphries would be a suitable substitute. In the end, Miss Bogan, probably at Humphries' suggestion wrote the essay on Ted. It was full of high praise and it must have pleased Ted for he had many copies made of Miss Bogan's essay which he circulated among his friends. What connection this inclusion of his poems in an anthology and these laudatory remarks by a prominent poet would have with his illness, how they could have caused or stimulated it, is not immediately apparent. However, Dr. Ian Shaw, one of the psychiatrists who examined Ted years later in Seattle, said that the periods after Ted had been awarded a prize (and he won a great many) were nearly always the worst times because Ted did not feel he deserved them. His pervasive sense of guilt made him feel unworthy within himself and this went simultaneously with a public show of pride and pleasure. It is just possible, therefore, that this first bout of illness may have arisen from the conditions set by Miss Bogan's praise.

Granting these obscure psycho-biological processes, the very qualities that made Ted a poet seem to have been the ones that made him ill, his sensibility and his energy. It is hard to imagine anyone learning how to be energetic or learning how to have sensibility. They seem to be inherited. If the poems are any proof of the strength of his memory, and I think they are, he was born with the sensibility. His native energy seems to have piled up inside him as a result of the abrasions of his youthful environment, an energy of resentment, rage, and fear, and to have been released by the shock of his father's death.

In many ways, Ted as a young man was a typical American of his generation. No member of a Junior Chamber of Commerce was more ambitious or more willing to work hard to attain his ambition. Saginaw was responsible for this set of mind and the *Tüchtigkeit* of his own family tradition. He was like the boy who sets out to be President—if he could not write the best poetry of his time, it was not worth writing any. Long before he had read Yeats and learned anything of his laborious methods of composition, Ted had rejected the notion of poetry that was current in schools and colleges then, that it comes easily in a burst of inspiration. He always thought his mind worked slowly and he knew without anyone telling him that if he had any talent at all, something no beginner can know, it would take years of effort, frustration, and technical experiment to bring it out. Until he made his final reconciliations in *The Far Field,* his career seems to have been an act of defiance, the poet as criminal, defying the hobbles of bourgeois custom, denying the ghostly expectations of his father and his family, these acts eliciting simultaneously a stupendous energy and God knows how much guilt.

His father's death was the most important thing that ever happened to him. Many youths can accept the deaths of fathers with some toughness and what grief they suffer does not rankle, but not Ted. The ambiguity of their relationship entangled his whole life at fourteen. (His mother supplied merely the conditions of that life, a much subtler influence that was to color his relations with women later.) The love and fear he felt for Otto Roethke were the deepest emotions he ever had and his complex feelings for nature were tied to his father, almost as if Otto working Ted in the greenhouse and taking him fishing and for long walks in the woods, had created the woods, the lakes, and the carnations. Ted once wrote in a letter that he had had "murderous" feelings toward his father. Many boys wish their fathers dead, not necessarily because of any Oedipal involutions, merely in a resentful flare-up after they have been slapped or beaten, but few have their fathers die with what must have seemed a dreadful promptness afterward. Ted would still have been enough of a boy at thirteen to fear that he had obscurely caused his death, and, even if he hadn't, the juxtaposition in his life of the wish and the dying would have been enough to make him guilty forever. His family wanted him to be a lawyer, and his entry into the Michigan Law School seems to have been a temporary accession to their wishes, but only temporary, for soon after that he wilfully and disobediently took up poetry, a career that his father could hardly have foreseen. How was Ted to explain this to him, being dead?

Otto Roethke seems to have been a lifelong presence in his son's mind. (Consider the vividness in *The Far Field* of "Otto," a poem written when Ted was past fifty years old.) He was a judge who could be wistfully appealed to but who could give no answer, render no decisions, and this may account for some of the persistent ambiguities. If, when Ted received praise or awards, he suffered privately because he did not think he deserved them, the suffering may have come from a fear that his father would have disapproved. (It is hard to believe that, had he lived, Otto Roethke would have disapproved of his son's winning a Pulitzer Prize, but all clocks stopped at his death and Ted could only remember him as he had known him.) At the same time Ted could see how his friends praised and envied his honors and publicly he could relish the acclaim. But he could always torment himself with the question: which was real, the blame or the praise? In fact, which was he, the disobedient son or the triumphant prize winner? It is not easy to live with such questions and this may explain why he could never gain honors enough, why, toward the end of his life he was looking toward the Nobel Prize. Perhaps one more might appease his father.

I am personally quite willing to believe that the episode at Michigan State Ted brought on himself. If he were to justify himself before his father, he would have had to re-create the world of woods and greenhouse his father had made for him (if only to show he could do it, to make himself equal); and if he hoped to break free entirely, to re-create himself in a mode he himself preferred, not that of the boy grown into a lawyer, but as a great poet, he was willing to use himself as a mine, to dig out, identify, and make images of his emotions, however painful, and follow, however tediously, the ramifications and possibilities of every metaphor before he could safely use it, to worry the beat and syntax of his sentences into an acceptable shape. And since the great poets whom he hoped to equal or surpass were then always ahead of him, none of his labors was enough. He thought he needed a new place to stand, a new way of looking at things, and he was willing to abuse his body to refresh his spirit.

Since, in Ted's individual case, there were obvious strains and pressures, both inner and outer, that preceded the later episodes, it may well be that these stimulated the biological changes that sent him into his manic states. The signs were obvious. It was as if a change in his metabolism occurred and his whole life moved to a more intense level, psychically and physiologically. He became increasingly excited, simultaneously cheerful and alarmed, eager to talk and talking incessantly, and full of extravagant projects. He indulged in eccentricities of dress like wearing three pairs of trousers at once, rubbers when it was not raining, sandals in the snow, and he had an old unblocked Borsalino hat with a wide brim he wore at such times. He would make dozens of phone calls to friends all over the country or even abroad—he liked to think himself rich during these times, rich and powerful. He slept little. In Seattle when he was persuaded to go to a hospital, he regarded himself as terribly strong, a kind of Superman, and once said to the attendants on entry, "You'd better tie me down, give me a mouth gag—I took on five docs at the last place."

In some of his attacks, he remained disoriented for some time. In others, after the initial sedation and the first few days of rest, he usually became quiet and rational and took an intelligent interest in the treatment as his ebullience dwindled. Dr. Horton says that he had an immediate rapport with other mental patients, no matter what their disorder. He had long talks with them and made them his friends. After these talks, Dr. Horton says, "He could always tell us the dynamics of the case. We would have hammered out a diagnosis in staff meetings. Ted would talk to the guy for half an hour, come in, and tell me exactly what his trouble was." When friends from outside the sanitarium visited him, Ted would introduce them seriously and without condescension to his new friends on the inside. (In his papers, there is a pathetic letter from Al "Silver" Buckles, recalling the old days in the hospital, and enclosing some rhymes he had written and thought Ted would be interested in.)

Ted always said, "I'm at my best when I'm slightly depressed," but his depressed periods were brief and shallow and seem to have been caused by exhaustion as much as anything else. Virginia Woolf was also diagnosed as a manic-depressive, but depression, suicidal depression, was where she lived and her manic phases were short, hectic, and terrible.

There is another feature of Ted's illnesses that seems atypical. He did not stop writing. He worked continually and many of his poems were written in hospitals.

During his "high" phases, he played three roles, the big businessman, founder of corporations and cartels; the big political manipulator; or he was the gangster, the friend of the Mob, the Syndicate, or sometimes their prey. These roles were not as sharply separated as I have made them in the interests of clarity, but it should be noticed that they were all figures of power in the community.

As an example of the temper of his mind at these times, I can

set down a letter he wrote me from St. Brigid's Hospital, Ballina-
sloe, County Galway, Ireland, September 12, 1960. (His first lines
show his reluctance to admit that he was mentally upset in any
way.)

Dear Allan,

Don't get your hopes up. I'm not here by grace of the peelers
—only for general check-up and minor surgery on varicose veins.

We've been jumping around with the local gentry. What a
country! The drunker you get, the bigger you are here. Brendan
Behan, of course, is now a has-been. There's a gin here called
Seager's. I'm trying to get a sign for your desk (of it.) (Pa.
Dutch syntax.)

What do you want in life, big stuff? You want a piece 1/10 no
more of a smash satirical review me and Hellman are co-
producing: words *and* music by me, "The Spittoon Song," "The
Saginaw Song," "The Song of the Devious Spielers," Etc. All
Irish cast with the last of the great pub-singers, James Coigne,
Bernard Tierney (the comic), and young Desmond O'Halloran
—these guys are uncorrupted by mannerisms, BBC, TV, bullshit.
Only 10 in the cast including me and the old lady who appears in
a couple of numbers, one skit, "On the Beach at La Boule" and a
modelling routine.

I don't do *all* music and words. Douglas Moore of ASCAP has
done one ballad and Bernard Tierney has a variation of "Mac-
Namara's Band." This isn't just bar-room talk, mac. Some num-
bers have been rehearsed until we're black in the face.

The damn thing will have speed, style, chi-chi—low budget,
no scenery—just goofy props, etc.

End of sales pitch. You can come in in units of $500—deposit
to account of Lamb Enterprises, Bank of California, Seattle, or
into my personal account there and you'll get a receipt from me.
But this aint arm-twisting—so another matter.

I wouldn't mention this to anyone else, possibly except the
schnooks out in Washington.

$64 question:

Could a ticket of Stevenson #1, Truman #2, and Old Lady
Roosevelt as Sec'y of State possibly win? Does the law say
Truman couldn't run for VP? If so, it's insane.

Other Items.

1. Fire Hoover and his top ten aides.
2. William A.C. Roethke as labor guy. Is that bastard tough *and*

powerful. His clients, Siegel, Cohen, everything on the West
Coast. Also NBC, ABC.

3. Chas. Odegaard as Sec'y of Commerce.
4. Archie MacLeish—Italy.
5. Seager & Roethke—Ambassadors to Russia and Eire.
6. Richard Wilbur and his wife to France.
   Warner G. Rice as Librarian of Congress.

Kick it around. It's the best political idea I've ever had.

> Love to Baba and Mary,
> Rattle-ass Roethke

Behind this would be: *Newsweek, N Yer, Esquire,* possibly
Atlantic Monthly. Kennedy can be beaten; or at least taught some
manners, the rich-Irish punk.

Since he always viewed everything ambiguously, even at the
best of times, with a kind of double vision, acting and judging the
act simultaneously, it is difficult to tell whether he means what he
says here, whether it is all fantasy, or, better, a joke. Certainly no
such satirical review ever hit the boards but he actually had
formed a corporation called Lamb Enterprises. Since he wrote a
similar political letter to *The Atlantic Monthly* as well as to
Robert Lowell, the campaign was much on his mind, and perhaps
he intended his plan to be taken seriously. His grudging praise of
his cousin, Bud, "labor guy") presages the eventual sinking of his
hatred for him and a reconciliation. However, his selection of
Charles Odegaard as Secretary of Commerce seems to contain ele-
ments of satire—Odegaard is President of the University of Wash-
ington. Professor Warner G. Rice was one of the teachers he had
admired at the University of Michigan, and at the time this letter
was written, Rice was acting both as head of the English Depart-
ment and as head of the General Library.

It is conceivable that after a stretch of hard work at poetry or a
period of domestic or social strain, he wanted a vacation, that a
hospital or sanitarium where he would be taken care of by
strangers to whom he owed nothing, where he could take off his
mask, where he could be utterly irresponsible, looked good to him,
not consciously, more with a side glance of his mind. In such a
place he could toy with the versions of himself he might have
become had he not become a poet, the rejected careers. His essen-
tial ambition could not allow them to be any but figures of wealth

and power and influence, but acting them out in a place where his actions could have few or no consequences may have been a form of sly play, partly or even wholly deliberate. He always retained a hold on objective reality, tenuous but present, and if a doctor found him spinning out some fantastic scheme and said to him, "Cut it out, Ted," he would cut it out and burst into laughter like a child caught stealing cookies.

Perhaps the final word should come from the psychiatrists who treated him since they will be accepted as the most trustworthy. Ted visited Dr. William Hoffer several times in London. Dr. Hoffer is a highly cultivated man, a pupil of Freud's, and he was greatly impressed by Ted both as a man and by his poetry. Ted told me once that Hoffer was the best psychiatrist he ever had. I asked him, why? He said, "Hoffer said, 'So you're a great poet, so you suffer.'" I told Ted he liked Hoffer only because he called him a great poet and he laughed. However, Dr. Hoffer elaborated his statement further to me, "I think his troubles were merely the running expenses he paid for being his kind of poet." Given the intensity of his vocation and the emotional costs of his methods of work, Dr. Hoffer seems to be saying that Ted's troubles were inevitable. And the first psychiatrist who ever treated him, Dr. Theophil Klingman of Mercywood Sanitarium said, "You can't cure a personality."

But all these conjectures may be false. The source may have lain in the chemistries of his blood and nerves.

Whatever the causes, he did not stop working when he was ill. His friends, his doctors, and his notebooks all attest to this. Well or ill, he wrote poetry or took notes for poetry nearly every day of his adult life. Poetry was the central fact of his life, and everything else, his states of mind, his friendships, enmities, his loves and hatreds, even his amusements, clung to it like filings to a magnet.

VIII

The First Book

After his discharge from Mercywood Sanitarium, Ted spent the spring and summer of 1936 at home in Saginaw, much of the time, since his sister was at the University of Michigan, alone with his ailing mother. He fired the furnace, shoveled the snow off the walk, and did other household chores. He played badminton a few times at the YMCA and once he had a date, a fiasco, for he wrote Peter De Vries, "God, maybe I'm just a poor soured intellectual, but it does seem that the average female has a mental life of a turtle." He continued to read miscellaneously—he was always reading—and it was not to acquire a fund of general knowledge; rather, like most writers, he abstracted and kept only what concerned him and let the rest slide out of his memory. He mentions the poetry of Léonie Adams; Tolstoi's *War and Peace;* the letters of Gerard Manly Hopkins to Robert Bridges; the English Literature of the seventeenth century in the *Cambridge History;* a novel by P. G. Wodehouse, *The Last of the Bodkins,* which he said was only fair. He said he was going to try out for a local baseball team when the spring finally came—he fancied himself as a pitcher.

He was not cheerful. Michigan weather is enough to depress anyone in the wintertime but he may well have been suffering a depression that followed his manic behavior at Lansing and Mercywood. His situation was, however, enough to worry anyone, convalescent or not. With his well-founded suspicion of academics, he was worried about his job, and with his mother aging and unwell, his sister still in college, and, granted his unthinking loyalty to them, a loyalty that operated regardless of affection as a duty he had to fulfill, he could easily foresee that he might have to support his mother for the rest of his life, and this might rob him of what is most precious to any writer—time in which to work.

He seems to have sunk into a gloomy stagnancy of mind which shows in his letters. He signs one, "Butch (Behind the 8-Ball) Roethke." In another he says, "I've been involved with gloom, a cold, a bum throat, and perplexing problems." In a third, "My inner life aint been much of late. And as for the great world of Saginaw—that is too harsh a reality to be faced." In another, "I've had a very gloomy and ineffectual week. Really did. Don't know what's the matter but I seem to have lost my drive."

About the middle of February, the Macmillan Company wrote and asked him if he had enough poems to make a book. He said he did not intend to submit a manuscript for at least two years. To feel that he had to say this must have depressed him further. He would be twenty-eight in May (and there is always that devil, Keats, dead at twenty-five.) True, his work had been printed in "the best magazines" and he had the sense of his own abilities a man of talent always has, but he seemed slow to himself and he knew he did not have a bookful of poems that would satisfy either himself or the critics.

By March 30, Ted had finished the reviews of three books for Malcolm Cowley which were printed in *The New Republic* during the summer: *Ideas of Order* by Wallace Stevens, *A Spectacle for Scholars* by Winifred Welles, and *This Modern Poetry* by Babette Deutsch. The completion of these essays shows that his mind was not completely flaccid but, then, he did not regard book reviewing as work in the way poetry was work.

After April 14 he received Dean Emmons's letter severing his connection with Michigan State and it must have seemed that the bottom had dropped out of everything, the poetry not coming and no job.

On May 25 he wrote Louise Bogan,

> . . . Just twenty-eight years ago little Theodore came into the world. Touching, isn't it? I've never really thought much about the passage of time over my flesh but this time it really gets me down. Twenty-eight and what have I done? No volume out and I can't seem to write anything. You can say what you want but *place* does have a lot to do with productivity. Hell, I don't care

what happens to me, whether I go nuts or my entrails hang out
but I can't stand being mindless and barren as I've been.

The *place* that had a lot to do with productivity was Saginaw, of
course. He had no one there to talk to about his work except during
rare visits from Peter De Vries, A. J. M. Smith, and John Clark.
Jobless and barren, marooned in the hot, flat Saginaw Valley, it
must have seemed to him that the world was elsewhere, his world,
the world of the poet. He managed to make a trip to New York
during the early summer where he saw Mary Kunkel, Rolfe Hum-
phries, and Louise Bogan. He also went to the tenth anniversary
party of the *New Yorker* magazine. Louis Untermeyer was also a
guest but Ted said he was too shy to go up and speak to him.

He had been writing letters all the spring, trying to get a teach-
ing post. On July 20, 1936, he wrote one more to Professor Theo-
dore Gates, the head of the Department of English Composition,
at Pennsylvania State College, and his application was accepted.
The fears that he would never work in an academic community
again were at last dispelled. Professor Gates told me, "I wanted
young fellows with ink in their blood. Roethke had won one of
those Hopwood Prizes at Michigan and he had published a good
many poems. I was favorably impressed with him." Ted had not
won a Hopwood Prize at Michigan. The prizes drawn from most of
a bequest from Avery Hopwood's will, which also provided for
the care of an aging green parrot, were not instituted until 1932,
over a year after Ted had left Ann Arbor. However, there is hardly
any doubt that he *would* have won a poetry prize if he had been
there. He knew this and so he had no compunctions about telling
Professor Gates that the award had been a fact.

Again this shy young man was faced with a new milieu. He had
to pack up, a monumental task for he could never travel light, don
his mask of tough camaraderie, make the journey, find a place to
live, assess his students, and, always withholding his deepest feel-
ings, try to discover colleagues whose minds he could respect,
whom he could talk to and drink with, and—this becomes part of
the pattern of his life from now on—to meet a girl he could fall in
love with. Once thus settled, he could work.

Penn State was to Pennsylvania what Michigan State was to
Michigan, chiefly an agricultural and engineering college and not

a bastion of the liberal arts. When Ted arrived there, State College was a town of about four thousand people and there was no industry, nothing there but the college. It is situated in almost the geographical center of the state in the Nittany Valley with the Seven Mountains to the Northwest and Bald Ridge to the south and east. It is beautiful country.

The college buildings are mostly of brick, grey or pink, and there is an alley of superb elms leading to the library which houses a collection of the writings of Joseph Priestley, the Englishman, once a resident of Pennsylvania, who founded the science of chemistry.

Ted took a room on the fourth, the top floor of the University Club on West College Avenue. It is a big building of pink brick with four huge white pillars in front. It is also next to the college power plant whose humming and puffing used to enrage Ted when he was trying to write. He immediately and effortlessly turned his quarters into a mess, so much so that any guest had to stand patiently until Ted cleared a chair for him to sit on, so much so that Ted refused to let the maid into it for the weekly cleaning—she would leave the clean sheets outside the door. It was in this room that Ted lost a pair of trousers and hotly accused everyone in sight of theft. A couple of years later when he was deep in the Augean labor of moving out, he found the trousers buried on a desk. He realized quite early that he was an itinerant and so did not attach himself to any of the rooms, apartments, or houses he lived in until he was married and living in Morris Graves's beautiful house in Seattle, but he could make himself comfortable and he liked the "U" Club moderately—they had a ping-pong table where he could play when the weather was wrong for tennis.

His students in the mass did not impress him, either with their backgrounds, their aims, or their eagerness to learn although there were individuals like David Wagoner whom he inspired and cherished. Most of them were going to be farmers, engineers of one kind or another, or scientists, and what he was supposed to teach them was Argumentation which prepared them, presumably, to write a coherent business letter or logical briefs for the debating team or legal cases. It is dry stuff to teach and Professor Gates says he was bored at first by having to correct freshman themes, but later he became extremely conscientious and loaded the margins with acute comments. In class he could not resist trying to light a fire under his students. He found ways to bootleg literature into his classes and make them aware of poetry. (After Philip Shelley arrived in 1939 to teach German, he and Ted were permitted to give a course in literature together, Shelley doing Rilke, and Ted doing Yeats and Auden.) On fine days he would leave the classroom and take his students out under the trees on the lawn, and this was considered rather daring. Soon he was well-known as a teacher and this meant to every student—the campus was that small. One day he snarled at a torpid class, "You've heard of casting pearls before swine, haven't you? Come on, you must have. Well, those were metaphorical pearls before metaphorical swine. But what *I'm* doing is casting real pearls before real swine." When the College started a building program, he said, "Penn State has an edifice complex." Professor Gates said of him, "He was one of my prima donnas. He used to bring poems to read me, his own things, but my tastes were formed too much earlier and I couldn't understand a word of them and I told him so." Gates liked him. He stirred the place up.

The "U" Club offered housing for bachelors and two of them, Steven Baldanza and Arthur Douropolos, were on the staff of the English Department. Ted became friends with them. He used to play tennis with Douropolos who was about half Ted's size and who would wait patiently, standing on the baseline, for Ted to beat himself by losing his temper. "That cagy God-damned Greek, I could kill him!" Ted would roar at the onlookers. Baldanza and Douropolos were as witty as Ted and they kept up a continual kidding of one another. When Ted's first book, *Open House,* came out and was on sale at the local bookstores, Baldanza did a sketch of Ted for a window display. When someone complimented him on it, he said, "Well, it's the best I could do with a sow's ear." Ted probably saw more of these two than any other single men.

Professor Lyne Hoffman lived across the hall from Ted at the "U" Club. He said Ted was moody and he was never sure, when they emerged from their rooms simultaneously, whether Ted was going to speak or not. This carelessness with the social amenities involved Ted in an amusing contretemps. He was a friend of Professor John Galbraith. Galbraith coached swimming. He had been a diver and Ted always respected athletes. Customarily Galbraith passed down a corridor in one of the classroom buildings every morning with an instructor named Gaskill. Gaskill was not a big man but he had fought amateur at 145 pounds. He would always say, "Hi, Ted," as they passed and Ted would merely grunt at him. This got under his skin and he grumbled to Galbraith, "If that big so-and-so doesn't speak to me, I'll. . . ." The next day Ted grunted at him again. Gaskill grabbed him by the lapels, and slammed him, as big as he was, against the wall and shouted, "God-damn it, speak to me. Don't grunt at me like a god-damned pig!" The next day when the passed, Ted said, "Hi, Bill" to Gaskill and grunted at Galbraith to whom he had always said, "Hi, Jack."

One day Ted found Galbraith standing by an open window in his office. He said he was trying to identify a bird song outside. "It's a vireo," Ted said at once and went on with great earnestness talking about birds, all kinds of birds, for maybe fifteen minutes but he broke off, saying, "Aw, shit, who wants to know about birds anyhow?" The mask had slipped for a moment, revealing the curious tenderness that was always there beneath, but he clapped it on again firmly.

After he arrived from Harvard in 1939, Philip Shelley became a good friend of Ted's and he took a flat in the Glennland Apartments where Ted lived after he moved out of the "U" Club. In a joint effort, he and Ted arranged to have W. H. Auden come and give a reading. Ted had been reading Auden's work for some time and he was very excited about meeting him. The year was 1941 and Auden came and stayed ten days. He says he and Ted hit it off at once and they remained friends. Although boxing was not at all in either Auden's or Shelley's line, Ted took them to see some College boxing matches.

Ted had many married friends on the faculty of whom Mr. and Mrs. Edward Nichols, Mr. and Mrs. Harold Graves, and Mr. and Mrs. Philip Aston were probably the ones he knew best. Graves was a professor of English and Aston of Physics, while Nichols was on the English staff. He was a novelist, a jazz enthusiast who wrote an appreciation of Bix Beiderbecke for a collection called *Jazzmen*, and it was through him that Ted first met David Wagoner, who was in the Navy V-12 program. In a recent letter Mr. Nichols gives some sharp insights into Ted's social life:

> My wife and I probably knew Ted as well as any of his married friends in State College. For one thing, my wife as chief department secretary used to type some of his material, and later

as an instructor saw him often around the office. This meant that
Ted knew us both well, which I think made him freer with us
than he might have been with other couples. Certainly we were
no intellectual outlet for him. He accepted our ignorance of
poetry, in spite of my B from Edith Rickert at Chicago about
which I kept boasting. The result for Ted was as much relaxation
as he was likely to have found anywhere else, compared with
personality difficulties he periodically ran into with others. The
friends who took him most seriously as a poet—and he deserved
to be taken seriously as a poet—ran into the hazard of having
Ted act like a poet, or sometimes worse, play his anti-poet role.
So the charm and wit my wife and I could enjoy in Ted was less
evident for them.

The Roethke that Ciardi was recalling in the *Saturday Review*
"obit," and that friends like the late Wilder Hobson so enjoyed
was the Roethke who would cook you steaks or veal scallopini,
messing the hell out of your kitchen but filling the rest of your
house with mad fun. We always liked his gorilla act, when he'd
go listing around a room with his long arms, hands cupped up-
ward, in a Tarzan swing. One time, after he and Beatrice were at
Bennington, and in the middle of a jazz session (on a visit to
State College) I tried to imitate his act, weaving around with
"I'm the best god-damned poet in the world!" Ted broke in with
a soft polite smile, "No, Edward, only in America." This was the
Roethke who could be so much fun and who could build up such
a store of affection in you that even when he was down (and
nobody at large could be downer) you were willing to drive into
town in response to a moody phone call at one A.M., pick him up,
bring him out, make him drinks, let him fester a while over the
lack of appreciation shown him by the department and the uni-
versity—in both of which he was dead right—then play him a
few sides of his favorite Beiderbeckes and early Armstrongs, and
finally a little-known record by a Chauncey Morehouse group
with George Brunis on trombone, which Ted always drooled
over. Well, my wife and I were never much good the day after,
but it seemed to help Ted. It was more like him to come in the
office singing *On the Alamo*.

Ted also saw a good deal of Philip Aston and his wife. Mrs.
Aston gave him a first edition of Eliot's *The Waste Land* and
earned Ted's perpetual gratitude. She noticed Ted's concern with
hands. He always noticed a woman's hands and urged her to take

care of them and he took care of his own. One day he came to help the Astons dig dandelions out of their lawn, bringing a bottle of Old Overholt rye, and a pair of gloves which he wore until the dandelions were dug. Mrs. Aston saw him socially discomfited only once. At a party he spotted a pretty girl, lumbered over to her, took her chin in his hand, and gazed down into her eyes. "Well?" he said. She flounced and said, "What do you think you are, a dentist?" And Ted was flabbergasted, silenced.

As we all do, perhaps, Ted seemed to keep his friends in compartments, social, tennis, and professional. Most of his friends at Penn State were social. Aside from Arthur Douropolos, his tennis friends were members of the varsity squad. (Ted became tennis coach at Penn State as he had at Lafayette and he was very proud of his pupils.) Philip Shelley knew as much *about* poetry as Ted did, and the two of them were the entertainment committee for visiting poets as they were for Auden. It was to Shelley Ted went when he wanted literary conversation but there were no poets with whom he could discuss his work—he had to depend on the rare visit from Stanley Kunitz or on trips to New York where he could see Rolfe Humphries or Louise Bogan. There was no one person with whom he achieved a complete social, intellectual, and emotional intimacy, possibly because there are few people who can combine a passion for poetry, tennis, bourbon whisky, the Detroit Tigers, birds, and Bix Beiderbecke, possibly because of a deliberate reluctance on his part, an instinctive withholding of himself for fear of getting hurt.

The girl he fell in love with was Kitty Stokes. She says, "I was Circulation Librarian at the time and spotted Ted at the desk as a difficult but interesting new faculty member. He asked me to dinner in October, 1936, I think, and I think I remember that he told me about the Michigan State breakdown and the months of treatment that first night."

Although Ted never kept his hands off women at parties, this seems to have been part of the mask. Poets were expected to be hot lovers and he was willing, even eager, to make the gestures. Miss Stokes, however, defines his relations with women he knew really well, "Any girl who hung around with Ted had to do a lot of mothering." Until 1940 when he took a flat in the Glennland Apartments where he lived, he saw Kitty chiefly in the evenings and on

weekends and she was soon known as his girl. She sensed the mass
of fear and guilt that burdened him and his constant, gnawing,
child-like need for praise, approval, and the knowledge that he
was loved and she supplied them. When they went to parties, she
remained unobtrusively in the background and let Ted have a
free hand. Ted was like a more boisterous Dick Diver—he could
take over a party, dominate it, make it go, and everybody would
have a lot of fun. This often involved him temporarily with other
girls but Kitty did not protest. She learned, perhaps painfully, that
he would return to her, and if he knew he had done something out-
rageous, the next day he would come to the library, make several
false starts maybe but apologize contritely in the end. She said it
was very hard to be angry with him for long.

He was beginning to think of himself as a gourmet cook and he
often cooked for his hosts in their kitchens as well as for Kitty in
hers. Philip Shelley says that Ted recommended a butcher to him
whom Shelley followed through jobs in five different shops. This
butcher told Shelley that Ted knew meat. Ted cooked a dinner for
William Carlos Williams and his wife ("we had a powerful lack of
interest in each other's poetry," Ted said) and for Katherine Anne
Porter and later told her of a good cheap wine. He was interested
in food and he was always trying to find good restaurants. One of
his first comments on Seattle when he went there was that there
were no good eating places.

In 1940 Kitty went on leave during the spring semester to work
at Swarthmore. Ted sublet her apartment and discovered he liked
the place. In the fall he rented an apartment in the same building
and they saw more of each other. He often took her to a restaurant
called "The Corner Unusual" or to drink beer in the "Rathskeller,"
a dark little place with brown wooden walls and a sign over the
bar, "Ask about Our Friendly Credit Plan and get a rap in the
mouth." In fine weather Ted liked to walk in the country and she
would go with him. She cooked a great many meals for him. She
often did his laundry and mending. Above all, she typed for him.
He never learned to use a typewriter, rather he wrote everything
out in green ink, sometimes brown, colors he said he adopted to
contrast with the blue or black used by students. He would write
out business letters and she would type them, lists of completed
poems, copies of reviews he had written or any critical notices

taken of him, various states of poems he was working on, and their final copies. He was very strict with her if so much as a comma was misplaced. He would not let her erase the mistake; it had to be done over from the start.

He brought student papers to her apartment to correct and talked to her for hours about teaching and the idiosyncrasies of different students. She said his marginal comments on the papers were copious and thoughtful. It was a measure of the trust he placed in her that he wrote poetry in her apartment for he knew it was then, if ever, he showed himself naked.

She made her own clothes and she would sit at one side of the room sewing, and he would sit at a table whose top reproduced in miniature the chaos of his own apartment, swearing and muttering, staring out the window, writing a line and crossing it out—he always used cheap dime-store notebooks—rocking back and forth and groaning. "It was like a woman having a baby," Kitty says. If he found a line worth keeping, he would read it to her in a loud cadenced voice and she would murmur approvingly. If she got a skirt ready to hang, she would stand on a box or a chair and Ted would put in the pins around the hem, and then return to his table.

In 1941 Kitty's mother came to live with her. She was an indomitable small handsome woman who did not think anyone, much less Ted, was good enough for her daughter. (Mrs. Stokes was not alone in this. Most of Kitty's female friends did not think so, either.) Ted's relations with Mrs. Stokes were in the nature of an armed truce but he continued to see Kitty almost as much as before.

One night in 1942 Ted stopped at Kitty's apartment and asked her to call a doctor. "I'm sick," he said. He would not have a telephone in his own apartment. He went upstairs and went to bed. Kitty called her own doctor who examined him and said, "He's too sick to be moved to the hospital." (There was no hospital then at State College. The nearest was twelve miles away at Bellefonte.) It was pneumonia Ted had, a much more serious illness before the use of antibiotics. The doctor hired two practical nurses for day and night duty. A few nights later one of the nurses stopped at Kitty's apartment and said, "The doctor says tonight will be the crisis and you'd better notify his family," but Ted had already told Kitty, "Don't tell the family. It'll upset them."

However, in view of the seriousness of the situation, Kitty sent a night letter to Saginaw which would reach Ted's mother the next morning when the crisis, presumably, would be passed, "Doctor decided today Ted has pneumonia hot serious fever will probably break tomorrow or Sunday Ted does not want you to know so write innocent letters I will let you know constantly Ted is at home with day and night nurses he likes and is quite cheerful he sends love." The next day the nurse came down distraught and said to Kitty, "I let it slip that you sent that night letter and Ted is very upset." The nurse was really frightened. She said Ted looked so ferocious and he said, "Kitty wouldn't do a thing like that. I told her not to tell them." Kitty went up to Ted, explained and soothed, and at last he calmed down.

One thing that emerges from this incident is the relations of the Roethke family one to another. They were always, each of them, trying to spare the others. There was a continual and conscientious suppression of any kind of bad news. This is kindness, certainly, but a kindness that becomes dubious when the bad news is startlingly and inadvertently revealed as it was here. Ted's doctors at Mercywood told him that he had to avoid worry as much as possible. His mother and sister knew this and they kept many things from him such as the state of his mother's health and finances, a leak in the roof, and he reciprocated.

Ted's concentration on his mental, physical, and emotional wellbeing was almost absolute. He was the most fascinating person he knew. He watched and listened to himself constantly and he became a life-long hypochondriac who was always taking pills of one kind or another but there was justification for this. The bout of pneumonia described here was one of three he had at Penn State alone. Also, after playing tennis, he used to complain to Kitty about pains in his knees and shoulders, apparently the first symptoms of the arthritis that plagued him later. "The weakness of the flesh" was a phrase he could take literally without connotations. And since, without being fully aware of it yet, one of the directions of his life was to know and unify himself, he came to learn not from anyone's precepts but from the scars of many illnesses that wholeness of being was related to the health of both body and spirit.

Fascinated as he was by all the processes of his life, he naïvely assumed that friends would be equally fascinated by their recital. When Kitty was working at Swarthmore in the spring of 1940 and during his summer vacations in Saginaw, his almost-daily letters to her set down minute shifts in his moods, spurts of cheerfulness, tiny irritations, moments of picayune despondency like his gloomy observation that he had missed getting a haircut the Wednesday before and would probably forget it this week as well. He writes from Saginaw:

> I made some pretty good butterscotch sauce, 1½ cups of light brown sugar, ¼ cup thin cream, ¼ cup corn syrup. Cook until a drop of it makes a soft ball in cold water. Don't overcook. My mother isn't much impressed by my cooking stories. She thinks it's sort of sissy, I guess. Well, Katherine, if I were a model person, I would be polite and cheerful but everything seems empty and futile, it really does. Call this adolescent if you like."

A list of requests he sent to her:

> 1) Can you get any dope on how bears' caves look and smell after hibernation? 2) Is that book *Culture and Christianity* in the library or ever ordered, Oxford Press, can't think of author? 3) Are there any books by Unamuno, that Spanish philosopher? 4) Make a double set of *Phoenix* if you have time.

And there is the sober observation he sent her while he was on a trip with the tennis squad, "I was a trifle sick to my stomach in Franklin, Pennsylvania."

Although Poland and France had been invaded and the Second World War had begun, Ted makes no comment on these in his letters for they were not part of his relationship with Kitty. That he was not unaware of these events is clear from two epigrams and an unpublished poem found in his notes. (The poem is undated, written uncharacteristically in blue ink, but seems to have been composed in 1941.)

SIDE LINE COMMENT

If I had a brain like Ambassador Bullitt,
I'd take each idea and carefully mull it.

If I were Senators Burke, Wadsworth or Barkley,
I'd try not to see everything through a brass hat, darkly.

THE QUESTION

The lavish and the mad our destinies appoint,
The good's fouled with the bad. The time are out of joint.
The gun prods in the back. The club finds out a skull.
When bellies hang too slack, the sensitive grow dull.
Oh, when will hate be gone, the blood begin to buck?
The foolish act atone and love renew its luck?

By 1942 Ted had been classified 4-F in the draft as a result of his stay in Mercywood so there was no question of any direct participation in the war.

Kitty says Ted put off accepting invitations on the chance that something better might turn up. He acted similarly about teaching jobs. Until his last years at the University of Washington, he never said he liked any place he worked as a teacher. His objections were always couched in the sheerest hyperbole—the staff, particularly the administrators were venal, stupid, and dishonest; the students were cretinous; the climate was unbearable; his quarters not fit for rats. These statements were spun out of passing moods of dejection but they seem to be signs of something deeper, a continual raging discontent with himself—his poetry was not good enough, and such as it was, by no means enough people, ever, said it was great. Perhaps somewhere there was the ideal post for him. He kept writing letters of application in hopes of locating it. While he was at Penn State, he applied to his alma mater, Michigan, to Hunter College, to the Edison Institute at Dearborn, Michigan, and eventually to Bennington College. Ted kept a very complete dossier at the Bureau of Placement of the University of Michigan and frequently wrote its head, Dr. Luther Purdom, asking him to keep his eye out for any good jobs that might be available. On June 6, 1938, he tells Dr. Purdom that he was the only national judge of the Witter Bynner Poetry Contest conducted by the College Poetry Society of America and at the installation of the Pennsylvanis Lambda chapter of Phi Beta Kappa, he was the official poet. He said, "With none of these activities am I impressed, but your office insisted that I keep my record complete."

Despite this persistent grumbling about his salary, his academic rank, and the general lack of appreciation shown him by the authorities, Ted was able to work hard at Penn State and it would seem that Kitty Stokes's calm encouragement made the right atmosphere for it. He published no poems in 1936, his first year at Penn State, but he published ten in 1937, sixteen in 1938 (numerically the most productive year of his life), twelve in 1939, and five in both 1940 and 1941. These were the years he was making the poems that went into *Open House*. "I know," Kitty says. "I typed most of them."

To one looking back over a man's career from the vantage point of hindsight, the development seems inevitable as if the event were the only thing that could have happened. To the man himself, struggling in the quotidian humdrum, the future cannot but seem murky. By the time he was at Penn State, Ted knew he was a poet, that, despite illness, lapses in confidence, harassments of doubt, his life would be devoted to it, and he had already lived a fair sample of that life. What he did not yet know was what *kind* of poet he would be. Yet to the later observer, it seems obvious. The excitement of life lay within himself, not outside, nor in anyone's past but his own. What struck him through his senses he transformed at once into signs of his own states of being, well or ill. It was himself he had to sing, not the circumambient world. He only used that.

Stanley Kunitz says he was not a really close observer, and, of course, he did not need to be since everything around him was useful to him only as signatures of himself. Lyne Hoffman says that he seemed to want to go everywhere, experience everything, but this seems a temporary aberration for, again, he did not need to since he already had nearly all the pertinent experience he was going to use in his work. (Ted was not a traveler, a sightseer. He rarely went anywhere he did not have to and the rare times he did, it was to see people, not the monuments or the natural beauties. Just after his marriage, with Auden's villa at Ischia lent him for his honeymoon, Ted dug his heels in and nearly refused to go. In none of his letters to me did he ever mention how anything looked but he always wrote about people.) To his contemporaries he often seemed merely selfish but to one who is looking for the poet, it seems that he was guarding his heart. But at this time he was not yet aware of this.

Kitty Stokes exercised a benign and stabilizing influence over him. She corresponded with his mother and sister and they hoped that Ted would marry her but he never seriously proposed. He said to her once, "If I ever ask you to marry me, don't do it. I wouldn't be good for you." He wanted all his girls to know each other and he asked Mary Kunkel, then Mrs. Jeremy Bagster-Collins, and her husband up to State College for a visit. Perhaps because they had a common interest, she and Kitty found they liked each other very much. It was on this visit that Ted, who always slept with his head wrapped up, offered a new clean blue baby blanket to Jeremy Bagster-Collins to wrap *his* head in when it came time to go to bed. Ted took for granted that if he did it, it was a universal custom. Later, he saw to it that his wife met Kitty and, later still, Beatrice Roethke and Mary Bagster-Collins became good friends.

Kitty says that the poets he read and reread at Penn State were Donne and Blake. While they were not, of course, unknown to him, his concentration upon them was new. Only a few touches of their idiom appear in the poetry he was working over then. Literary influence takes time to absorb. There seems to be a time lag between the reading of a work and its use as a kind of model, and further it is likely that only the works one reads for pleasure are the ones influential. Ted's tastes in English poetry were catholic except for the Augustans, and he read poetry gladly, good or bad. If it was bad, he grew angry and seemed to take bad lines almost as a personal insult. If it was good and he was reading it aloud, his voice would change with excitement. At the end, with the same enthusiasm and language with which he would applaud a good boxer's left hand if he were watching him in the ring, he would applaud the poet as if he were present and saying it fresh before him. It is hard, therefore, to see Ted making a study of the poets who influenced him and consciously lifting metaphors and conceits for his own use as Eliot suggests. The poetic references he makes in the poems of *Open House* are chiefly to the work of poets he had been reading for some time, Elinor Wylie, Léonie Adams, Louise Bogan, Emily Dickinson, Rolfe Humphries, and Stanley Kunitz. In fact, Kunitz, in pointing out the feminine delicacy and precision of some of these poems, suggested to Ted that he quit reading lady poets; he was giving the coarseness and vitality of his own nature no outlet. This surprised Ted because he was not aware he had taken so much.

By 1939 Ted decided that he had poems enough to make a

book. Stanley Kunitz put them in order and suggested the book's title, and with a characteristic mingling of eagerness and trepidation, Ted sent off the manuscript. It was turned down by Henry Holt and Company and by the Oxford University Press, to whom Ted wrote and asked for the readers' comments because it was hard to get objective criticism, and the letter contained the implication that the Press had kept his manuscript six months. In 1940, it was accepted for publication by Alfred A. Knopf.

Like Yeats and Joyce and Hemingway, Ted was alert to the importance of managing his career. He did not believe in casting his work out and letting it find its own level. He had worked as hard as he knew how on these poems. They were as good as he could make them and he was going to see to it that as many people read them as possible, and not only the public in general but the right people, the writers and critics. In February, 1941, he wrote to J. B. de la Torro Bueno at Knopf's, enclosing three hundred and thirty names of friends and professional acquaintances and will send a list of former students and "other people" shortly, and this will be followed by a list of newspapermen, critics, and booksellers who would be interested.

Ted was acutely conscious of fellowships, awards, prizes, and he suspected that a word from the right person would always be helpful in getting him one, so he did not scruple to cultivate the right persons. (He often found that he liked them.) This cultivation was not brash but subtle and indirect. An example: during the summer of 1940 Ted and I met at a writer's conference sponsored by Olivet College, then under the aegis of Joseph Brewer. The principal movers and shakers were John Peale Bishop, Sherwood Anderson, and Katherine Anne Porter. Ted and I spent a very pleasant afternoon drinking beer with Anderson but that was not what Ted had come for. He had already cooked a dinner for Miss Porter, and through her he met Bishop. Ted had a copy of *Open House* in manuscript and he prevailed on Bishop to read it and give him some criticisms. On March 7, 1947, before *Open House* had been published Ted wrote this letter to Miss Porter:

Dear K.A.P.:
If you have occasion to write John Bishop, please tell him this: Auden referred to him as one of the two really good critics of poetry in America. There's so much malice and backbiting going on that I like sometimes to pass on praise if it doesn't have to be

directly. I'd tell him myself except that he might think it boot-
licking. Matter of fact, I've never thanked him for being so
decent last summer . . . Well, my damned book is out Monday.
Say a little prayer if it isn't too blasphemous.

Sincerely,

Ted Roethke

PS Bravig Imbs calls you one of the great amateur cooks of the
world. My God, when I think I presumed to cook for you!

This letter shows considerable sophistication. With its com-
pliments cut away, the gist of its intention seems to be, "Please
get John Bishop to review my book." If this seems to be too harsh
and skeptical a statement, I can only say that I was led to make
it by reading dozens of similar letters among Ted's papers. But he
was not quite so self-centered as this makes him seem. He did not
want an audience of his fellow poets only. (In a sense he already
had that.) He wanted all his life to be widely read, and since he
grew up in it, he was aware of the almost corrosive apathy of the
public at large, aware and oppressed by it and he wanted to
explode it if he could. Poetry, he believed, should have an ac-
knowledged civic place in the life of his time and a large part of
his work as a teacher was an unremitting labor to create an
audience for it. As a poet he was quite properly determined not to
go unheard. He had done some public-relations work and he knew
the techniques of attaining publicity. If he employed them to push
his own work into public notice, it should be remembered that he
generously pulled the work of other poets along with him.

Early in March, 1941, *Open House* appeared, in blue cloth, with
the title and the poet's name in gold on the spine. It was dedicated,
"To my mother," and it contained forty-seven poems in five
groups.

The gap between a book's appearance and the first reviews is
the worst time and Kitty Stokes says Ted was nervous and filled
with anxiety but he needn't have worried. Most of the reviews
were good and those that contained adverse criticisms tacitly
acknowledged that this was the work of a genuine poet and not a
beginner.

Here are some excerpts from reviews that Ted kept. In a
parenthesis it says "Compiled by K. M. Stokes."

W. H. Auden, *Saturday Review of Literature*

Mr. Roethke is instantly recognizeable as a good poet . . . Many people have the experience of feeling physically soiled and humiliated by life; some quickly put it out of their minds, others gloat narcissistically on its unimportant details; but both to remember and to transform the humiliation into something beautiful, as Mr. Roethke does, is rare. Every one of the lyrics in this book, whether serious or light, shares the same kind of ordered sensibility: *Open House* is completely successful.

Louise Bogan, *The New Yorker*

The first book of a young poet with a real sense of lyric style, a fine, bitter wit, and a feeling for the small and medium-sized as well as for the large doings in the world about him.

Yvor Winters, *The Kenyon Review*

Roethke has no desire, it would seem, to write poetry which, in the language of a distinguished contemporary, is sufficiently ambiguous to be self-explanatory. His thought is clear; the feeling of the poem is his personal realization of that importance . . . Roethke is ashamed neither of having subject matter nor of the kind of subject matter he has, and he writes in a style that is good in this period and would be good in any other.

Rolfe Humphries, *The New Republic*

. . . the book is not padded with practice pieces, poems whose chief value was in the exercise; Roethke has been quite severe in his selection and every specimen is *per se* valid.

John Holmes, *Boston Transcript*

The wholeness of *Open House* demands comment. Mr. Roethke has built it with infinite patience in five sections. The first is personal pronoun; the second, the out-of-doors; the third is premonition of darker things—death among them; the fourth is the purest of metaphysical wit, something very rare in our time; and the fifth contains still another side of this poet's nature, the human awareness of which he has become capable in his recent development.

Elizabeth Drew, *The Atlantic Monthly*

Theodore Roethke is unlike most modern poets in the sense of inner security and certainty which his poems communicate . . . Whether he is writing light satire or descriptions of natural scenes, his poems have a controlled grace of movement, and his images the utmost precision; while in the expression of a kind of gnomic wisdom which is peculiar to him he attains an austerity of contemplation and a pared, spare strictness of language very unusual in poets of today.

Babette Deutsch, *Decision*

Most of the poems here deal . . . with the interior landscape. He is sensitive to its subtler aspects. He writes with particular acuteness about the mind as awareness grows upon it.

The excisions from these reviews were made by Ted himself, and the remainders show what he wished to keep either because he liked the praise or because he thought others would be impressed by them. Keeler's Book Store at State College gave him a cocktail party where he autographed copies of *Open House* but he seemed shy and ill at ease doing it. The store had a big window display and they sold over a hundred copies. Harold Graves gave him a big party on the night of publication and a man named Burne Helme generously presented each of the guests with a copy of the book.

He was launched and successfully but it was not like him to be satisfied. He alternated between feelings of awe that he, Theodore Roethke from Saginaw of all places, had done this thing, written a book you could hold in your hand, and grumblings because the praise was not high enough.

It is important to notice that Stanley Kunitz with Ted's help arranged these forty-seven poems and gave them the order that John Holmes praised; that is, the poems were written first and the order imposed later. Ted was not consciously exploring himself or the world and he did not yet have a unifying theme—he was merely writing poems as they came to him. There are two poems, however, in *Open House* that offer strong hints of the future, "Prognosis," and "Premonition."

In "Prognosis," he is already using filial tensions, but the suffering they caused him has not yet been elaborated or their ramifications explored as they will be in later works.

As Louis Martz points out in his essay "*A Greenhouse Eden* (*Theodore Roethke, Essays on the Poetry,* edited by Arnold Stein, University of Washington Press, Seattle and London, 1965) Ted

did not include "The Premonition" in his later volumes of verse
and he says:

> One can guess why Roethke did not include the poem, for it is
> quite unlike anything else in this early volume: the frank
> reminiscence, the utter naturalness and simplicity of the lan-
> guage, the subtle use of terminal assonance (especially of the
> "er" sound), in place of formal rhyme; the shimmer of implica-
> tion in place of the hard conceit; the evocation of a mystery
> instead of the sharp precision of idea. Roethke was in fact em-
> barrassed by the open display of feeling here; ten or fifteen years
> ago, in discussing this poem, he said he winced in reading that
> cry, "Oh, that was long ago!" The exact word he used was, I
> think, "corny." But now this seems the one poem of *Open House*
> that clearly points the way home, to Roethke's truest manner,
> the cultivation of the inner force of memory. It points to the
> greenhouse memories that form the still point of his deepest
> imaginative existence, and it finds its fulfilment in Roethke's
> posthumous volume, in the poem entitled simply "Otto"—his
> father's name, the name of the greenhouse owner, protector and
> procreator of greenness.

THE PREMONITION

Walking this field I remember
Days of another summer.
Oh that was long ago! I kept
Close to the heels of my father,
Matching his stride with half-steps
Until we came to a river.
He dipped his hand in the shallow:
Water ran over and under
Hair on a narrow wrist bone;
His image kept following after,—
Flashed with the sun in the ripple.
But when he stood up, that face
Was lost in a maze of water.

IX

The Lost Son and
Other Poems

Bennington College lies in the Vermont hills not far from the town of Bennington. It was founded in 1932 after years of planning. The students who applied for admission were very carefully scrutinized and once admitted they had, in the beginning, academic carte blanche. They told the college what they wanted to learn and the college would try to teach it to them. Later, however, it was found that seventeen-year-old girls do not always know what they want to learn and some required courses were introduced. Aside from lectures and seminars, each girl had a tutor who supervised her intellectual development as a whole and assigned work in areas where she seemed to be ignorant. Otherwise the college was not in the least paternalistic. A distinguished faculty had been assembled and at the time Ted was teaching there, Kenneth Burke, Francis Fergusson, Peter Drucker, William Troy and his wife, Léonie Adams, Karl Knaths, Stanley Hyman, and Martha Graham were among its members.

The town of Bennington was split between Old Bennington (founded in 1761) on the hills above the Walloomsac River and Bennington proper, the industrial town in the river valley which made paper and textiles, not a very pretty town as New England towns go but there were many shade trees and it was quiet. By the 1940s Old Bennington had become a summer resort like Manchester. While there were some fine new houses, the *ton* was established by the old ones, many built in the Eighteenth Century, glowing white in the shade of magnificent elms. In the Historical Museum are preserved some red coats, Hessian mitres, a brass cannon and Colonel John Stark's flag from the Battle of Bennington in 1777. In the Old Burying Ground lie the bodies of Colonel Baum's Germans and Stark's Vermonters. History here means the history of the Revolution. Ethan Allen was a local man and the only notice I ever heard Ted pay to these famous victories was his gleeful repetition of Allen's behavior at Ticonderoga. The history books say that Allen beat on a door of the fort and intoned, "Open in the name of God and the Continental Congress." The local tale, however, which may have come down by word of mouth, is that Allen beat on the door and shouted, "Open the door, you goddamned British sons-of-bitches, or we'll kick it in." This delighted Ted.

He was again fortunate in the natural setting of the place he worked. From the campus of the college almost any way you turned offered a beautiful view of the hills. In the fall they took on a marvelous purplish-red color from the turning leaves. Winters were deep with snow but there were many blindingly bright days, and the springs covered the hills with varying tints of Green that shaded to blue with distance. As he did everywhere he lived, Ted went for long walks through the countryside and once I met him carrying a tall plant with both hands keeping the earth carefully packed around its roots. It was a mountain rhododendron, he said. He had found it on some hillside and he planted it again near Shingle Cottage where he lived.

On April 1, 1943, Ted began a leave without pay from Penn State and he came to teach at Bennington. It was the culmination of one of his characteristic periods of restless dissatisfaction, which was intensified by the fact that he had had a book published and favorably reviewed and so *deserved* something better than his teaching post at Penn State where he complained his abilities went unrecognized. It was not that any one place or position had attracted him; he was propelled outward by his own revulsion.

As I have said, he had written many letters of application to colleges and at Christmas time in 1940, he went to the annual meeting of the Modern Language Association at Indianapolis. Ostensibly the purpose of these meetings is to acquaint college teachers of the humanities with the state of criticism at the time. A two- or three-day program is filled with readings of critical papers and it is an honor to be asked to give one. In practice, however, the MLA meetings are a job mart. Heads of departments with a roster of instructors or assistant professors to fill give cocktail parties to which these young men come as his guests and under cover of social amiability are shrewdly assessed and perhaps hired. There are also the malcontents like Ted who are looking for a change.

At Indianapolis Ted sold a poem. Morton Dauwen Zabel bought "Reply to Censure" for *Poetry Magazine.* In a letter Ted thanked him for some criticism of the poem Mr. Zabel had given him and then said, "It is difficult for me to know how to act at M.L.A. meetings. I try to be honest and friendly but perhaps succeed only in being silly." This is his official manner to an important professor. It *was* difficult for him to know how to act, for the sight of so many academics all in one place filled him with rage and contempt which he dared not display and the exercise of the necessary hypocrisy was a strain. He wrote me more candidly of the Indianapolis meeting,

> I really knock myself out at those meetings. Why the hell I go is beyond me. Maybe some vague hope that a biggie will give me a better job.
> The aesthetics section was a howl: the Allen Tate protégées were going cross-eyed counting the pimples on each other's ass. God, what an I-love-me bunch!

Ted did not find the place he was looking for at Indianapolis, and the next thing that occurred to him was to ask for a Guggenheim Fellowship. A Fellowship is awarded chiefly on the strength of one's recommendations, and once Ted had decided that he wanted one, he went after it with his usual energy.

During the last two weeks of August Ted was at the School of Creative Writing sponsored by Middlebury College at Breadloaf, Vermont. While he was there he met Robert Frost, Theodore Morrison of Harvard, and Bernard De Voto. De Voto suggested that he write Dr. Henry Seidel Canby, send him a copy of *Open House,* and if he was impressed by the poetry, ask him if he would write a Guggenheim recommendation. Ted did this in a very polite letter. Dr. Canby replied that he liked the poems and would be glad to give Ted his support with the Guggenheim

Foundation. In a letter written November 18, 1941, Ted respectfully urges him to send the letter and briefly sketches his project,

> A series of poems about the America I knew in my middlewestern childhood has been on my mind for some time; no flagwaving or hoopla, but poems about people in a particular suburbia. Poems in *Open House* like "Highway: Michigan," and "Night Journey" represent a beginning.

In 1940 a brother-in-law of Peter De Vries, Professor Carl Burklund of the University of Michigan Engineering College's Department of English, published a volume called *New Michigan Verse* (University of Michigan Press, Ann Arbor). Along with some work of A. J. M. Smith and John Malcolm Brinnin, it included ten of Ted's poems, "The Light Comes Brighter," "Highway: Michigan," "The Heron," "Feud," "Long Live the Weeds," "Autumnal," "No Bird," "To My Sister," "Interlude," and "Slow Season." Ted was flattered when Burklund asked to include his work, but he had a few misgivings also because he did not want to be known as a regional poet. In his preface Burklund makes a statement about the civic importance of the artist that Ted absorbed and used later, in varying forms, himself: "It is my belief that any art achievement of a state or given area has a significance no less pertinent, let us say, than its industrial achievement . . . Artists may not be more indispensable to a commonwealth than engineers or scientists but neither are they less so . . ."

On February 7, 1942, Ted made his first application to Bennington in a letter to William Troy, the critic, who was teaching there. Since there was no academic rank at Bennington and no formally arranged departments, Troy was as nearly a head of an English Department as the college had. Ted says he can offer energy, teaching ability, and a background of experience that more conventional candidates might not possess. He then gives a *curriculum vitae* and a list of people who would recommend him and ends by saying he will pass through New York (where Troy was then) in April on his way to an appearance at Harvard. The letter aroused interest at Bennington and it led to his being hired there.

On April 7, 1942, Ted gave one of the Morris Gray lectures at Harvard, one of the first plums that fell to him after the publication of *Open House*. He saw Robert Frost again and met F. O. Matthiessen and Philip Horton, the biographer of Hart Crane.

In a letter to Stanley Kunitz written in July, Ted says he is still at Penn State, "We kept right on this summer with the accelerated program," and he says that Kitty Stokes is in summer school at Ann Arbor. He sends some poems to Kunitz for criticism, among them "The Return," which he says no editor wanted apparently and also "the mud and slime one." On July 14 Kunitz answered him from his farm at New Hope, "After "The Return" (which I like more and more), I like "The Minimal" best. You're a great fellow with bugs and bogs."

Both the poems mentioned were later published in *The Lost Son* and the fact that Kunitz saw them as early as this shows that Ted's manner is changing. He is beginning to use his own past in concrete detail, freshly.

In the early fall of 1942 he went seriously to work soliciting recommendation for a Guggenheim Fellowship. On September 13, he wrote to William Rose Benét, whom he did not know, at the *Saturday Review of Literature*. He sent him a copy of *Open House* and said that he wrote at the suggestion of Dr. Henry Seidel Canby and hoped that some of the pieces might interest him sufficiently so that Benét would be willing to write in his behalf regarding a Guggenheim Fellowship. (Apparently Benét did not comply.) He also wrote to Peter Monro Jack, formerly one of his teachers at the University of Michigan, who was then one of the principal reviewers for *The New York Times*, and on October 5, Jack replied that he would recommend Ted for the Guggenheim "if you wish but I have already recommended José Garcia Villa with all my heart." Baffled, Ted wrote to one friend he was certain he could rely on, Rolfe Humphries, who wrote back on September 17, "Why, sure. Of course put me down on your Gugg. application and best of luck." By this time Ted was obviously worrying about the whole matter and he sent a copy of his own statement of his qualifications for the Guggenheim to Humphries to be criticized. Humphries replied on October 6,

> It is hard for me to give you advice. This sounds a lot better to me but I am not the Guggenheim people, and I suppose some cunning is involved. I think you should dwell a little longer on

the affirmative side; then your negative statements would sound a little less like scathing satire which might be taken to heart in the wrong way.

There is a question as to whether Ted needed to be so meticulous about this Fellowship. He was superbly qualified to receive it by his work alone, but since his own opinion of his work swung in this wide arc from "matchless" to "worthless," he was not a reliable judge of it. I do not believe that he cynically thought awards and prizes were never given on merit alone but had to be connived at; rather I believe with Dr. Shaw that he always feared he did not deserve an award, however much he may have wanted one, that he, the guilty son faced with the awesome patriarchal power of a foundation, had to strain every resource to please it. It is not beyond probability that all this anxious letter writing were simply magical acts of propitiation.

But the propitiation failed. When the list of awards came out in the spring of 1943, Ted's name was not on it.

When he arrived in Bennington in April, 1943, the weather was still chilly. Ted was given Shingle Cottage as his living quarters but he complained that he was not feeling well and the cottage was too cold. For the first few weeks he stayed in an apartment in the Commons Building.

This slight illness may have been a manifestation of fear, or, more properly, stage fright. He was now a member of a faculty of artists, critics, and scholars, many of whom had formidable reputations, all extremely well-read, well-traveled, and worldly in ways his former colleagues had seldom been. They were intellectually sophisticated and in conversation did not limit their remarks to cautious statements about their own fields but sparklingly and irreverently invaded others'. Bennington would seem to have been the intellectual milieu Ted was looking for but the question must have dogged him, was he up to it? His students, many of whom were very pretty, a circumstance upsetting enough in itself, were of a social class Ted had rarely mingled with, girls who already had or would soon make New York, Washington, or Charleston debuts, who had traveled abroad, gone to private schools, and had the clothes and manner of the rich. This stirred all sorts of atavistic and Middle-Western antagonisms in Ted, his ambiguous fear and admiration of the rich, his ambiguous fear and admiration of the East, and it made his pedagogical manner at first more harsh but simultaneously, since he was on trial and his students were girls and attractive, more earnest. I was standing in a corridor as he was finishing the last class of a term. He said, "Well, I guess that's all. Don't turn into a lot of little bitches before next September." The girls, of course, adored him and it was at Bennington that his reputation as a great teacher began to burgeon.

He made friends very soon with Mary Garrett (now Mrs. John Woodburn), who was Dean of the College. She had a beautiful apartment on the campus and Ted spent a great deal of time there. She offered him much the same support to his ego as Kitty Stokes at Penn State. (He did not break it off with Kitty on his departure. He continued to write to her and they remained friends the rest of his life.) Mary Garrett often cooked for Ted and he for her and nearly every Saturday night her apartment was the scene of a faculty party. It was a measure of the dedication of this group that, as much as they tried to avoid it after a hard week, the chief topic of conversation was the students, how to teach them, how to bring them out, and many a little girl would have been flattered, perhaps frightened to learn how seriously her quirks and vagaries were taken by her teachers.

A little later Ted came to know Kenneth Burke and he was always a little in awe of him. Burke's days on *The Dial* and *The New Republic* were behind him. He had already published *Attitudes Toward History* and *The Philosophy of Literary Form* and he was beginning work on *A Grammar of Motives*. Although he wore it lightly enough, he was prodigiously learned, certainly, except for C. S. Lewis, the most learned man I ever met. His conversation was brilliant—everything he touched he illuminated. And his taste was impeccable. Ted was often with him and, more than any teacher he ever had, Burke increased his intellectual range. Ted once said, "I used to act as a feeder to Burke with kids," and in a recent letter to me, Burke said, ". . . I was one of Ted's Papas."

During the college term Burke spent Thursday, Friday, and Saturday at Bennington and the rest of the week working at home in Andover, New Jersey. When he was on the campus, he lived in a small upstairs room in Shingle Cottage while Ted occupied the floor below, so it was easy for them to meet and for Ted meekly to receive Burke's tough-minded criticism of his work.

In 1944 James Turner Jackson came to teach at Bennington. He had been a brilliant student of mine at Ann Arbor. I had aroused Ted's interest in him and he got Jim a place on the staff of Bennington, teaching English. In his senior year at Ann Arbor, Jim had suffered a mental breakdown and had spent some time at Mercywood Sanitarium. Since they were both, so to speak, alumni of Mercywood, this made a bond between them, and Jim became more intimate with Ted's mental and emotional trials than anyone there.

Bennington had only about four hundred students then and it was small enough so that Ted's faculty acquaintance was not limited to literary people. Inevitably he would have had to talk about economics with Peter Drucker, psychology with Eric Fromm, painting with Karl Knaths, the dance with Martha Graham, or sociology with Lewis Jones or George Lundberg. This sharpened his awareness and kept him alert to other fields of interests than his own.

It was at Bennington that Ted evolved his famous course, "Verse Form." He had talked to Léonie Adams (Mrs. William Troy) about what courses he was best fitted to teach there, and in a letter to her just before he arrived, he sketches out a "Possible Course in the Analysis of Poetry," and he says of it,

> If the sole consideration were teaching efficiency, this would be the best possibility for me. Such a course would be a chance to range around in time and yet concentrate on individual poems; to deal with minor or special writers for whom I have a real enthusiasm (Vaughan, Marvell, Herbert, Clare, Beddoes, Lawrence, Hardy, and the like and introduce little-known people. I have rather good files on Kunitz, John Betjeman, and some of the Canadians like A. J. M. Smith.) Actually, such a course would provide a real supplement to existing courses, it seems to me.

He was too modest. His course became probably the most important literary course in the college. He worked himself and his students very hard. He demanded that they read more intensively, more widely than they had ever read before. Poetry was a

vocal and aural experience as well and he devoted agonies of
concentration trying to get them to *hear* the poems in all their
complexities. In composition he winkled out of them short lyric
poems by cajolery, flattery, and threats better than they them-
selves or anyone else had thought them capable of, and each in
her separate way sensed that love was the wellspring of his
teaching.

The process exhausted him. After a day of teaching he seemed
numb and vague, and at the end of the term, a wreck. On the days
he taught he used to cook himself a big breakfast. The coming
strain would take hold on the way to class and he would step
behind a tree and let the breakfast come up. Mary Garrett asked
him why he bothered to cook such a big breakfast if it wasn't
going to do him any good. "Doesn't everybody shoot their break-
fast?" he asked in mild astonishment.

The students, inundated by vast surges of Ted's vitality, came to
think of lyric poetry as the most important human activity and
they tended to let their other work slide so that they could labor
over a poem that Ted might find acceptable or even praise. One
of my students was also taking "Verse Form" and I asked her,
"Why do you write such lousy short stories for me and such good
lyrics for Ted?" She said soberly, "I'm afraid he'll hit me."

In an undated letter to his cousin, Gilbert Gaum, from this
period, Ted sets down his beliefs and his practices in the teaching
of literature:

> . . . but the best teachers don't teach it as a "subject" at all (as
> body of information, as "culture," etc.) instead as experience
> (and not tippy-toe Gustonianism) but the complete assimilation,
> the mastery of complex texts: getting the whole of what appears
> on the page or on the canvas. This includes bringing to bear on
> the material the best thought of the past (in criticism, for in-
> stance, Aristotle, Coleridge, etc.) as well as modern insights
> (Freud, Groddeck, Marx, Richards, Burke, etc.). It includes
> questions of value (granted almost as dubious a word as culture)
> and taste (the area where the hacks and boobs are always
> weakest) Etc. etc. As to my particular function, put briefly, it is a
> constant effort to recover the creative powers lost in childhood.
> This is hard to do; takes patience, luck, insight into each student;
> hard work; means for the student, learning by doing. But it can

be done without ghosting or becoming a spiritual or intellectual papa. Every year I have not one but many students tell me they learned more from such a method than any previous course in literature (or often anything else). All this is over-simplifying a complex subject. But I can't go into it at any greater length. I hate writing letters when I have other things on my mind. (Matter of fact, one of the administrators here has urged me many times to do a book on teaching. But why? I'd rather write one lyric than a hack book. And I don't want to get a name as an administrator, which is what those books lead to, eventually.)

The hell with it. Teaching at its very highest is too much like the dance. Once the moment, the class, is over, it's all down the rathole. For instance during the spring semester, for about six or seven weeks, I was really hot, if I do say so myself, in all three courses, classes conducted, paced, and often brought to a real pitch of excitement with genuine insights off-the-cuff, hot improvisational rides, etc. And the kids getting really good at what they did. This is not just performance or hysteria—it's making use of every possible means to move students ahead intellectually and even at times, if you'll pardon the word, spiritually. It's a teaching method in which you're always trying for short cuts, trying to make jumps from one plateau of achievement to another, a method that uses suggestion a great deal but it's still specific, that makes great use of the associational forces of the mind.

Again, Ted is too modest. As a statement of his teaching aims and how he realized them, this letter is certainly accurate but it is hardly a description of a "method" that anyone else could use, for Ted was unique. At that time there was hardly another teacher of the writing of poetry in the country who knew modern poetry as well as he did, who had the experience of writing it, who had the faith in the latent creative powers of his students, and who loved it as much. Perhaps he was recalling his own school and college days, the sadness and frustration of having no one to talk to, or who could talk to him, and generously he was trying to prevent this sadness and frustration in his students.

Classes were staged quite informally. Many of them were held in the living rooms of the dormitories, the girls sitting cross-legged on the floor or lolling in chairs or divans, not dressed up at all, but bare-footed, in blue jeans and sweaters or sweat shirts, with their hair hanging, smoking endless cigarettes. Or if the weather were warm, Ted might take them all out on the grass. In an ordinary college, the formal arrangement of the classrooms, with the rostrum for the professor, and the students sogged in neat rows of chairs facing him, imposes a certain restraint, and paradoxically, since the rostrum is a little stage, often elicited an actor's performance from Ted (there was a good deal of the ham in him). At Bennington, students were not compelled into attitudes by rigid arrangements of furniture, and the *illusion* was created of a group of intelligent friends, one of whom happened to be older, more experienced, more knowledgeable than the others, gathered together to talk seriously about literature. Although there were certainly long monologues delivered, they were explicatory. There was little of the lecture about them and students felt free to interrupt, to argue or deny, and because of this freedom, excitement was generated, not least of all in Ted himself, who, as he said, "knocked himself out" every time.

But it *was* an illusion. He knew that very few of the girls had any real knowledge of literature compared to himself, and any interest in it, compared to his, was, except for the rewarding few, slight and only occasional. He also knew (but did not mind) that there were few young men in the neighborhood to divert them. Usually Bennington girls saw Williams men on weekends but this was wartime. Most of the Williams men were in service and their places taken by Navy V-12 men whom the Bennington girls did not care for. The display (the gift, really) of the tremendous vitality Ted showered on them in his teaching attracted the girls, and since vitality is always magnetic, they fed on it, and out of his classes came relationships rather different from the expected liaisons between teacher and pupil.

In 1944 when I was teaching at Bennington, I used to see him coming up to the Commons for lunch after his morning classes, disheveled, swinging wearily from side to side to ease his already painful knees, his face hanging and expressionless, paying hardly any attention to the bevy of young things around him. I once asked him, "Why do you knock yourself out so?"

He replied with a snarl, "Ah, I know it's lugging pork up Parnassus"—here his face brightened—"but you get 'em up there once, they see what it is. They're better then than they'll ever be again."

He was out to create people anew, to implant or uproot, re-arrange, abrade if necessary, their sensibilities, to tear down and trample on all familial and social veils between themselves and the world as he saw it (he could be contemptuous enough, sometimes even publicly, of their origins, the long coddling and the money, contemptuous and admiring at once), and expose their little naked spirits, lift them up with love or drag them by sheer force of will up to the level where they could confront the most important thing in the world which was, of course, poetry, confront, comprehend, and sing it themselves.

"Verse Form" was a shattering experience and no student of Ted's ever forgot it.

It was at Bennington that he perfected his teaching style and gained confidence in it. "Style" is the right word, for he came to know more and more exactly what he was doing. He disdained no pedagogical trick or sleight to gain his ends. Since he believed that all children are creators and that these powers had been stunted by their lives since, he rejected no one. There was always something there if he could reach it. And many is the little debutante crippled by her upbringing to look only toward The Marriage and the photograph in *The New York Times* out of whom he drew a beautiful poem. And it was characteristic of Ted that he felt such poems not only justified the race but conferred a real distinction on the poet. Beatrice O'Connell, the beautiful girl whom he later married, was in his classes there for two years, and she says the principal emotion Ted inspired in them was awe.

Ted taught at Bennington on renewed leaves from Penn State from 1943 until 1947. He lived alone in Shingle Cottage most of the time except for Kenneth Burke's semiweekly stays, cooking his own breakfasts there, eating lunch at the Commons as well as dinner if he did not eat in Bennington—there was one very good restaurant with a chef from the old Lafayette Hotel in New York. While there were plenty of tennis courts, there were not many players who could give him a good game. He depended mostly on walking for exercise, and once, Jim Jackson says, he shot baskets in the gymnasium in the Carriage Barn:

> It was late one night. Ted discovered that the PA system (left over from some drama or dance activity) was still operating, whereupon he began to boom out first random doggerels, then some of his recent lyrics. Meanwhile I dug up a basketball and

started shooting baskets, more or less idly. Ted now swung into a mock broadcast of The Big Game; introduced himself to the crowd and—the game now hanging in the balance—announced he would suit up and enter the contest in person. He gave over the mike and sportscast to me and began bounding up and down the court, his Jackie Gleason style rather grotesque in appearance but effective in getting the ball through the hoop.

During the free winter terms he went home to Saginaw or, as he did in the winter of 1945–1946, stayed at Shingle Cottage working. Occasionally in the winter or the short summer holiday he would get down to New York to see friends or editors.

In such a small college as Bennington the faculty inevitably became better acquainted with their students than in a larger one. Many of these girls were very attractive and Ted was not immune to their attractions. He lived alone. He did not know how to type. Often girls would volunteer to come to Shingle Cottage and type for him. Friendships and affairs grew out of such and other meetings. In the fall of 1945, President Lewis Jones received an odd letter from the mother of one of the students. She said that she had at last decided to let her daughter marry "this man." (It was not until late in the letter that "this man" turned out to be Ted, but it is very doubtful that Ted had proposed marriage.) She said she had been set against the match but that her daughter was so importunate she was assenting. President Jones did not like the look of this. Teachers at the college were hired on a year-to-year basis and Mr. Jones decided not to ask Ted to return. Both Mary Garrett and Jim Jackson think that Ted had somehow learned of Jones's decision. Ted was very conscious of his dossier and, since he did not know the reasons Jones would assign for not rehiring him, he could foresee some black mark on it, and this would worry him.

To counterbalance this worry was the satisfaction of a Guggenheim Fellowship. His second application had been successful and he was awarded one in the spring of 1945 but he did not intend to assume it until a year later. He would have a year of free time in which to work.

Early in the fall of 1945, there is a curious entry in his notebooks: "Why do I wish for an illness, something I can get my teeth into?"

The most important results of his years at Bennington were the discovery of his true materials for poetry and the breakthrough in style that accompanied it.

Ted came to Bennington with a solid reputation as a minor poet, a reputation founded on short lyrics that followed what was then the "metaphysical" fashion, highly-polished, succinct, studded with conceits that expressed a "wisdom" that he sometimes did not feel. Seen in the perspective of all his work, they were his school pieces, written one at a time as they came to him, the major themes of his later work stated certainly but still fallow and unrealized in them. From a hard-boiled prudential view of his career, a view Ted took anxiously and constantly, he knew it was time to come up with something new. As Jim Jackson says, "With considerable accuracy, I think, Ted assayed his touch with the discursive, the expository, the 'abstract-logical' and found it wanting. Routine at best; often dipping down to the mediocre."

As early as 1942 while he was still at Penn State, he was working along the line of what came to be known as "the greenhouse poems." ("The Minimal", which Stanley Kunitz had seen earlier, was published in *Harper's Bazaar*, November, 1942.) Ted seemed to be feeling his way very tentatively, only half-consciously, back to his early life in Saginaw. All any writer has to work with is his own experience. (I do not know what critics mean when they say a poet has "transcended" his own experience.) Ted had been using his—many of the poems in *Open House* had Saginaw "subjects"—but in bits and pieces. He had not yet taken an overview of his life as a whole, possibly because he felt himself committed in some way to short lyrics.

I believe that coming to Bennington stimulated the change (and again half-consciously, he may have suspected it would and wanted it). Leaving old haunts may have meant shedding old habits of thought and feeling that were soiled by repetition. Poetically it may have meant a breaking out of the short lyric. (After the composition of *The Lost Son*, Ted saw the process as one of getting himself "loosened up.") And if his coming to Bennington did not of itself thrust him back into the contemplation of his old childhood life, it certainly signaled some change in his work.

But, given his ambition, his intense desire to be accepted by the established, the orthodox critics, any changes in style or in his attitude toward his material would be a gamble. (He could not change his material. His childhood with its attendant figures had been "given" him in more profound ways than he yet knew.) He was sophisticated enough to know that any new original work might be suspect to the critics and misunderstood by his small public, that it would probably be called immoral or unintelligible and therefore disesteemed. But he made the gamble and not in a careless riverboat fashion; rather, I think, he believed he had dispersed himself, making observations on Life in his short lyrics. Now there was a pull, subliminal, irrational, toward a unity of self, and instinctively he knew where he had to go to discover it.

In 1944 Ted published one poem, "Night Crow"; in 1945, none. These were the years of gestation. "Much surge, much lassitude," Jim Jackson says. On days when he was not teaching, he moped around Shingle Cottage alone, scribbling lines in his notebooks, sometimes, he told me, drinking a lot as a deliberate stimulus (later he came to see alcohol as a depressant and used to curb his manic states), popping out of his clothes, wandering around the cottage naked for a while, then dressing slowly, four or five times a day. There are some complex "birthday-suit" meanings here, the ritual of starting clean like a baby, casting one's skin like a snake, and then donning the skin again. It was not exhibitionism. No one saw. It was all a kind of magic.

At last one day, Kenneth Burke came into Ted's rooms and Ted read him two of the "greenhouse poems." "And I said, 'Boy, you've hit it.' And I kept demanding more. As far as I know Ted's gong struck then, when he hit that greenhouse line," Burke says. The next year, 1946, he published "Carnations," "Child on Top of a Greenhouse," "A Field of Light," "Flower Dump," "Forcing House," "Fruit Bin," "Moss Gathering," "Old Florist," and "Weed Puller." He had found his vein.

Of this period when he was breaking through into his new style, Jim Jackson writes:

> Ted never talked form or method much in my presence.
> Rather, at Bennington during *The Lost Son* gestation, he talked
> endlessly of *the long poem*. Meaning by this, as I finally came to
> see, not the long poem as any particular verse-form, past, pres-
> ent, or future, but as *entry* into the poet's whole lifelong ex-

pression (segmented, of course, for certain practical as well as aesthetic reasons). Thus, the long poem viewed as a fiction-writer might view "the extended narrative" which is his life's work, sometimes put down in single portions, sometimes in more direct continuities called trilogies, tetralogies, and the like. Here the meaningful and feelingful co-exist; the short or long "floating" lines commingle, whether as "prose" or "verse" and there is a growing, continuing awareness of being your own source, of the uniquity of your material and—even more!—the assurance that the very process of probing the self constitutes an exploration of all human knowledge. The same qualities of expressiveness hold for story or lyric, or letter to a friend or even memo to a business associate. Ted sensed a tyranny, then a drudgery, then a lethargy in the verse-forms of his own earlier practice, which just prior to *The Lost Son* period was beginning to drain the heat and blood from his "line." He hoped to revivify that "line" so that it would remain *at all moments* abloom from his lips, soft, fiery, and discursive all at once. *The Lost Son* happened to be the best available "staging-area" for the launching of the new line.

Prior to the start of *Son* . . . Ted made a "brief" for each verse in progress. An analytical sub-structure; a reasoned-out girding of his thoughts which could then, ideally, submerge itself in the "secret joinery" of song. (And quite naturally at this time he utilized existing and traditional verse-forms, stanzaic patterns, etc.) Proof? At Bennington, at that genesis-interlude of the "great change," his poems in their rough drafts startled me over and over again by their obvious duo-structure: the legal or the logical co-existing side by side with the intuitive, the associational: the former being most in evidence in the presence of certain abstract nouns, generalized epithets or crudely personified ideas, which almost without exception disappeared in the later drafts. These abstractions were at once so out-of-tune, so alien in their feel and texture, in the context of the associational or "internal landscape" as you call it, that I can remember often bursting out to him in immediate questioning or objection to their presence. To which Ted's quick reply and fairly casual defense was, "Sure, sure, but it's not going to *stay* in, for God's sake! It's just something left over from the thought stage of the piece. The thinky-thinky."

Considering Ted's immersion in Yeats's work during these years it may well be that he had come close to adopting Yeats's practice of writing out a prose version of the poem he was working on as a preliminary means of educing all that could be done consciously and rationally, and then throwing himself trustingly on his intuitions.

By the autumn of 1945, Ted was in a fever of creation. He had found his "line" and he had already finished some of the greenhouse poems and set down a great many lines that, refined and given direction, would later go into *The Lost Son*.

Again Jim Jackson's comments are illuminating:

> *Lost Son* was written in huge swatches. With run-on chants, dirges coming forth pell-mell. Sense of continuity uppermost at all times—even though particular poems in *Lost Son* were later detached and presented as individual poems.
>
> . . . poems were organized structurally along simplest lines of Place, dramatic shift-of-event, etc. (These simple structural placements remained unchanged from rough through final drafts.) The theme was left to take care of itself!
>
> . . . in rough-draft the long poems appeared to be in free verse (or rather, a line closer to what William Carlos Williams calls *versos sueltos*, loose-limber verse with enough exactness and repetition in measure to avoid free-verse's monotony; very strongly cadenced except for the great clinkering presence from time to time of those abstract nouns I've previously mentioned. Like Blake in mid-career, Ted was no longer satisfied with the lyric as his sole form of expression. He had didactic and symbolic fish to fry—again like Blake—and for them the lyric didn't suffice. Blake hoped to merge poet & teacher; so, at times, did Ted.

It was at this fruitful time that Ted entered a phase of manic excitement that was a prelude to his second mental episode. He had gone ten years without any but the ups and downs of cheerfulness and dejection that were normal for him. To have recognized the onset of a second attack—and he did recognize it, for he relished the immense manic vitality of the beginning, tried to preserve it and keep it under his control—certainly frightened him with the realization that his balance was so precarious that he could lose it without trying.

The students and most of the faculty had gone away as usual for the winter term but Mary Garrett and Jim Jackson had remained. It was soon clear to them that Ted was not well, and after several days of persuasion, they were able to take Ted, just after Christmas, to the Albany General Hospital. He was given shock treatments there which terrified him—"they'll turn my brain to jelly" —and after a few weeks of care in the hospital, he spent a couple of weeks at the Leonard Nursing Home in Albany.

When Ted was discharged from the nursing home near the end of January, 1946, his manner was quiet but it was not the calm of total recovery and Jim Jackson accompanied him home to Saginaw.

Ted had with him the old unblocked Borsalino hat, and on their arrival in Saginaw, he took Jim around the town looking for another one like it, ransacking the clothing stores, introducing Jim to clerks he remembered from years before but never finding the mate. This seems to have been a little run of acclimatizing himself, of getting used to the town again (perhaps, after the illness, it seemed strange) before he put himself to the trial of meeting his mother and sister (who, he may have feared, would seem strange to him also). Jim saw him safely installed at home and went back East.

His family, deeply troubled that there should have been a recurrence of his illness, could see that he was not wholly well. While he would often say, "You're not to worry about me," and while it was obvious that he was working hard, he would often seem unable to stop talking. "Don't interrupt me. Let me talk. I can't be interrupted," he would say. The talking would go on half the night sometimes. June Roethke had become a high-school English teacher by this time, and, since her mother was not well, it was she who had to listen. She typed the new poetry and his voluminous correspondence as well, and she got very little rest. She taught every day and acted as confidante and secretary at night. Exhausted as she was, she felt very sorry for him, sorry and resentful simultaneously. Ted also walked in the house for hours without rest, sometimes at night, upstairs, downstairs, and back again. Each has his own way of buckling down to the blank inimical paper. Ford Madox Ford more restfully played solitaire.

As his habit had become, Ted was dosing himself with pills

without a doctor's advice. Jim Jackson sent him a supply of pheno-barbital from Woodstock, New York, where he was visiting Mary Garrett and told him he could probably get more if he needed it.

It was in this condition of only partial stability that Ted was working on "The Lost Son" and the other long poems of his second book, "A Field of Light," "The Long Alley," and "The Shape of the Fire," but he was at home, the fountain of memories, and the greenhouse was there and the field behind it.

Since he was now, in the spring of 1946, assuming the Guggenheim Fellowship which had been granted him the year before, it may be interesting to look at Ted's "Plans for Work" which he submitted with his application:

> I have in mind the following projects:
>
> (1) a dramatic-narrative piece in prose and verse about Michigan and Wisconsin, past and present, which would center around the return of Paul Bunyan as a kind of enlightened and worldly folk-hero.
>
> (2) a series of lyrics about the Michigan countryside which have symbolical values. I have already begun these. They are not mere description, but have at least two levels of reference.
>
> (3) a series of lyrics for song and dance, the music to be composed by Mr. Gregory Tucker and the choreography by Mr. William Bales.

The first project is hardly to be taken seriously. He wrote Rolfe Humphries that, in contrast with the care he took with his first Guggenheim application, he had waited until the last day before the deadline to apply and had whacked up his projects in a hurry. He really did not intend to do anything about Paul Bunyan. The second project seems to refer to the greenhouse poems which he already had in hand and which were followed by *The Lost Son*. As early as 1944 both William Carlos Williams and myself had urged him to try some long poems and the suggestion coming from such different sources may have impressed him. The third project is interesting. It is part of his effort to expand his field and gain a larger audience. He keeps turning over plans for a verse drama (as he will say at the end of *Open Letter*). He was always anxious to have his poems set to music and eventually did have many of them but this particular plan seems to have come to nothing. Gregory Tucker was resident composer at Bennington and William Bales was the male complement to Martha Graham there.

Usually Guggenheim fellows travel abroad and Ted told Rolfe Humphries that he might go to Ireland and Catherine De Vries that he would visit Mexico and South America if his mother were well. It is doubtful if he would have made any of these journeys. The impedimenta he felt his daily life required, the mass of papers, books, notebooks, as well as his clothes would have been hard for a single person to keep track of and he seems to have realized this. When he did go abroad, it was with his wife who looked after tickets, passports, reservations, baggage, everything. So he went nowhere on his Fellowship. He stayed in Saginaw and worked on the poems that were to go into his second book.

The ultimate sources of a work of art lie too deep in the artist's mind to be accessible to explanation. There are, however, visible circumstances attendant at the time which may change or stimulate the artist's practice and adorn the work. One was Ted's desire to make a poem that would be for him wholly new. Another was his apparent readiness to leave old models and to change his poetic diction in response to fresh influences.

Louise Bogan, who gave a reading of her poetry at Bennington in 1944, says that during the Bennington years before *The Lost Son,* she recalls talking with Ted a great deal about Yeats and lending him books on Ireland, histories and travel guides. She says, "He went into the Irish literary situation very thoroughly." It is her opinion that it was Joyce, not Yeats, the verbal exuberance of the Joyce of *Ulysses* and *Finnegan's Wake* that influenced Ted in *The Lost Son.* He also assigned to his students research papers about Ireland and its literature and he learned much from them but, except for the attention paid to Joyce, this Irish influence and Irish lore were being laid up for the future. He was later to absorb so much of Yeats and employ so many of his devices that W. H. Auden, when I asked him if he could remember any specific advice he had given Ted, said, "Yes, I told him that Yeats was becoming a kind of rhythmic tic with him and he'd better watch it."

Another source of influence on *The Lost Son* was *Mother Goose.* My daughter had a complete *Mother Goose* we used to read to

her. Ted borrowed it (and never returned it) and he used to give
the verses back to her piecemeal, dramatically. His favorite was:

> "Hinx, minx, the old witch winks.
> The fat begins to fry.
> There's nobody home but jumping Joan,
> Father, mother, and I.

Jim Jackson writes:

> Two lines immediately come to my ear, recalling that period
> of "break-through" when *Open House*—in method and verse-
> form as much as in content—was being superseded by *The Lost
> Son:* the first is Blake's clarion opening of "The Marriage of
> Heaven and Hell": "Without contraries there is no progression."
> The second is from W. C. William's "The Desert Music":
> "How shall we get said what must be said?
> Only the poem.
> Only the counted poem, to an exact measure:
> to imitate, not to copy nature, not
> to copy nature
> NOT, prostrate, to copy nature
>   but a dance!

The greenhouse poems, many of which he had finished before
he was hospitalized, are firmly based in his childhood in Saginaw.
Some like "Big Wind" and "Child on Top of a Greenhouse" are
poetic elevations of definite events.* In many there is the presence
of a protagonist but he functions usually as a commenter on
natural processes, and in some poems, like "Carnations," he is
absent entirely. The protagonist, or, taken biographically, Ted, is

---

* I owe to Mrs. Mortensen, Ted's cousin, the account of the background of *Big
Wind.* She said, "One night the wind blew all the water out of the Saginaw River."
I said, "Oh, go on. How can wind blow the water out of a river?" She said, "It did.
It blew it all out into Lake Huron. The water pressure went down to nothing all
over town and Otto had these greenhouses full of carnations. No water, no steam
to keep them warm. It was November and if they froze, he'd lose his whole crop.
So they got a man from the Wickes Boiler Co. and he hitched up a pipe to the
vat of liquid manure and pumped the liquid manure into the steam pipe. It stank
to high heaven when it got hot but they saved the carnations."

Still dubious about the power of the wind, I went to the files of *The Saginaw
News* and discovered there a photograph taken the morning after the storm. The
water was indeed gone from the river; boats were careened on their sides; and
only a few puddles were left in the riverbed. This has happened two or three times
in Saginaw's history when the wind was right.

not the center of these poems. They can be read more or less objectively. This is not true of *The Lost Son*.

He was hard at work during the spring of 1946 and, as he finished a poem, he would send it out to a magazine. He also submitted a group of them for a Houghton-Mifflin Poetry Fellowship. A letter he wrote to the magazine, *Word Study*, in April, 1946, is interesting,

> I have written this poem, "The Apteryx," as you will see, solely for possible use in your publication or for use as advertising copy. In either case, it is submitted only with the understanding that you pay for published material or for use of the idea. If it is bought to be used as advertising copy, it must be understood that the line rate is higher rather than lower and that my name must not be used on the copy unless I can check the lay-out.

This shows Ted's tough business manner. He had been a publicity man. He knew all the tricks, and, characteristically, he wanted his business correspondents to know, too. With important editors who were merely going to publish his poetry and not use it for advertising, his manner was more ingratiating.

On May 27, 1946, Ted received a letter from Houghton-Mifflin about his application for the Poetry Fellowship,

> Your project came so close to getting the award, was spoken of so favorably by Horace Gregory and Ferris Greenslet, that I know Mr. Greenslet, as well as the rest of us, would be happy to see it when it is completed.

A disappointment and Ted did not take them lightly. It is reasonably certain that the epigram about Horace Gregory, already mentioned, was composed after the reception of his letter.

Another dispiriting rejection came in July, 1946, from *Horizon*, Cyril Connolly's magazine in London,

> But really we are looking for the poems which have something immensely moving about them without caring much how or why it gets there. It seemed to us that your poetry was in a way very American in that it just lacked that inspiration, inevitability or quintessence of writing and feeling that distinguishes good poetry from verse.

Since some of his submissions to *Horizon* had been the greenhouse poems which he was proud of, this letter made him wrathy and he was still fulminating against the "god-damned limeys" when I saw him later in the summer.

He came down to spend a weekend at my place. I was living on a farm then near Onsted, Michigan. I picked him up at a bus station late one afternoon in a light shower of rain that made the roads slick. He seemed quiet, slightly depressed. We had barely sat down with drinks in our hands when we heard a loud metallic thumping outside in the road. (I know nothing that shows the impermanence of the modern auto better than the noise they make when they crack up. It doesn't sound *serious*.) We all ran out of the house. In the ditch across the road lay a sedan on its side, and as I approached, it sounded like a cage of wild animals, yowls and thumps. I opened the door to the front seat and out scrambled a mama, terribly excited and voluble but unbleeding, and a papa who seemed shaken. I opened the door to the back seat and three little kids climbed out whole. But all the time I had been hearing a high steady screaming. I looked down into the back seat and saw the rear of a little baby. Its head had gone through the window and when I climbed down in, I could see a spine of glass leveled at the baby's Adam's apple. I couldn't break the glass with my heel for fear of cutting the baby's throat, so it was a matter of working the kid very gently back and forth to get it past the spine of glass. It took about five minutes, the baby screaming with remarkable power the whole time, and when I got it free, its little face was a mask of blood from a scalp cut. I handed it up to someone and got out myself just in time to see the mama wrapping its head up like a melon in a baby blanket. I asked her if I could take her and the baby to a hospital but she said, "Nobody's going to take my little baby away from me." She was in shock and I thought of slapping her to bring her out of it, but a crowd had gathered and I was afraid they would say, "Look at that man hit that lady," so I merely walked away. Someone drove off with the whole family.

Ted had been watching this from across the road. He said, "I got to get out of here. I can't stand this."

"But it's all over," I said. "Come on in; let's have a drink."

"I got to get out of here," he repeated. He seemed gloomily agitated.

I tried to talk him out of it—we would have big prime steaks for dinner, chicken Tetrazzini tomorrow, and so on but nothing would do. He had to leave and I drove him back to the bus. He had ridden a hundred and fifty miles to get there and he stayed only half an hour. It was the baby's face covered with blood that did it.

One of the matters we talked about driving to the bus station was the possibility of his getting work at Ann Arbor where I had returned after teaching at Bennington. Ted knew many of the staff there and they knew him; in fact, he had been a student of some of them. With the confidence given him by his Bennington experience, he was disturbed that Michigan might not value him highly enough. He told me he would accept the rank of Associate Professor and take seven thousand a year. I said I would see what I could do, but it was no good. Professor Louis Bredvold, the head of the department, had heard of his stay in Mercywood eleven years before and thought him unstable. There was also an odd kind of institutional self-deprecation at work—since Ted was a Michigan man and they had known him, they did not believe he could possibly be as good as his reputation.

In the years 1946-1947, as fruitful as they were for him, Ted was nagged constantly by worry about a teaching job. Technically he was still on leave from Penn State and he kept up a cordial but intermittent correspondence with Professor Gates there (by this time he addressed Gates as "Dear Ted"), but he did not want to return to Penn State for good because he thought he had outgrown the place. He seems to have suspected that President Lewis Jones was not going to ask him to return to Bennington when his Guggenheim Fellowship was finished and he may have been tired of the students there. At least he was viewing them with his characteristic double vision as this letter to Catherine De Vries on December 14, 1946, shows,

> Do you ever read *Junior Bazaar?* In October there was an article on Bennington by one Leo Lerman. For your convenience I shall quote p. 223, "In literature the shouting's about Thomas Wolfe, Faulkner, Dostoevsky, Dylan Thomas, W. H. Auden, Theodore Roethke, and Kenneth Burke. About poet Roethke, a member of the Bennington faculty now on a Guggenheim: 'He'd break his neck for talent. He's the best teacher we ever had. He takes more time and trouble than anyone we know.'

> Touching, aint it, the cynical little bitches getting so lavish?
> But even so I doubt that I'll go back—at least for the present. I
> told Penn State that I'd come back Feb. 1. Somehow I feel that
> I've got something bigger to do than teaching little girls but
> what the hell it is, I don't know. For a time I was brooding
> about the West Coast. But of late the idea of being closer to
> N.Y. has appealed to me. But I'm not very good at pulling
> strings. Too bad, too, because I'm a really good buy now, as a
> teacher and writer, loosened up, I am, a 30-game winner, etc.

Ted's brooding about the West Coast led him to write to Pro-
fessor George Lundberg at the University of Washington in
Seattle. Ted had known him when he was teaching sociology at
Bennington and he mentioned "your laudable and oft-repeated
plan of getting me out to the Coast some time on one of those
lecture series or some such." He also made inquiries about a place
at U.C.L.A. from Professor F. P. Rolfe of the English Department
there. Although he was sure of his abilities as a college teacher by
this time, he became anxious enough in May, 1947, to apply to the
U.S. State Department for a post as Cultural Attaché. None of
these applications came to anything and reluctantly he went back
to Penn State in February, 1947.

In spite of his worries, the work on the poems that were to make
his reputation continued in Saginaw through the year 1946, with
his sister patiently doing the typing and acting as his secretary.
His social life was quiet, a little tennis, and some evenings with
Buzz Morley and other friends. On May 8, 1946, he sent William
Carlos Williams a manuscript copy of *The Lost Son* and a letter,

> Dear Dr. Bill,
> I have been reading over your letter to me written in July,
> 1944, and the later one about the set of short pieces I sent you in
> which you made the comparison with James Stephens. It goes
> without saying that these letters meant a good deal to me and
> have helped me, I believe, in the laborious process of getting
> really loosened up.
> But here's a long one which I think is the best I've done so far.
> It's written as you'll see right away, for the ear, not the eye. It's
> written to be heard. And if you don't think it's got the accent of
> native American speech, your name aint W. C. Williams, I say
> belligerently. In a sense it's your poem, yours and K. Burke's.

He's been enthusiastic about it even in its early version. My real point, I suppose, is that I'm doing not one of these but several: with the mood or the action on the page, not talked about, not the meditative T. S. Eliot kind of thing. (By the way, if you have an extra copy of your last blast against T. S. E., do send it to me. I can't seem to get a hold of it anywhere.)

Do let me know what you think of this long one when you have time. You had more to do with it than you think.

The tone of this letter seems absolutely sincere and it shows who Ted thought had exerted the immediate influences on *The Lost Son* and the poems following it.

Now that he had a second book ready, his dissatisfaction with his publisher grew the more he thought about it. He wrote a letter to Knopf's asking if the firm would consider bringing out a second edition of *Open House* with a different jacket bearing some of the notices which had commended the first edition. Knopf's did not reply and perhaps Ted knew they wouldn't. The letter may have been a pretext for breaking off relations. In a letter to Diarmuid Russell in which he seems to be mulling over the possibility of letting the literary agency of Russell & Volkening represent him, he makes his complaints against Knopf's very plain,

My first book, *Open House*, published March 10, 1941, had a printing of 1000 copies and these are just about sold out, I believe. There were no advertisements anywhere, not even institutional ads or group ads with other books as in *The Times* or *The Herald Tribune*. The Knopf publicity man refused to take an ad costing $6.00 in the Lafayette College alumni magazine which would have reached some hundreds of my former students. I was told later that I had made a mistake by mentioning that I had done various kinds of publicity for colleges and J. Robert Crouse of Cleveland, one of the founders of N.R.L.A., now the Edison Institute.

While there seems to have been some personal friction, the principal cause of his discontent was neglect, what seemed to him a patent demonstration that he was undervalued.

It was two of his former students at Bennington who lured and guided him to a new publisher, Sarah Moore, the daughter of Douglas Moore, professor of music at Columbia, and Judith Bailey who had recently begun work as a reader and editor for Doubleday & Co. At a party at Sarah Moore's which seems to have been at Christmas time, 1946, Judith introduced Ted to John Sargent, now president of Doubleday but then a young editor. Sargent had already read and admired Ted's poetry. The two hit it off when they met and Sargent became one of Ted's best friends in New York. Shortly after this Ted left Knopf's and went with Doubleday. Ken McCormick, one of Doubleday's principal editors, says, "When we saw Ted's new book, we knew we didn't have anyone on the staff who could criticize him or edit him, really. His stuff was too good."

In February, 1947, he wrote Catherine De Vries that he had put together "the new book, twenty-five short and three long poems. A beautiful book it seemed to my prejudiced eyes—and also to the two canaries who typed it."

In February, 1947, Ted went back to Penn State to teach for the spring semester. Although he said to Professor Gates in a letter that his loyalty to Penn State bordered on the fantastic, this seems to have been mere courtesy. While the friends he made there remained his friends and admirers the rest of his life, he had in a manner of speaking used the place up—it was full of memories of his work on his first book and by this time he had finished his second. To return to Penn State at all seemed a step backward but it was something he had to do, for he had no other job. He continued writing and, although he had his usual apprehensions about finding another place, the semester was in terms of his mental equilibrium a peaceful time. As far as he could ever feel good about his own work, he felt good about *The Lost Son*, and since the publication date had not been set, his fears of what the critics would say had not yet begun to bite.

In September, 1947, he writes Catherine De Vries about his summer,

> During part of June I was in Michigan; then went to Bennington for a day, then to Yaddo for most of July and parts of August. In early August I went with Robert Lowell up to Breadloaf to visit Frost and give a reading at the School of English. Then we went to see some mad friends of his (Lowell's) at Ipswich. Later I taught at the Univ. of New Hampshire Writers Conference; stopped at Bennington again; then to Yaddo; then to West Cornwall, Connecticut; then to New York, then State College, then home.

That except for a few stops in Boston, etc. is the summer. I had a lot of fun; caught quite a few bass; was croquet, tennis, ping-pong and eating champion of Yaddo (these intellectuals are not much competition.)

But I wrote only one piece: 52 lines. The last part, however, is quite wonderful . . .

Beside Robert Lowell, Ted's friends at Yaddo were J. F. Powers, Bucklin Moon, and Hans Sahl, who later translated several of Ted's poems into German. They drank with him, went fishing with him, and furnished the competition in the different games. Lowell says that Ted played croquet with a handkerchief over his head knotted at the four corners to keep the sun off—his hair was thinning even then, and that he was a serious, even grim contestant who played to win. When Ted usurped the bathroom for too long a time, Lowell and Powers would bang on the door and shout, "*Ordnung! Ordnung!* Papa is coming!" It was his first acquaintance with Lowell, whom he was later to pay the compliment of fearing as his chief rival in American poetry.

At West Cornwall, Connecticut, he visited Jeremy and Mary Bagster-Collins at Yelping Hill, their summer place. Ted and Jeremy Bagster-Collins played tennis every day and Mary Bagster-Collins said, "Once I was shelling peas beside the swimming pool and I could hear them on the court. They swore horribly all the time. It was really fantastic." Ted seems to have enjoyed himself that summer.

After long but friendly wrangles protracted by Ted's finickiness with John Sargent and Ken McCormick about type, paper, format, jacket, end papers, and publicity for the new book, Ted saw it published on March 11, 1948, after he had gone to the University of Washington. It was entitled, *The Lost Son and Other Poems*.

Whatever anxiety and trepidation Ted may have suffered while waiting for them were dispelled when the reviews came out. They were all good, as these excerpts which Ted made and preserved himself demonstrate:

Louise Bogan in *The New Yorker*,

> In the long poem that gives the book its title, he plunges into the subconscious as into a pond, and brings up all sorts of clammy and amorphous material. He often frames it in the language of the adage, the proverb, the incantation, and the nonsense rhyme . . . "The Lost Son" is written with complete

conscious control. The effects have been manipulated as all art is manipulated, but the method aids in the understanding of the material instead of befogging it. Throughout true emotion gives the chosen style coloration and shape. The pattern of "The Lost Son" is ancient and satisfying as well—the pattern of light-found-after-darkness. The poet rises, at the end, to the surface of his obsessive dream to see the world in the light of day . . . Roethke is full of virtues that are instinctive or that can be acquired only with great difficulty.

Babette Deutsch in the *New York Herald-Tribune,*

Here, as in no other recent book of poetry, the darker workings of the auditory imagination are palpably recognizeable . . . This younger practitioner has an ear for these cadences, the aural virtues that reach out and lay hands upon the nerves of the listener . . . The shifting rhythms unite with the homely images taken from childhood memories of root cellars and greenhouses to produce unusual and powerful effects . . . What emerges at the end is a history of a man's soul.

If the long title-poem is the richest in significance, the more accessible short lyrics should not be neglected. They, too, have a delicate music, and, what is rarer in contemporary verse, a tenderness that is quite clean of sentimentality.

Robert Fitzgerald in *The New Republic,*

There is a long poem in four sections that rises to a more universal occasion than most of Berryman's and has, I think, important merits. The earth, meaning damp dirt, slimy roots, sticks and stones, is something that the dead, and children, are closer to than anyone else except rare farmers and greenhouse keepers; Roethke's unique sensibility seems to combine the intuitions of all these. His short lyrics have been mildly good, but his long poem is of another order. It is, among other things, a skeletal evocation of the mystery and wild fear in a real experience of that earth which is "filth a fairing" behind every life. The handling of the rhythms is original and sure, the form abstractly or dreamfully dramatic, with choral jingles and sharp, eerie back-chat in an earth tongue of Elizabethan energy,

These flowers are all fangs. Comfort me,
  fury.
Wake me, witch, we'll do the dance of rotten sticks.

There were many more reviews, all filled with praise from other magazines and newspapers.

The Lost Son and Other Poems is an amazing work. In retrospect its thematic links with his earlier poems are plain enough but no one could have foreseen the abrupt freshness of language, the new, vivid, free-ranging associations he made into his symbols, or the use he put to a native democratic assumption, that if he plumbed the depths of himself, he would find there the fears and ecstasies of all men. With a heroic insouciance he seems to have taken the euphoric slide and skitter into a bout of illness, its terrors and despairs, the slow emergence from it, and made them somehow into Louise Bogan's "ancient and satisfying pattern—the pattern of light-found-after-darkness." If his earlier poems seem muted by other voices, he sang out in this book with his own.

X

Working Methods

About the time of the composition of *The Lost Son*, Ted's poetic practice became fixed and it changed hardly at all from that time forward. It will be illuminating to draw on the different sources of information now available and set down what it was.

He said to me and to many other people, "I'm always working," and I never saw him when his pockets were not filled with loose bits of paper—even on the day he was getting an honorary doctorate at the University of Michigan—old envelopes, or if these chanced to fail, he would use paper matchbooks. On these he would write down striking words or phrases he heard in conversation. I have seen him bring out the paper when the words had barely been said, and if this interrupted the speaker's flow, Ted seemed oblivious; or he would break into his own talk to write down a phrase that had occurred to him whether he had said it out loud or not. One time Richard Humphreys was walking with him in the country near Harbor Springs, Michigan. They were talking steadily and not about poetry. Ted stopped abruptly, fished some paper out of his pocket, and wrote something on it. Humphreys asked, "What was that you wrote?" Ted showed him a list of disconnected words. "I just heard a rhythm," he said. Like other poets, he had, beneath his daily occupations and amusements, a fundamental awareness of the materials of his craft.

Periodically he would transfer the contents of his pockets to his notebooks but these scraps were not his only source—he seems to have sat down and written in the notebooks every day. These were cheap dime-store notebooks. Only a few were the expensive leather-bound ring-lock kind used by college students. Ted never saw all his papers collected during his lifetime, but if he had, I think he would have been astonished at the amount of paper he covered. There are over two hundred of these notebooks alone in which he set down his private jottings, not to mention others containing more than twelve hundred poems by other people he had written out by hand as aides-mémoire. "You can't remember a poem unless you write it down," he often said. There is also over a ream of paper in loose sheets covered with poetry whose function I shall discuss presently. Added to these are the drafts of his prose writings and fair copies of them to be given to whatever typist he was using at the time, and the thousands of letters of his voluminous correspondence, a total, I should say, of several million words. Of all the lines of poetry he wrote, a rough guess would estimate that only about 3 percent were ever printed.

When he first started to write poetry in the early Thirties, he did it in what most people would consider to be the conventional way, that is, the germ of a poem would occur to him. This might be a single luminous word, a coherent line, or merely a string of words picked out at random but set in a rhythmic order that appealed to him. Gradually in the notebooks would appear an accretion of relevant lines, with many false starts and crossings-out, and slowly the "subject" of the poem emerges to an observer. The beat of the line and its length are often determined by the first coherent line he sets down; other times by others. The rhyme scheme, if any, appears later. The main point here is this: his earliest practice was to work on one poem at a time. He would continue to work in the notebooks until one can see that the conception of the poem was complete in his mind, however rough it looks. Then he seems to have left the notebooks and worked on loose sheets of paper, adding, cutting, and refining until the poem was done. Then it was given to a typist and, if he were satisfied with it, sent away to a magazine at once. (He did not keep poems by him and lay them away for several months to see if they would improve by neglect.)

If, however, he had any doubts about the piece, he would take or send it to one of his poet friends, in these early days, Rolfe Humphries, Stanley Kunitz, John Holmes, or Louise Bogan, and such was his own ambivalence toward his work, he did this very often. If he and his friend were face to face and the friend made some definite criticism or suggested a change, Ted was apt to damn him as an insensitive clod whose effrontery in daring to complain of this poem was insupportable, and then collapse and humbly make the changes. When at last the poem, steeled by these criticisms, satisfied him, he would send it off. Like an oyster he had a high rate of irritability with editors but he never thought their criticisms would result in pearls, and while he was grudgingly willing to change the punctuation or, more rarely, a single word, he would howl down any major changes, withdraw the poem, and submit it elsewhere. Until he had Diarmuid Russell of Russell & Volkening as an agent who would perform the agent's chore of making many submissions, it took only two or three rejections for Ted to become discouraged and lay the poem permanently away. And even with an agent, he liked to deal with editors himself.

About the middle of the Thirties after Ted went to Penn State, the character of the notebooks begins to change. Where the first ones contained nothing but poetry and a few addresses he wanted to remember, in these he begins to write down titles of books, excerpts from some of them, mostly critical and philosophical works, remarks on abstractions such as love, anger, hatred, sharp, always sharp criticisms of contemporary fellow poets, descriptions and assessments of social situations in which he had recently taken part, and, increasingly more frequent, aphoristic observations of himself. Letters are begun and stopped halfway. He may keep a diary for three or four days with the emphasis not so much on what he does as how he feels. (On two widely separated days in these, there is the single entry, "Frightened.") But there is always the poetry. It dominates the notebooks, and these other items are merely interspersed. We can see him set down a phrase he knows is good and later see him try to work it into poems, sometimes years later. "A sidelong pickerel smile," for instance, appears first in 1938. It shows briefly in drafts of other poems but is cut. It finally comes to rest in "Elegy for Jane" in the 1950s. "The paralytic stunned in the tub and the water rising" was set down in 1937 and not used at all until "The Meadow Mouse" in *The Far Field*, his last book.

When he begins work on the greenhouse poems in the early 1940s, one last dimension is added to the notebooks, memory, the memory of his childhood. He writes little accounts of boyhood scenes. He asks himself questions, "Who were the old women in the greenhouse? What did they do? Tying strings to wires? What else? Their skirts swinging." (This seems to be the first returns that led to "Frau Baumann, Fran Schmidt, and Frau Schwartze."*) There is a good deal of this searching of his past and it is the past of his earliest years. He leaves his high-school and college years alone, and all the years after. He does not recall his hours of play, his playmates or his days at school, his music, painting, or dancing lessons, his frequent illnesses, the Christian Endeavor meetings or the rides in the Buick—these may not have been recallable. They seem to have no meaning for him. What has been burned into his memory and what he writes about are always himself, his father, his mother, more rarely his sister, the greenhouse and its flowers and its working people, the field behind it, the fishing trips with his father, and his own rambles in the game preserve and along the rivers. Instinctively he remembers the period and the area that has been charged with his deepest emotions.

Since he saw the years of the greenhouse poems as a time when he "loosened up," he loosened up inevitably in his notes. The notebooks of the Thirties were always dead serious; now he begins to write funny, even scatological doggerel occasionally; concoct witty apothegms; wisecracks; jokes.

From this period onward, he writes lines of poetry, one, two, three at a time, and they are not lines for any poem he has then in mind. Occasionally he rings a line he thinks good; a few pages later, another, and so on until maybe thirty pages later, we see six or seven of the ringed lines written consecutively and it is clear that a poem has started. He has abandoned his habit of working from an inkling toward a conception and writing lines to support it. His practice has changed—now he lets words or lines themselves suggest or evolve into a conception. And his critical tact lies in perceiving just which lines, juxtaposed, will become coherent, and ultimately take shape as a poem. He rereads his notebooks constantly, sometimes dating the rereading, and many poems are

---

* Mrs. Mortensen says that no Frau Schmidt ever worked in the greenhouse, although Frau Baumann, Frau Schwartze, and Frau Zeiler did. Ted may have forgotten Frau Zeiler or he may have adopted "Schmidt" to suit his rhythm.

mosaics of lines written months, even years apart, gathered from different notebooks. He now sees all of his life that is memorable as capable of being turned into poetry, a great flow of it, but he seems to have had a pointillist memory—small echoes, single lines. His problem was not to compose these lines, find images, metaphors—he had thousands of those—but to find ways of making poems out of this huge store of lines. One of his notes is: "What I want is themes."

Once he had decided—and it seems to have been a hard-won decision, weighed and judged, and not at all quick or serendipitous—that these limited areas of his childhood were to be the sources of his work because he coolly saw them as having drawn to themselves the deepest emotions of his life, he did what nearly every writer of talent does: working out of absolute conviction and sincerity, he enlarged, enriched, and dignified them until they became symbols for the whole of life.

Better than any comment, a selection from his notebooks will show how his mind worked and what his concerns were. (Most of the poetry is left out.)

Written between November, 1930, and February, 1931

> This is a subtle grief, a care
> That catches at me unaware,
> A grief too difficult for tears
> That ravages my greenest years
> And chills the proud and secret heart
> Before its generous hours depart.
> Since I am young, it does not find
> Sufficient mastery in the mind;
> Since I am careless, it can be
> As treacherous as ecstasy
> And though it leaves, it will return
> To mock me with a savage scorn
> A fear too shameful to confess,
> A terrible child-loneliness.
>
> The rage defines the man.

Notebook, 1942

> Meister Eckhart, St. Theresa of Avila, St. John of the Cross, St. Francis of Assisi.

Notebook, 1944

For ten years I played roaring boy when I was really frightened boy.

I'd rather be vulgar than cold.

Yeats' career in part so managed, so stagey, a kind of gentleman racketeer. There were two magazines in which he would not appear, some rich women to whom he would not toady.

What a small talent I have after ten years work.

The error of Rimbaud: the world is chaotic, therefore I must be.

Notebook, March, 1944

The new resolutions: I will take walks, start a new notebook, work with my hands. What am I worrying about?

Why do I hunt for something to hate, something to annoy me?

How terrible the need for God!

The paradox of destruction: I (protagonist) can no longer be good. I am bored with the moral course, yet anything otherwise produces anxiety.

A gnawing nervousness of one who has learned to keep down the worst concomitants of . . .

I'm old and I'm tired and I'm bored . . .

Time to myself—and when I have it . . .

The state of wanting to kill everything one loves, cut off more than the nose to spite the race. (Sic)

To wish for an illness—for something to come to grips with, a break from reality.

Or to eat—and again to forget.

Notebook, January, 1945

Afraid? Why, hell, I've been afraid all my life—dogs, thunder, my cousin . . .

God save us all from the mad technician
From the drawing board that erases half a city
That kills and . . .

For some reason this illness seems to have shaken loose powers: I am alive with ideas, some bad, no doubt, but there is more vehemence, more energy, more contempt, more love.

Make poetry the reflection of your life.

Do I repeat the egg?
Hunch me another, fat one.
(Not used but in the new style of *The Lost Son.*)

Titles: The Long Alley, The Whole Flower, The Stones Sang, The Root, A Green Bough, The Root is Green, The Fire and the Rose, The Root of the Rose. The Lost Son.

To go back is to go forward.

You know, Louise, I was really hurt at the time that you gave me only such a brief notice on that first book.

Notebook, August, 1945.

I'm willing to drink or insult people but I'll be damned if I'll play games.

Words are not to be wallowed in.

What was this greenhouse? It was a jungle and it was a paradise. It was order and disorder. Was it an escape? No, for it was a reality harsher than . . .

When I can't stand people, I give them a fictional character. Hence my calling you, Bucko.

Wait. Watch. Listen. Meditate. He'll come when. No, I know he wont come. He doesn't care about me any more. No, I mean HIM, the Big He, that great big three-cornered Papa . . .

Nine pages later:

That stillness became alive.
A lively understandable spirit entertain me.
I was no longer alone.

I hate the external world. Don't you understand that?

Notebook, January, 1946

Stood in a far field.

My whole life a struggle against cyclic disturbances?

Notebook, July, 1946

An old woman's acquiescence, her wisdom.

The long journey from the interior.

Random Undated Notes

The notion of emptiness generates passion.

I am beside myself, sitting by you.

I used to think it was all right to be a woman; but it isn't.

Yes, it's possible to create a true natural order simply by putting down things repeatedly.

Can't we make this discussion a little more disorderly? I'm not rich but I'm glossy.

Love is the true surprise.

Slowly the speech of the dead is beaten into praise. An eye walked there, wily as an adder, making a new place pure. Even I can be a mother, giving birth to my father.

The fallacy: there's something to be learned in sinning.

In the ponds of her being, I was the happiest fish;
A cherub dropped in the lap of love.

My attacks of false humility have taken a turn for the worse.

By taking he began to give;
Astonished, found himself in love.

I write about myself, cunts, and God—so, in that order . . .

If a man lives badly he becomes a woman; if she lives badly he becomes a brute.

She: I'd like to get married but it's so vulgar.

What's the winter for?
To remember love.

I live in a country, the land of the free.
Did I eat my mother?
Did my mother eat me?
Or was this devouring done mutually?

The heart's core, you will find, is most intractable material.

To love objects is to love life.
The pure shaft of a single granary on the prairie,
The small pool of rain in the plank of a railway siding.

Innocence is a thing of the spirit, not the body.

I'm sick of women. I want God.

For we need more barnyard poets, *echt Dichter* of *Dreck* and *Schmutz,* poets who depart from the patio, the penthouse, the palladium.

Where true beginnings move
The mind, and make their spring.

All bushes can't be bears.

If you can't think, at least sing.

Am I too old to write in paragraphs?

I need to become more learned in the literature of exasperation. In my worst state, once I think of my contemporaries, I'm immediately revived.

Who loved his life can love his death as well.

I always wonder, when I'm on the podium, why I am there: I really belong in some dingy poolhall under the table.

She: You ought to be interested in other people.
He: Why? They're even worse than I am.

I was betrayed by my own hardihood.

By light, light; by love, love; by this, this.

I don't know a thing except what I try to do.

Sure I'm crazy
But it aint easy.

What words have good manners? None.

I feel like a pig; but there are worse ways to feel.

I have all kinds of inner security; what I need is outer security.

I seek first and last that *essential* vulgarity I once thought charming.

For the mind is always hunting resemblances, seeking out correspondences, snatching for pieces of the supreme puzzle—like a hand plunged into an active mist—plucking; a hoof raised, pawing more than ground.

I am proud to suffer: to know I can and can make it something else.

Mr. Randall, what's this about sleeping on a board to improve your rhythm?

From Rilke I learned there are themes other than light.

Flesh, flash out of me.

A breath is but a breath
And the smallest of our ties
With the long eternities;
And some men lie like trees,
The last to go is the bark,
The weathered, tough outside.

There is no one ideal, no end to this matter of making noise that
rhymes.

I'd like to be sure of something—even if it's just going to sleep.

Of all pontificators, those who prate of poetry are the most
tiresome—including those aging Sapphos who speak as if they
had invented integrity.

I'm so poor I can't subscribe to my own downfall.

In the very real and final sense, don't *know* anything. That is
what saves me from you, dear class, and from ultimate madness.

> In every man there is a little woman.
> The teacher needs his students to stay human.
> Suppose you master one cliché—
> You're a step beyond the horse: a horse's A.

Anything that's longer than it is wide is a male sexual symbol,
say the Freudians.

O Mother Mary, and what do I mean,
That poet's fallen into the latrine—
And no amount of grace or art
Can change what happens after that.

So much of me already gone to death.
An old wood rich in glory, a true grave,
A lake with swans in the large mind of love.

XI

The West Coast

Ted became a member of the University of Washington faculty through the good offices of Professor George Lundberg, the distinguished sociologist whom he had known at Bennington. Lundberg recommended Ted vociferously to Professor Joseph Harrison, the head of the English Department. Lewis Jones, former president of Bennington, and in 1947 president of the University of Arkansas, also wrote an enthusiastic letter in his behalf, and on a visit to Reed College, Oregon, his alma mater, for a conference of educators, met Harrison there and talked Ted up personally. Some excerpts from Jones's letter are prophetically interesting:

> I can say without any hesitation that Professor Roethke was one of the best teachers we ever had at Bennington. . . . Roethke did a marvellous job of breaking through the inhibitions of his students and we had a great burst of creative writing activity under his influence . . . Roethke would spend an endless amount of time helping individual students with their writing problems and was very good at teaching just plain English composition. You are, no doubt, familiar with Roethke's writings. He is extremely complex, temperamental, and a somewhat eccentric person . . . If the University of Washington can take his somewhat eccentric personality, it will acquire one of the best teachers I have ever seen in operation. I have always liked Roethke and admired him, although I must confess that his intensity has sometimes led him into clashes with his colleagues. On the whole, however, he is an easy person to work with and can get along with anyone who has a true appreciation of sound literary values—he does not, however, tolerate fools gladly . . . I haven't

been on the U. of W. campus for a long time, but my guess is
that Roethke would find a place there and I can guarantee that
if you get him you are in for a renaissance of interest and
enthusiasm in creative literature.

On August 21, 1947, Lundberg wrote Ted an amusing letter,
telling him that a small house in the University district had been
found for him and continuing:

> As for transportation out here, you will find that trains go as
> far as Missoula, Montana, after which you go by 24-mule team
> to Spokane and then walk the rest of the way. You should pick
> up an Indian squaw for a guide as Lewis and Clark did and she
> will take care of you the rest of the way . . . When you arrive, if
> you send up the proper smoke signals, Chief Seattle will conduct
> you to your lodgings . . . If you get near any towns that have a
> railroad in the near future, you might ask for a folder known as
> a timetable, which may be had free in most railroad stations . . .
> These remarkable documents, if you can read them, will tell you
> all about trains, Pullman fares, exactly how much different types
> of service cost. But all of these services are best suited to people
> of human and normal proportions—I suggest that you get a box
> car where you can stretch out. You can easily live off of the dead
> buffaloes the train will kill as it picks its way westward. Bring
> a full set of shooting irons because the Indians will be sniping at
> you from every bush and street corner.
> What's this I hear about your griping about salary? Since
> when did poets begin to get paid in this world? Man, get your
> mind on higher things. Who steals your purse steals trash, etc.

The "griping about salary" refers to Ted's protest that Washing-
ton's first salary offer was too low. On August 22, 1947, the presi-
dent of the University, Raymond B. Allen, wrote to Ted at Yaddo
saying that his appointment as associate professor of English had
been approved "at a salary of $5004 ($586 a month) on a nine-
month basis, effective September 16, 1947." The offer was less
than a hundred dollars higher than the first one but Ted accepted
it. The Washington authorities did not know it but it was a fore-
taste of things to come.

On Puget Sound with two big lakes inside the city, Seattle has
a beautiful natural site but it is hilly and spread out. Ted did not
own a car then, and lodgings near the University were necessary

if he were going to walk to the campus. The house at 4337 15th Street, N.E. suited him and he stayed there two years. (In 1950 he bought a car "right off the floor," as he said, of an agency in Saginaw, a new green Buick Special. He called it, "The Flying Juke-Box" and "The Death Car." He drove it in progressive degrees of delapidation, the rest of his life.)

They say he was quiet, circumspect, and diffident at first, and probably, since he had worked at state universities, wary. Undoubtedly he felt the need to assert himself—he usually did in new social situations—by way of getting himself properly established and he found an early opportunity. When he learned that his teaching program included a course in the writing of fiction, he went roaring down the corridor to the office where courses were assigned. Mrs. Jerry Lee Willis, a teacher in the English Department, was in charge. Ted was loud, wrathy, and profane. It was hardly complaint, she says; it was defiance. (It was true that Ted did not like to teach fiction. He had never written any and, lacking any real experience with it, he did not feel himself competent.) Mrs. Willis soothed him with a course in poetry.

A few nights later, having learned that Mrs. Willis was a widow, Ted asked her out to dinner. They became friends and, from then until his marriage, she knew him better than any woman in Seattle. Ted did not confide much more of himself to women than the care of his ego but this was not a small task and many found it fascinating. More than to his male friends whom he often sensed as competitors, he frequently revealed himself unmasked and offered women the untidy parcel of his fears, his essential tenderness, and his boisterous laughter, and while he certainly relied on Mrs. Willis's kindness and tolerance, he was no more "faithful" to her than he had been to Kitty Stokes.

A letter to Eddie and Eleanor Nichols, dated January 26, 1948, shows Ted's early impressions of Seattle and sets up one pole of his continual ambiguity:

> The job is cushy; now only two courses, both by permission. 30 (or is it 29) students in all, 7 hrs. a week. I teach fancy: vigor and style. But so what? The town, its mores (so *damned* genteel —the pioneers are all dead or in jail)—the town, I say, is the worst bore in the U.S.: not a decent restaurant, nothing but beauty parlors and "smart" shops and toothy dames with zinc

curls. A damned matriarchy, worse than State College in that respect, only you don't hear the bitching about Money.

The weather is pretty good. I played tennis outside Sat. & Sun. Salmon fishing, etc.

Still, I feel restive. Maybe the Guggenheim undid me for working.

I was in New York for New Year's, came back a week late. I may fly East when the book comes out (March 11). Doubleday is frankly peddling it as the best book of verse of the year. That's true but it is naive to think that the committees (those old farts) will come to that conclusion. However, who am I to complain?

Douglas Moore wants me to do a kids' opera, the libretto, and I may do it.

In NY I drank some Dutch beer with Wilder Hobson . . . Wilder played his trombone with a dame in the next apt. on the piano. She was really good and he did better than I ever heard him.

Auden has sent the MS of the book to Eliot. Nothing will come of this! . . . if you know people who buy poetry, tell them about you-know-what.

Love,
Ted

The other pole of Ted's ambiguity can be seen in a piece that seems to have been written as an essay:

The campus is a riot of wonderful natural life—as well as new buildings and old. There is no need to barber and pamper the landscape; everything grows green and strange—the rhododendron, holly, hawthorne, horse chestnut, pink and white dogwood, Japanese cherry, Scotch broom, and the ever-present evergreens. Even the stones and sides of trees bear a fine mossy sheen. In one corner of the University area, across from a block of apartments, is a rich thicket, dripping and dense, mossy and dark. At the other end rise the usual frightening monoliths to science; but somehow you feel that the natural—and the human —worlds are not going to be overwhelmed.

A casual and prodigal place—and a place of no nonsense. You can smoke anywhere, in class, in corridor, even in the wooden buildings. Apparently the feeling is, if these burn down—well, we'll build better ones.

And the campus dress has the same easy sensibleness. There is none of the straining for effect, the hats and gloves, the high heels, the double-fox furs of the Twenties, when all the co-eds seemed to be trying to look like Peggy Joyce or Mrs. Harrison Williams, and the boys were all junior executives complete with black suits and stuff collars. Now, for the girls, on week-days, knitted sweaters, skirts, saddle-shoes, gabardine trench-coats seem always standard. But even this classic norm does not confine the personality of the Washington co-ed; there are variations, pleasing to these old eyes, in color and fabric, in head-scarf and hair-do.

And when they take pen in hand, on an examination, these Washington students, after they get over a little initial stiffness, can get off good remarks with the same unstudied casualness that marks their daily life.

It might be remarked in passing that Ted barely notices the University buildings in his description but he lists spontaneously the flowers, trees, and shrubbery. For him, natural growths, each species, had characters as sharp as people. Another note: after Bennington, "students" meant girls to Ted and those old eyes spotted two or three he became quite intimate with.

Soon after he had become part of the Washington English staff, Ted won the first of his many prizes, the Eunice Tiétjens Award. She had been an associate editor of *Poetry Magazine* and the magazine gave the prize in her memory. It carried an honorarium of $100. Ted was properly grateful, though not superficially overwhelmed, for both the honor and the money, and it spurred him into a course of action that was not only characteristic but later became habitual. He began to maneuver for a promotion and a raise. It was a tricky business: the full professors of the department had to vote on his admission to their number and Ted had not bothered to ingratiate himself with all of them. He prodded his friends into spreading encomiums where they would do the most good, but as the voting day approached, it was not at all clear that the promotion would go through. Ted then threatened to quit. The threat seemed to work, for in April, 1948, he was made full professor and he was given a raise of $999.

While Ted certainly wanted the promotion and the raise on his own account, his motives were not entirely selfish. When a university was led or forced, if need be, into taking notice of a poet and in the most practical way, by bestowing rank and cash, the cause of poetry everywhere was advanced, he believed. These were prizes wrested from a hostile environment and, if they were not signs of its total conversion, they were at least its acknowledgments of value.

Money was important to Ted not only for the prestige it gave him and because it paid his living expenses and allowed him to indulge his tastes for thick, prime steaks, imported ale, and an endless number of new books, but also as a means of redeeming his family's fiscal honor. Nearly everyone who knew him well has heard him rage or grumble about the loss of the Roethke family fortune. And the fortune grew larger as he grew older. He was never precise about the extent of this treasure nor about the way he was done out of it, but there were dark hints of treachery, skulduggery by trusted relatives when he himself was too young to know what was going on, something criminal to do with the sale of the greenhouse after his father's death, and even, in his more expansive moments, with the loss of the ancestral Prussian villages.

When he was in one of his manic states, he concocted many plans to regain what to him was a lifetime's financial grubstake out of which he had been mulcted. Jim Jackson, who heard the story many times, has listed them:

    a. His familiar Big Business fantasies, forming corporations and cartels, making use of his cousins, Bud, and Chester Biesterfield, who was head of Dupont's patent division.

    b. His notions of somehow rigging and rarifying his teaching situation salarywise (one example: royalties paid by the college based on high student demand for his services) so that his professional compensation would increase enormously. Not by step-raises small or large but by such leaps and jumps that it might have been cheaper for the college or university in question to offer him a percentage or "cut" from its total "take" as a way of keeping him. (Here the birth of the teacher as a sort of academic entrepreneur.)

    c. His later dreams of stage appearances, lecture tours, verse-vaudeville turns and the like.

There was no Roethke family "fortune." A plausible source of Ted's references to it may have been this situation: Ted was thirteen years old when the greenhouse was sold. He probably heard his father and mother discussing its sale and the various asking prices mentioned, any one of which would have been several thousand dollars, and to a thirteen-year-old boy, fifty thousand, say, would have seemed an immense sum, a fortune, in fact. This sank into Ted's impressionable mind and remained there. And its evaporation was not caused so much by the chicanery and double-dealing of relatives, if, indeed, any of it was; rather, it was that Ted's mother used it, invested it, eked it out over the years to put him and his sister through college and to support herself.

People do not, however, act on truth; they act on what they believe to be truth, and the fortune burned in Ted's mind, lost, irretrievable, but an indispensable prop to the aristocratic past he was trying, like Yeats, to construct for himself. What is most interesting in this agitation over money is that while he was constantly demanding more pay, writing letters to find higher-paying jobs, and devising extravagant schemes for the sale of his poetry, he never wrote a line of poetry which was designed to make money. He could have descended into cliché and written a "popular" kind of verse which would have made him more money than his own did; he could have written middlebrow literary essays for magazines; he could have written fiction;* or composed the play he was always threatening to. He could have, that is, if it had been merely money he wanted but it was not. His real aim was recognition, and, without giving it a thought, he knew that in Twentieth Century America, recognition did not spring from evanescent words of praise from his peers, however lavish or gratifying. Recognition meant titles, prizes, and heaps of dollar bills. Money was merely one of the signs. The proof of this, I think, is clear: his complicated schemes for making a fortune and his gnawing regret for the lost one were merely fantasies.

In 1948, Ted got a letter from one of his Bennington students,

---

* While he was at Bennington, Ted had a small library of books on how to write fiction. It affronted him to learn that short-story writers sometimes got a thousand or two thousand dollars for a single story, that a best-selling novel might make its author a hundred thousand while he got so little for his poetry. He said he was going to write fiction, himself. (He never did, of course, except for a couple of bad comic pieces in his notes where he imitated the style of S. J. Perelman.) I said to him, "Would you buy a book on how to write poetry?" He snorted with contempt. "Then don't buy books on how to write fiction," I said.

Judith Bailey, who was then living in Paris. She told him of a new magazine, a quarterly issuing from Rome, *Botteghe Oscure*, that was looking for good new poetry. Almost simultaneously, he received a letter from its founder and editor, Princess Marguerite Caetani, who said that John Lehmann in London had spoken to her about Ted's work and asking him to send her some. Soon after Ted made the first of his many submissions to "La Princesse Caetani di Bassiano." Later he addressed her more correctly as "La Principessa."

A long and charming friendship came out of this. Princess Caetani was born Marguerite Chapin in Philadelphia and in 1902, somewhat in the manner of a heroine out of Henry James, she went to Paris to study singing with the famous tenor, Jean de Reszke. Among the students and musicians of her circle she met a handsome young composer, Roffredo Caetani, Prince of Bassiano. They fell in love and were married.

They settled at Versailles and were frequent hosts to a distinguished group of writers, among them, Paul Valéry, Valéry Larbaud, the translator of Joyce, Alexis Léger, (St.-Jean Perse), Léon-Paul Fargue. Out of dinner-table conversation the idea for a magazine emerged, for which Léger suggested the title, *Commerce*—"commerce d'esprit." Princess Caetani, full of enthusiasm, undertook its financial sponsorship and became its working editor, handling all the submissions and correspondence herself but appealing to Léger for final literary judgments. *Commerce* did not concern itself much with criticism or scholarship, rather with the best contemporary poetry, fiction, and essays it could find in France, and it continued from 1924 until 1932.

In 1932 the Caetanis left Versailles to live in Rome or at their country house in the Roman campagna, Ninfa. They were an ancient family—the earliest tomb of the line lies in the grottoes of the Vatican. One ancestor was Pope Boniface VIII; a later one corresponded with Stendhal. And Ninfa was in fact the ruins of a medieval city. They refurbished part of it and the Princess made a beautiful garden on its grounds, using a stream that once filled the moat. Stone pines and avenues of cypresses formed a setting for mimosa, camellias, magnolias, lilacs, and lilies. It was here that she entertained her friends, writers and artists, at Sunday picnics. These began when the Second World War was barely over, as soon as the Allied armies had possession of Italy, and these gatherings stimulated a beginning to the revival of European art. All her friends from all over Europe who could get there and the new Italian writers were her guests, and out of these occasions came the suggestions for another magazine which evolved into *Botteghe Oscure.*

The Caetani palace in Rome was in the Via Botteghe Oscure near the Circus Flaminius. The Spanish embassy occupied the ground floor, and the Caetanis, when in residence, the rest of the building. It was from here that Princess Caetani issued the magazine with the help of a few assistants. She was eager to see the work of young writers. She read their writings herself, criticized gently and tactfully, and paid enormous prices for whatever she bought, sometimes so large as to be in the nature of subsidies. Unlike many of the wealthy, she was amazingly generous and personally so. Her letters to her contributors, warm-hearted, candid, and graceful, are never businesslike. They contain inquiries into the health, general well-being, and finances of the recipient, and often she would impulsively insert a large check if she thought her correspondent needed it. Sometimes things got into a muddle but everyone was gladly patient. She wanted *Botteghe Oscure* to be an international magazine—*Commerce* had been French, printed in French—filled with the best work of her time. She expended floods of emotional energy, tact, and determination to get it and she did.

Prose was represented by such writers as Alberto Moravia, Calvino, Arpino, Carson McCullers, Truman Capote, Elizabeth Bowen, L. P. Hartley, Rilke and Brecht, Paul Valéry, Camus, and André Malraux.

She published the first printed version of Dylan Thomas's *Under Milk Wood* as well as poems by W. H. Auden, E. E. Cummings, William Carlos Williams, Vernon Watkins, Robert Lowell, René Char, W. S. Merwin, James Agee, W. D. Snodgrass, and Ted himself.

To any of her contributors who were traveling on the Continent, she extended the most lavish hospitality either in Rome, Ninfa, or her apartment in Paris, and she arranged catalytic meetings between writers from different countries and backgrounds which often proved to be stimulating to their work.

Botteghe Oscure made heavy demands on her time and strength, and its publication was discontinued in 1960 when Princess Caetani was eighty years old, yet she continued to correspond frequently with her contributors whom she regarded, of course, as friends.

Ted called her "the last of the great patrons," and he wrote her,

> Even if I don't write, you remain in my mind, actively, as a symbol of graciousness and of another kind of ordered life, in which art matters. You deserve letters even better than those Rilke wrote to his Countesses (and how he loved to roll a title on his tongue) or that Yeats wrote to Lady Gregory. I have *thought* of such letters but am a Prussian (by descent) and can't write them. Alas for me—not for you.

Her personal and financial encouragement were very important to Ted in the years following his first submissions in 1948 and, aside from his Irish experiences, she was, in a sense, what Europe meant to him. She epitomized in the style of her life, its history, its taste, and the variations of its culture, yet she was, at the same time, an American whom he could approach without strangeness and it is significant that he joined her with his mother as the suggestive background for his poems, "An Old Lady's Winter Words" and "Meditations of an Old Woman."

As can be seen from the scattered references, Ted was now personally acquainted with the chief American poets of his time, and had become friends with some of them. He had assessed their work, compared it to his own, and found himself confident that he was their equal, if not their superior. He had been printed in Europe and, while he realized that it was too early to speak of a European reputation, nevertheless a beginning had been made. Recognizing the slowness of his development, he felt that the Tietjens Award, while certainly welcome, had not come soon enough. As early as his Bennington days, in the spring of the year when the Pulitzer prizes were announced, he would complain loudly and bitterly that he had not been given the one for poetry. Simultaneously and somewhat pathetically, he was ridden by gnawing doubts that his work was any good at all and that his career, such as it was, was only an elaborate deception. Who was he, a Saginaw Valley boy, the son of an immigrant greenhousekeeper to aspire to the grandeur of writing poetry? But he kept these doubts buried within himself and they were revealed only to his psychiatrists. To be whipsawed between the maintenance of this confident persona and the encouragement of the doubting self was a constant strain.

He soon won over his students and the renaissance of writing on the Washington campus that Lewis Jones had predicted was not long in coming. After his varied experience he was perfectly sure of himself before a class and he knew what he was doing. He demanded probably more reading and writing than any of their other teachers and in class his aim was always to bring them to such a pitch of excitement about poetry that they would speak without thinking, spontaneously, off the cuff. (When they did this he could gauge how much of his teaching had sunk in.) What gave him his power as a teacher was, I think, a candor and sincerity that was absolute, and students feel this. Proof lay in his remarks about his own struggles with poems he was currently working on. Later they would see these poems in print somewhere and this would give them a sense of participation, for Ted always said he learned from students, that teaching was no good unless he did. Out of their naiveté and relative ignorance they often said fresh things, opened a new point of view for him that helped him. He was grateful and he said so. Some of his early pupils were Carolyn Kizer and James Wright and somewhat later David Wagoner, whom he persuaded the English Department to hire as a teacher. Ted's influence on his students came more from their heightened awareness of their own uniqueness, a new sense of the language as an instrument, and from infusions of his own vitality than in any stylistic imitation. As he said many times, he did not try to be a Papa.

His mature range of reference and the knowledge and alertness he expected from undergraduates can be seen in these notes from one class session, taken by a student and preserved in Ted's papers under the title (in his own hand) "Class Goodies":

> Thomas Moore
> John Moore
> Marianne Moore   (Freudian slip—Marilyn Moore)
> Douglas Moore

Sir Thomas More

Nicholas Moore

Start Robert Graves

Read Rosalie Moore—Yale Series

Words in a Violent Ward:
    In heaven, too,
    You'd be institutionalized.
    But that's all right,
    If they let you eat and swear
    With the likes of Blake,
    And Chris Smart
    And that sweet man, John Clare.
                    T. ROETHKE

Poetry—memorable speech
    —when you make a joke
    —curse effectively
    —give a cat its right name
"Hotter than god damn blue hell."

"Stick out your can—here comes the garbage man."

"Language starts in the compost heap of life."

    Poetry editor of *The New Yorker* is good—Howard Moss.

    See Hillyer's *Collected Poems*.

    Notice texture and quality of vowels.

"Wild and slow and young,
    She moved about the room."

"When the crocuses poke up their heads in the usual places."

"Pickety-fence rhythm."

    Seager—*The Inheritance.*

    Look up Stendhal

    At party, to Roethke, "Do you do something, or what?"

"Poets are tough."

    Miss Gould: "What do great poems say? They say—change your life."

    Rilke—"A sick man, clung to by other sick people."

". . . a disgusting piece of self-love."

Poets of disgust, contempt:
  Pope   Sitwell
  Earl of Rochester   Swift
  Baudelaire   Lawrence

"A snake lay coiled in oozy triangles." Kipling

"The snake lay coiled like excrement" Lawrence

"It shouldn't happen to a hitch-hiking dog."

"You think by feeling."

"Emotion is a thing of reason."

"A tear is an intellectual thing
And a sigh is the sword
Of an angel king."
             BLAKE

". . . the rational and intuitive together—man at his highest."

Angst

"slow relaxing skeletons."

Auden, master of epithet
See his *New Year's Letter*

Use initial alliteration
Kunitz: "The thing that eats the heart
      is mostly heart"

Read some Russian fairy tales

Make use of two-syllable prepositions

Eros contrasted with Apollo

Gestalt

"Art is not life
And cannot be
A midwife to society"

Try to build up tension

Read Tennyson

"The love of the beautiful will keep man alive."

"Jokes, stories, and poems unite humans."

"Form is a sieve." AUDEN

Locked couplet example:

"He who shall teach the child to doubt,
The rotting grave will ne'er get out."
BLAKE

Don't pontificate

"Swift's servant beat him.
Now they use
A current flowing
From a fuse."

The Oxford Book of Light Verse

"Never love unless you can
Bear with all the faults of man."

Learn to manipulate the caesura

Periodic sentence—verbal phrase comes at the end.

Poems New and Collected   Rolfe Humphries

Anthology of Irish Verse

The Faber Book of Modern Verse

"Edward Arlington Cemetery."

The natural order of things is usually best

"Eternity is now."

Becoming—study the Catholic, Indian, Platonic views

Sonnets
    from situation to the exception, from generalities to par-
    ticulars, string of metaphors, thesis to antithesis

Need for some kind of climactic end

A bogus heroic tone comes easily

"What are your feelings on religion?"
"Point one—I think God is just fine."

Take on material when you're ready for it

Come Hither   W. de la Mare

". . . like in the army, if you're any good, you don't carry
anything."

Gunsel—homosexual killer

To break a cap—to fire a gun

Miss Emma you aint momma—morphine

You have to learn lingo

Selected Poems   W. C. Williams

Look up Louis, not Allen, Ginsberg

In order to write good stuff you have to hate adverbs

"Eliot—he's sort of wormy."

Belloc—*Cautionary Verses*

Boeuf Bourguignonne

Liebfraumilch

Heart's Needle   Snodgrass

Editors: "Look! We can't use this! This is good!"

Look for jazz rhythms in Hart Crane

Animism example: stones singing, leaves saying

The chief lesson is to learn to cut.

Use interjections to loosen up verse

Zulfikar Ghose *This Landscape, These People*
"England like an antique in a glass box."
"Breathing into the air like a woman's hair."

Irish: Kinsella, Montague, R. Murphy

A. E. Housman is soft, used inverted sentimentality, dead diction, though has some passages of ravishing movement

"The ability to remember things is related to the ability to create."

Fears of the artist—once you've done a thing well, you have to do it again, and differently

If you have the ability to see and write sensual detail, you're in business

"Even his heart wishes to bite apples."

R. Wolfe—went entirely mad and had the delusion that his penis was a radio station

"When I blow this whistle—I want it so quiet you can hear a rat pissin' on that cotton."

Lowell *Quaker Graveyard in Nantucket*

Particularity will keep you from sentimentality

To students from little high schools in the apple orchards, in the wheat fields to the east, small towns in the mountains and along the straits of San Juan, poetry, the whole of literature no longer lay dead on the page to be patronizingly dissected by scholars; it leaped up alive, a stern delight.

Since Ted did not like to get up in the morning, he fixed his classes in the early afternoon at one and two o'clock, no later because some of his students had to work then at board jobs. Beer could not be sold on the campus and after his classes Ted often went to The Rainbow, a beer joint half a mile away. Troops of students followed and the class, for all intents and purposes, since he talked the same in class or out, continued, sometimes after a hamburg or two, until late at night. Ted liked students, and if the Bennington girls had adored him, his impact at Washington was deeper and more exciting. He represented the whole world of art to them because he made it real when he talked; he convinced them of its importance, and proved to them that poetry, and by implication, paintings, sculpture, and sonatas were possible to make.

In 1948 Robert Heilman succeeded Joseph Harrison as head of the Washington English Department. Because of his long distrust of all academic persons, Ted felt that any one of them had to prove he was a "nice guy" before he would accept him, and at first he regarded Heilman with suspicion. Some years later Ted wrote a letter recommending him to the Guggenheim Foundation for a fellowship and with startling candor, he said that at first he thought Heilman a "time-server" and "political hack," but as he came to know him better, he saw that he was not only honest and decent, one of the ablest administrators he ever knew, but an acute critic and he was proud to be his friend. It is a good thing Ted gauged him correctly, for Heilman was always one of his kindest, staunchest friends and admirers and he defended him against any attack that was made on him.

Whether it was the stimulation of a new setting, the West Coast with its opulence of natural life in its almost English climate, or whether he felt that he had been idle too long (and "idle" meant not that he had not been writing but that he had gone too long without publishing a book), Ted worked in the years 1948 and 1949 with what seems to be an almost frantic assiduity. In a letter from Saginaw where he spent the summer of 1949, he says, "I spent all summer thrashing and sweating to break through into a new style," and he filled more notebooks and more loose sheets with poetry in these two years than in any period of his life. On

sheer bulk he would have had to average four or five pages of
poetry a day. Ted had no facility: everything came hard, and this
labor was done in the face of his teaching, the hours he spent with
students, his reading, which was increasingly mystical and theo-
logical, and what time he took for his social life. He published only
three poems in 1948, including "Praise to the End!" in *Botteghe
Oscure,* and one poem in 1949, "Unfold, Unfold," which was trans-
lated into Italian.

Slowly taking shape out of this mass of writing were the poems
for two projected books, *Praise to the End!* and *I Am! Says the
Lamb.*

Ted believed that he should experiment continually with the
language, that each new book of his should be written in a new
style. In the notebooks where he is working toward the poems of
Praise to the End!, short lines predominate; long lines are few. The
only poet of his contemporaries whom he always praised in the
privacy of his notebooks was one who had no literary influence on
him whatever, E. E. Cummings. He respected Cummings because
he "blew up the language," and he thought this a mark of genius.
In the notebooks where we can see that he has formed his concep-
tion of "I Need, I Need," Ted seems to be making a like effort:

> Tell me, tufty, where is far?
> It's the wind keeps me waiting.
> Why is how I like it.
> Diddle we care couldly.

In the midst of attempted lines for "Where Knock is Open
Wide," we find:

> A piece of a mouse
> The cat wouldn't eat.
> A hat is a house;
> I hid in his.

He discards the first two lines here and puts the last two into
"I Need, I Need."

On January 5, 1948, Ted sends the poem "Praise to the End!" to
Kenneth Burke with a brief explanatory outline of it:

Put crudely
1) Act
2) Reaction to act (quiet, sense of impotence)
3) Song: reasons for act
   reaction again
4) Two flashbacks related to act, then the present again.
5) Sublimation (The fact that there are few human symbols here isn't accidental.)

Simultaneously Ted was working on the poems that went into *I Am! Says the Lamb*. This is a book for children and many of the poems are about animals. Ted's relations with children were not paternal, or even avuncular nor patronising because they were unfinished adults, rather he seemed to feel an awe (which he seldom showed them) of their fresh perceptions and instant easy creations. I have seen him with my own daughter—his effort was not specially to be kind but to understand her. Of course, children responded; there was an immediate rapport. Mrs. Max Nicolai, the wife of a lawyer whom Ted made friends with quite soon after his arrival in Seattle, says that once Ted was at their house and she missed him. She called but there was no answer. Puzzled, she went upstairs to look. She found him in a bedroom with the door shut, reading to her three children, who were all as quiet as mice.

Ted did not have any pets as a child, and in his poetry up to this time, he acknowledges the existence of only a few animals, dogs, cats, moles, rats, and such, but in *I Am! Says the Lamb* he uses comically such large and esoteric beasts as gnus, sloths, yaks, hippopotami, bears, and others. As I have said, he was always, when he was feeling good, witty and playful, and he seems to have wanted to show this side of himself in verse, a side which heretofore had been dissipated socially or buried in epigrams and wisecracks in his notebooks.

His interest in animals may have been stimulated then by one of his students, Lois Lamb. She grew up apparently on a farm in Central Washington and had not only great knowledge of animals but an affection and an odd kind of intuitive understanding of them that fascinated Ted. In 1949, when he was at Pinel Sanitarium, he and Lois Lamb conducted a series of "experiments" with a flock of turkeys on the sanitarium grounds.

In 1948 and 1949, Ted finished enough of the children's poems to

make a two-page spread in *Flair* magazine, the short-lived publica-
tion edited by Fleur Cowles. Their submission and acceptance
was arranged by a former Bennington student of Ted's, Phoebe
Pierce, (she was probably the "Sweet Phoebe" mentioned in
"Words for the Wind" and at Bennington she was the roommate
of Beatrice O'Connell whom Ted married). She acted as a kind of
unofficial agent for Ted and the spread was published in the issue
of March, 1950.

He had great hopes of making a lot of money from *I Am! Says
the Lamb*. There was talk and some negotiations begun for a comic
strip and a movie short based on the poems. Musical settings for
some of them were written by Ben Webber, Douglas Moore, Gail
Kubik, and others. In his effort to get poetry heard rather than
read, Ted wanted to have cheap records made of these poems read
by himself and inserted into a flap pasted to each copy of the
book. (He tried to persuade Ken McCormick of Doubleday to do
this with *The Lost Son* but the plan seems to have been imprac-
ticable.) It was true that the poems were widely published in Eng-
land and America during the Fifties but, when Ted says they were
"danced to all over this country, and broadcast (without pay-
ment) over all major networks," he was probably exaggerating.
He did not seem to expect a great deal of money from his serious
poetry—although he told me once he had rather appear in *The
Ladies' Home Journal* than anywhere because they paid the most,
a statement which I doubt—but in these children's poems he con-
vinced himself he had a gold mine. Yet it should be noticed that
the wealth was to come from the different promotions of the book
—he had not cheapened himself so far as to write "popular" verse.
It was up to the publishers, producers, musical directors, and
others to *make* it popular.

In these early years at Washington Ted was in full career. He
was working as hard as he could at the two things he liked best,
writing and teaching. His reputation as a poet was growing (but
not fast enough to suit him) and his students were eager, intelli-
gent, and appreciative. Aside from Mrs. Willis and his students,
he had made friends among his colleagues, Arnold Stein, Angelo
Pellegrini, Jackson Matthews, Nelson Bentley, Solomon Katz,
Heilman not quite yet—Ted was still a little suspicious—and he
often played tennis and drank with Max Nicolai, who later be-

came his lawyer. In 1949 he wangled a teaching post for Jim Jackson, who came to Seattle and resumed his old friendship. It takes determination and luck for an artist to surmount the variety of obstacles which society—and he himself with unwitting inadvertence—can throw in the way of a period when he can work effectively, eat well enough, have friends to drink with, and be bothered by only petty everyday worries. But Ted managed it.

The summer of 1949 he spent in Saginaw with his mother and sister. It is hot in the Saginaw Valley then, hot and damp, and Ted seems to have worked much at night; not that it is much cooler then but it seems so with the sun off the rooftops. Something of his manner of working after the breakthrough of *The Lost Son* comes from Judith Bailey. She says she believes that Ted actually abused his mind by concentrating on single objects for so long at a time, and she says he would also take deliberate flights of free association—she saw him stand and stare at a refrigerator handle one night and begin, "Refrigerator handle—Frigidaire—air-hose— snake. . . ." It went on for half an hour with incredible quickness. Any object, a refrigerator, a tree, a house, seemed to be to him not only itself but the sum of the associations he could wreathe around it, a microcosm, in fact, and out of these exercises came his symbols and many new word combinations.

Shortly after he returned to Seattle, his friends, especially Robert Heilman, noticed that he was acting with a strange exuberance. They thought he had had a wonderful summer. Jim Jackson was not so sure—he had seen this before. One day late in October Ted asked him to go shopping with him. Jim says Ted started spending money like a drunken sailor—the favorite purchases in these states were wallets and typewriters. "I could usually abort the bigger sales and get his money back to him later," Jim says. He could see that Ted was at the beginning of another manic phase. (He always felt rich when he was "high.") Ted wanted to go to Jerry Willis's apartment. Jim accompanied him and left him with her. Ted said he was going to a party at the Heilmans' that evening and he wanted a clean white shirt. She went out and bought him one. She says he was talking a great deal, but he seemed cheerful and she had never seen him ill, so there was nothing for her to recognize. He went on to the Heilmans'.

Late in the evening after a period of rushing volubility, he started throwing things around the Heilmans' kitchen but they were all of metal, tin pie plates, saucepans, and the like—nothing that would break. (This may indicate the tie that he always had with objective reality.) Heilman was baffled and somewhat frightened. He called Dr. Edward Hodemacher, who watched and listened to Ted a few minutes and called the police. When they came, he cautioned them to go easy, that this was not an arrest, and he told them to take Ted to Fairfax Hospital. Ted did not go willingly—he protested loudly enough—but he offered no violence.

At Fairfax the diagnosis was "hyperactivity and disorganized behavior," and after a period of sedation, Ted remained in a similar but diminished state, active, talkative, fairly cheerful. Jim Jackson saw him every day, ran any errands for him that seemed wise, put the damper on silly expenditures, and carried messages for him. Ted was terribly worried about his situation at the University, and between them, Jim and Robert Heilman were able to give him some reassurance; since he had begun teaching that quarter, his pay would continue until the end of it certainly. Jim said he continued to write in his notebooks, working on the *Praise to the End!* poems, and he kept up, as he always did in sanitariums, a heavy correspondence, sometimes writing to people who had not heard from him for years. Since institutional food was unsatisfactory, he sent out for prime beefsteaks and cases of ale, and this ran his bills up. Jim says he wandered around through the place wearing his Borsalino hat and a hospital gown and soon made friends with all the other mental patients and he would introduce them to Jim as equal to equal with the greatest courtesy.

On November 28, 1949, he was transferred to Pinel Sanitarium where he first met Dr. William Horton who was struck by his obvious intelligence and sensitivity, and the difficulty of treatment simply because of this.

Ted stayed at Pinel until March, 1950. The second quarter of the academic year began in January and he was given leave without pay. This angered him but he knew his anger was useless since he was already practised in the impersonal actions of institutions. His bills had been high, often running over $1000 a month, and they had nearly exhausted his savings. His problem was simply how to live for the next few months until the fall semester began.

He did not want to throw himself on his mother's bounty, so on February 28, 1950, he applied to Henry Allen Moe of the Guggenheim Foundation for a renewal of a grant. He says,

> I should like this letter to be a re-application, and I am hoping there is some way or special emergency fund whereby, if this renewal is now possible, that I might be granted money for a six-month period.
>
> My situation is this: As of January 1, 1950, I am on leave without pay from the University of Washington. My expenses during recent months have been very heavy and I am now using money from savings.
>
> I expect to be in the East on or before April 1, probably at Yaddo. I intend, during this six-month period to:
>
> a. Complete the sequence of longish poems. There are now eight. The last, "I Cry, Love! Love!" will appear in the Hudson Review. But two earlier ones are yet to be done before the cycle of ten is finished. (Some elegaic poems are to appear in the *Kenyon Review* this spring.)
>
> b. Complete the sequence of poems for children: a total of about fifteen. Four of these are appearing in *Flair,* and such musicians as John Verrall and Douglas Moore are writing settings for some of them. Jean George is doing illustrations.
>
> c. Complete a three-act poetic play: a *playable* intense tragedy based on experiences at Bennington. This has been blocked out, act by act, and some model sets have been made. Many individual scenes of this play have been written. I believe the language of some passages to be an advance over any previous work.

He encloses excerpts from the best reviews of *The Lost Son.*

His list of projects shows that the two books were approaching completion but he never did finish the play or, indeed, any play. Scattered through his notebooks are lines of dialogue, speeches and replies, but they are disjointed and it is impossible to extract from them any consistent line of action.

He wrote this application a month before he left the sanitarium. It is not, however, to be taken, merely because it makes perfectly good sense, as evidence of his response to treatment or progress toward "recovery." Early in January he was gathering a collection of his students' work and he wrote to David Wagoner at the Uni-

versity of Indiana, asking for tear sheets of any poems he might
have for a possible little anthology to be published by the Univer-
sity of Washington Press. As long as he had something definite to
say or a reasonable request to make, Ted could always write a
perfectly rational letter no matter how "sick" he was. The fact that
he could do this says quite a lot about the nature of his episodes.

His application was granted and the Guggenheim Foundation
awarded him a second Fellowship in the spring of 1950. After
leaving Pinel, Ted went East to Saratoga and spent some time at
Yaddo.

While he was at Yaddo, John Brinnin wrote him that Dylan
Thomas was in the country and wanted to meet him. Long before
he came to the United States, Thomas had said that Ted was the
only American poet he wanted to meet because he admired his
work more than anyone's except possibly Robert Lowell's. (Ted
played poetry the way he played tennis, competitively, although
he was always making formal disclaimers that he did this. He
was like Hemingway. To view literature as a contest to be won is a
Saginaw Valley, Middle-Western, American set of mind, and
throughout Ted's career he saw Lowell loom larger and larger as
his chief opponent.) The admiration was mutual. While he was at
Bennington, Ted had praised Thomas's work to me and recited "It
was my thirtieth year to heaven" with great feeling.

After Thomas's death, Ted wrote an elegaic essay about him in
Encounter and he tells of this first meeting:

> I first met him in 1950 in New York. John Brinnin had written
> me twice that Dylan Thomas wanted to meet me. I found this
> hard to believe but when I came down from Yaddo in May, still
> groggy from my own private wars with the world, it seemed to
> be so.
>
> Someone had lent me an apartment uptown; he was staying
> downtown on Washington Square. We sometimes alternated;
> one would rout out the other, different days. He had been built
> up to me as a great swill-down drinker, a prodigious roaring boy
> out of the Welsh caves. But I never knew such a one. Some
> bubbly or Guinness or just plain beer, maybe; and not much else.
> We would sit around talking about poetry; about Welsh picnics;
> life on the Detroit river and in Chicago (he greatly admired
> *The Man with the Golden Arm*); the early Hammett; and so on.

Or maybe bumble across town to an old Marx Brothers movie, or mope along, poking into book shops or looking into shop windows.

Earlier in the *Encounter* essay, Ted says:

> . . . I had come to think of him as a younger brother; unsentimentally perhaps, and not protective as so many felt inclined to be—for he could fend for himself against male and female; but rather someone to be proud of, to rejoice in, to be irritated, or even jealous of.

When Ted gave his affections to anyone wholly, as he did to Thomas, making hardly any of his customary reservations, he had to claim kinship, they had to be family affections. (Later he told René Char that he regarded him as an older brother.) Ted talked to me about Thomas several times and it was very plain that, as a man, he liked Thomas better than any other poet.

This third episode of mental illness seems to have surprised Ted. He did not tell even Jim Jackson that he had planned it or induced it as he had with the two earlier ones. It may have been the result of overwork in the two years preceding. The fruits of these years, poems that were to make up *Praise to the End!* and *I Am! Says the Lamb,* were appearing in a great many magazines, sixteen of them in 1950 alone.

One of them, "Elegy for My Student Jane," appeared in the summer issue of the *Kenyon Review.* It is, I believe, the first of his poems to have its whole origin on the West Coast. Jane Bannick was a student of Ted's for only one quarter. She was thrown from a horse and killed. Ted had not known her very well but this fatal accident stimulated him to write this beautiful poem, more a formal elegy than a lyric expression of grief. He may have been influenced also by Lois Lamb, who had fallen from a horse the previous summer and described the fall and the attendant fears to him in detail. The poem later appeared in many anthologies and in German and Spanish translations.

In September he bought his first car and drove it cross-country back to Seattle. The journey impressed him deeply. It was the first time he had experienced the breadth of the continent except in glances from a train window. He writes in an unsent letter just afterward:

Here I don't know just how the material will be resolved but
for next or possibly later book will be a happy journey westward
—not along the Oregon Trail but on Route 2; in a word, a
symbolical journey in my cheap Buick Special toward Alaska
and, at least in a spiritual sense toward the east of Russia and
the Mongolian Plains whence came my own people, the Prus-
sians, those poop-arse aristocrats, my father called them, who fed
their families into the army or managed the hunt for Bismarck
and Bismarck's sister—all this in Stettin in East Prussia, now
held by the Poles.

Grandiose? Perhaps but it's already more than a plan and
will, I believe, have a real imaginative order without the support
of the boring footnote or the pretentious allusion.

His uses of geography and history: to lead him home to his
father, and ultimately, since they became identified, to his Father.
Toward the end of his life this journey appears in his notes in
another context.

With his tedious sense of insecurity, Ted seems to have felt that
his illness and absence, even on a prestigious Guggenheim Fellow-
ship, had damaged his standing at Washington. He still harbored
vague resentments toward Robert Heilman because it was he who
had called a doctor and started the whole train of events that
landed him in the sanitarium. He got into correspondence with
Professor Gordon Ray, then head of the English Department of
the University of Illinois, who wrote him about the possibility of a
post in Creative Writing, "All I can say is that should a professor-
ship materialize, you will certainly be very seriously considered
for it." It is plain that he did not feel himself settled in the West.
In November, 1950, he is writing Barbara Jones, Lewis Jones's
wife, at Fayetteville, Arkansas, that he has used her husband's
name without his permission as a reference on a Fulbright applica-
tion. Ted asked for a place in Italy, but this did not go through.

He seemed to be completely well in the autumn of 1950, and he
was working and teaching but not quite at the same level of in-
tensity as in 1949–1950. He had asked the English Department to
install book shelves in his classroom so that he could reach out and
find a quotation easily without interrupting himself, and there
were several hundred books in this collection. He could not keep
his students from turning into disciples. His vitality drew them
to him and seemed, since he believed it so passionately himself,

to guarantee the truth of everything he said. He saw them not only in class, in conferences, and at the Rainbow Tavern; he went to their parties.*

Since Ted knew and liked his students so well, he assumed, probably correctly for most of them, that their enthusiasm matched and their abilities approached his own, and his examinations were, from his point of view, searching, but from an objective point of view, fiendish. (For a question on one of them, lists of eight nouns, eight verbs, and eight adjectives were given. "Select five of each and write a short lyric using them.") Recently Miss Elizabeth Bishop, who taught poetry at Washington, was using Ted's old classroom. She told me of an inscription written, perhaps with a nail file, in the paint on the underside of one of the bookshelves, "Died, June 8, 1952, in an exam of Ted Roethke's," and the student's name signed.

On January 18, 1951, Ted sent the manuscript of *I Am! Says the Lamb* to his agent, Diarmuid Russell, and said:

> The book of twelve longish poems is also done, will send it soon. William Carlos Williams went into a real lather and says they represent something unique; they embody many important metrical discoveries; they're so ahead of their time that it will be years before they'll be imitated.

*In the piece on Richard Selig in *The Poet and His Craft*, Ted writes, "Once when we were both in our cups at an ex-GI houseboat party, I thought he went too far in his contempt for some of the more naive people present, and I gave him a mild, glancing poke in the jaw—the only time I have ever struck a student. He hit me back, somewhat less mildly, and then the usual virtuous fellows intervened.

"But the effect was salutary. From then on, Richard condescended to no one, in class at least, and indeed often went out of his way to defend some hapless innocent in the cockpit of a course called, "The Writing of Verse."

Had I not talked to students who were guests at this party and saw the incident, I would not have believed this account. It is true that Ted was a pretty good boxer and he would often shadow-box in public, sometimes surprising the secretaries in the English Department by going into a crouch and out of it raining lefts and rights on the unoffending air. But I never saw him hit anybody or even come close. His wife says he once knocked a son-in-law of Allen Tate's down at a party in New York and was so appalled at what he had done that he left the party at once, so there must have been twice in his life when he actually let fly, but I still find this next to incredible. He was too fearful. The boxing was merely part of the mask.

At the end of the piece on Selig, he says, ". . . beneath the mask of bland cunning and ferocity—all too frightening and real—was a tender and compassionate man who might have become one of the fine ones of his generation, to say the least." With only a slight change of adjectives, this would do for a description of Ted himself, and perhaps Ted's sympathy and praise were elicited by this recognition, for Selig did not make it—he died of leukemia at Oxford.

In spite of his genuine friendship with John Sargent and Ken McCormick, he seems to have felt no special loyalty to Doubleday as a publishing house, for he says, "If we are going to do business with Doubleday . . ." and he sets his terms in his usual businesslike way: retain English rights; no remaindering; an advance even though four of the twelve poems are from *The Lost Son* (then out of print); both books to be released in the fall; retain all recording, music, movie rights ("a possibility of an animated cartoon deal— some of the kids' things when Gail Kubik gets back from Italy in the fall"). Although Doubleday accepted *Praise to the End!* for fall publication in 1951, *I Am! Says the Lamb* was not so successful, for Russell wrote Ted on December 8, 1951, "Eight publishers have seen the children's poems." None had accepted them and Ted had to shrink his dreams of wealth but he did not yet abandon them.

One of his traits which cannot be stressed too often is his unfailing kindness to younger poets. While obviously genuine and spontaneous, this encouragement links up with his continual effort to find a larger audience for poetry, to give it an importance in our communal life. On June 22, he writes John Brinnin from Saginaw,

> I was lying here leafing through *Modern Poetry* and suddenly came on those lines beginning, "Goodbye, godfather, sons go on their own, etc." and I read through to the end with a real sense of excitement (not looking up the author). Then, of course, I read the whole piece several times. I felt ashamed, ashamed that I'd never got into the poem before; those evocative "O's" at the start seemed to throw me off. You're really with it in that piece; the true charge. It goes beyond your (almost excessive) skill with the language: breaks through the rhetoric.
>
> Now, Jesus, don't take this amiss or think I'm condescending or something. The list of contemporaries I can stand is so short that I feel impelled to praise as well (albeit clumsily) as I can. Really all the best,
>
> Ted

The poem was "The Worm in the Whirling Cross." Later he and Brinnin became much better friends.

Although he got to Maine to visit Wilder Hobson and to Connecticut for a stay with Mary and Jeremy Bagster-Collins, Ted spent most of the summer in Saginaw, where he said the heat and his hay fever made life intolerable, working over details of *Praise to the End!*, which had been scheduled for publication on November 8. Half an issue of *Poetry* was devoted to student poetry from the University of Washington and half from Paul Engle's Poetry Workshop at the University of Iowa, and Ted insisted that the Washington poetry be placed first in the magazine.

On October 24, 1951, he writes to Babette Deutsch,

> By now you should have a book . . . I hope the whole thing gives you a jolt, a bounce, a kick, a bang or whatever it is . . . As I said, I did some different things this summer, and one at least breaks through into something else, I think. I only wish I could read & work for about five years at this point instead of having the hoorah & hullabaloo of teaching. (As I try to teach, at any rate) I've sublet a biggish new house out in North Edmonds (four bedrooms), fireplace in my bedroom . . . living room looking out over the Sound. But oddly enough, it's lonely and I resent the 30 minutes drive each way. Maybe like old Willie, I'll collapse into matrimony around 50. But there are no vivid prospects at the moment. "The parish of rich women"—yeah, but to hell with them.
>
> This time I don't even want to think about the damn book. It's done and as good in that kind of thing as I can do, and I figure nobody else has dug into that particular vein, so that's that. I can't get "competitive" about it, or aggressive (I know you once thought I was, a bit, and I guess you were right.) Forgive.

On November 8, 1951, *Praise to the End!* was published by Doubleday. The title was taken from Wordsworth's "The Prelude," Book I, and the book was dedicated to William Carlos Williams and Kenneth Burke. It contained thirteen poems and was eighty-nine pages long.

The reviews were good but none of the reviewers had that air of excited discovery that greeted *The Lost Son.* Ted was now an established poet and this more temperate tone was one of the penalties he paid.

Here are some excerpts from reviews Ted preserved:

Selden Rodman, *New York Herald-Tribune,* December 2, 1951

> In its present form, at least, Roethke's verse communicates nothing except to the reader who is willing to surrender himself

to the music of suggestive incantation and join the poet on his
somnambulistic return to the nursery. The words, as a descrip-
tion of Roethke's eery garden of forced growth would have a
double meaning; and to those who demand more (or less?) of
poetry, Roethke answers:

"Reason? That dreary shed, that hutch
for grubby schoolboys!
The hedgewren's song says something else."

In their quite different ways, Blake, Yeats, and Whitman made
the same response.

Richard Eberhart, *The New York Times*, December 16, 1951

Roethke gives us the new, age-old excitement of a true poet
uttering the feelings, the meanings deepest in him, in his own
peculiar way, driven by compulsive force.

The verse is an incantation, a celebration—and it is often
playful. Roethke is an interior monologist forever inviting the
soul to the Self. He has delved into obscurest childhood and in
mature complexity has drawn up marvels of tonal simplicity and
penetration, gnomic flashes, witty self-criticism, curious neo-
logisms, all bestowed with fountain-like exuberance. His ver-
balism suggests Swinburne but a more resilient Swinburne of
the times.

Louise Bogan, *The New Yorker*, March 15, 1952

Roethke has added several long poems to passages from *The
Lost Son,* published a few years ago, and these additions accent
his original theme—the journey from the child's primordial
subconscious world, through the regions of adult terror, guilt,
and despair, toward a final release into the freedom of conscious
being. Roethke's description of this progress attaches itself to a
recognizeable myth and legend hardly at all; his renditions of a
sub- or pre-conscious world is filled with coiling and uncoiling,
nudging and creeping images that often can be expressed only
with the aid of nonsense and gibberish. But it is witty nonsense
and effective gibberish, since the poet's control over his material
is always formal; he knows exactly when to increase and when
to decrease pressure, and he comes to a stop just before the
point of monotony is reached. Behind Roethke's method exists
the example of Joyce, but Roethke has invented a symbolism, in
his searching out of these terrors, marginal to our consciousness,
that is quite his own.

In the year 1951, *Poetry Magazine* gave Ted its highest award, the Levinson Prize. Recognition was coming, but, for Ted, too little and too slowly. In fact, there could never be enough of it, for enough would have meant that it would have had to outweigh the guilts and terrors of his mind and these seemed to be without limit.

The desire Ted had expressed to Babette Deutsch of having a period free from teaching when he could read and write led him, in the spring of 1952, to approach the Ford Foundation with a request for a grant.

In one section of his Ford application he said he wished to be able to have time to read philosophy and theology. The reading that he had done in the mystics, which had been continuous but desultory since the late Thirties, was becoming more important to him, but it is hard to tell from his notes—he hardly ever mentioned this in his letters—whether this was spontaneous, for the good of his own soul, so to speak, or whether it was a conscious mode of deepening the content of his poetry, rather the former, I should think, because Ted was, in odd ways, a believer. He was not, after his days at the Presbyterian Sunday School in Saginaw, a regular communicant of any church, although his wife says that when he was entering a manic phase, he liked to go to church and once she had to prevent him putting a hundred-dollar bill in the collection plate. He also had the quirk of crossing himself frequently. Often before a tennis game, he would kneel and cross himself quickly, and when he visited the grave of Chief Seattle, he knelt in the grass and did it seriously. But these are the superficies of devotion, almost, perhaps, a jesting relationship with the sacred. His real concern with his belief shows most clearly in his poetry where a profound desire for a personal wholeness grows clearer and clearer, a desire for harmony with all created beings, and an elevation of his father, the dead god, into an identity with God.

The Ford Foundation grant came through and Ted had the pleasant prospect of free time from June, 1952, until September, 1953.

As a part of his hectic schedule, on April 10, 1952, Dylan Thomas gave a reading in Seattle, a brilliant success, as nearly all Thomas's readings were. Ted introduced him. Few readers have

the intuitive understanding of poetry and none Thomas's magnifi-
cent voice. (A compliment Ted cherished and repeated time and
again was Thomas's statement that Ted was the best poetry reader
in America. Coming from Thomas, this was the accolade.)

Their meeting was not as quiet and sedate as the earlier ones in
New York. Arnold Stein gave a party for Thomas after his reading.
He and Ted appeared together quite late in the evening. Ted
brought a girl and Thomas, the wife of his Seattle host. With them
they had a case of champagne which they hid in Stein's shrubbery
so that only they could drink it. At parties Ted usually ran the
show or sat in a corner and sulked. This time, however, he gladly
relinquished the center of the stage to Thomas, who gave a long
recital of poems, his own and others', climaxing it with a long
poem composed extempore. Arnold Stein says that it was one of
the most amazing performances he ever heard, and Ted was
loudest in the applause. Ted did not seem to feel that Thomas
was a rival in any way and he demonstrated a kind of proprietary
pride in him as one would in a younger brother.

Ted was changing. In his letter to Babette Deutsch, he said that
he was lonely in his house in North Edmonds. This is perfectly
possible despite the fact that Jim Jackson lived nearby and, by
this time, Ted had a great many friends in the English Department
and in the city. However, when he hints directly after this that he
may when he is fifty "collapse into matrimony" like Yeats, it seems
clear that it is a woman he is lonely for. Ted was forty-five at this
time—he had five years to go but he did not wait them out.

XII

Marriage and
The Pulitzer Prize

The year of 1952 seems to have been a period of mounting confidence. Ted had weathered his third attack, emerged from it full of plans and energy, and he did not yet, apparently, think that any one of his attacks were any but isolated incidents and he always hoped each one would be the last. *Praise to the End!* had received good, if not desireably superlative, reviews, and on February 27, The National Institute of Arts and Letters in a communication signed by Van Wyck Brooks notified him that he was the recipient of a grant of $1000 "for your creative work in literature." The actual grant read:

> To Theodore Roethke for the vigor and originality of his style, the subtlety of his versification, and his faithful devotion over many years to the art of poetry both as a producer and a teacher.

On July 22, he was notified that he had been nominated for honorary membership in the International Mark Twain Society. The fact that Ted had little connection with Mark Twain (except for the one we all have, reading *Tom Sawyer* and *Huckleberry Finn*) must have made this honor more pleasant since it showed that he was becoming a public figure. The Society had a most impressive list of public figures as sponsors and vice-presidents: Winston Churchill, the Duke of Windsor, Bernard Shaw, Franklin D. Roosevelt, Thomas Mann, and, rather a surprise, Field Marshal Viscount Wavell.

These honors, this money, together with his Ford grant must have put Ted's mind as much at ease as it was ever likely to get.

Twenty years before, if he could have foreseen them, he would have jumped up and cracked his heels with delight. Now he found them mildly exciting but actually no more than his due and he settled quietly in at home in Saginaw for the summer.

Any period of work for a writer is apt to be uneventful and Ted's was calm and peaceful. He seems to have been specially interested in reading the works of Paul Tillich and Reinhold Niebuhr (whom he had met at Bennington) while continuing his study of the Christian and Eastern mystics.

He had arranged for Richard Eberhart to take his place at Washington while he was on leave. He was always vain of the stature of the people who filled in for him. Auden had followed him at Bennington and on his various leaves from Washington, Louise Bogan, A. J. M. Smith, Stanley Kunitz, Léonie Adams, and Rolfe Humphries acted as substitutes.

In August Arabel Porter of the New American Library bought five of his children's poems for use in *New Yorld Writing*, and in September, Rolfe Humphries some poems for an anthology he was making for Ballantine Books, Inc.

John Brinnin had become director of the YM-YWHA Poetry Center in New York and on November 4, 1952, Ted said in reply to a letter from him:

> I have long since decided that it's not worth while for me to open my trap for less than $100 *to me* . . . About that date: I'm taking my basic pattern from what I did at Reed College last spring—about forty or forty-five minutes reciting and palaver and gags *without* books and then some of my own things *with* books. I was loose, the kids reacted well, and they've already asked me back. But the chief thing that concerns me with your people is *what not to do* in a humorous way. I tend to get to get too rambunctious, start imitating contemporaries, etc. This, if people do not know you, I realize may be catastrophic . . .

The date set for the reading at the Poetry Center was December 4, 1952, and although he did not know it, it was to be an important one in Ted's life.

Ted had been hard at work reading and writing, holed up in Saginaw since June, and he was becoming restless. He had been living cheaply at home and all this Ford money seemed to be burning a hole in his pocket. On November 8, 1952, he got a letter from Cynthia Colby, secretary to the Poetry Center, saying that

Dame Edith Sitwell usually stayed at the St. Regis in New York and that a letter marked "Hold" would probably reach her. Dame Edith had singled Ted out for the highest praise in a book she had written about American poetry. He had written to thank her and an epistolary acquaintance had sprung up.

On December 1, 1952, he writes her from Saginaw:

> Dear Edith Sitwell,
>
> I have, somewhere among my papers, a lengthy screed to you in longhand but I *can't* find it.
>
> It said the obvious: that I was delighted and proud to get your spontaneous and generous words; that the whole letter was getting dog-eared from being carried around and looked at so much; that my sister even took it to her school for a private showing to her special friends, etc. We've done everything, so far, except frame it.
>
> I loved the story about the elephants. Herewith is a poem, "The Partner," which has a line about them. I hope you will like all four pieces of this sequence in a formal vein. I daresay I give old W.B.Y. too much in the first one: actually the rhymes, as you will see, go back to Ralegh and Sir John Davies—a kind of plain bald style with (I hope) some colloquial bounce.
>
> This year I'm on a fellowship and will be in New York on December 4 for a reading. I do hope you will still be there and that there will be time and occasion for a private gabble.
>
> Guess what *Praise to the End!* sold: 550 copies. I certainly mean a great deal to the people of my own country.
>
> No, John Lehmann never sent me a copy of your American anthology. And, alas, apparently he has no interest in publishing *Praise* either, for Diarmuid Russell, my agent, has said nothing about any such possibility. I hope he decides to, eventually.
>
> This is a poor return for your wonderful letter, but it carries my warmest wishes to you and your brothers. I hope very much that I shall see you.

The poem he sent to Dame Edith is one of the sequence, "Four for Sir John Davies."

On the same day he wrote to Dylan Thomas, who had then less than a year to live:

> Dear Dylan,
>
> A guy in East Lansing showed me a copy of *The Listener* with a comment by Martin Armstrong indicating that you had read three poems of mine over the B.B.C. Naturally, I was pleased to

hear this; and now the *Collected Poems* has come. Thank you very much. I am proud to have that book.

Not to be tiresome—but I am wondering whether it would be possible to get a copy of the recording made at that time. One is usually made, isn't it? If this is at all practicable, I'd be most grateful if you would put the proper wheels in motion to see that I get one, along with the date of the broadcast which I need for the University files. Please ask whoever is responsible to send me a bill for I am not trying to be a free-loader about this.

It is not vulgar or idle curiosity or vanity that prompts this request. I want very much to find out what you hear in those rhythms: I can be taught something by that and maybe jogged into new effects later.

Karl Shapiro asked me for a piece on *In Country Sleep*. One afternoon I did a short up-boil: a prose poem in wild rhetoric which will either make you laugh or make you sore. I wanted K.S. to clear it with you first but he said, in effect, don't be naive. I did send the proof to John Brinnin who thought there was nothing objectionable in it. I certainly hope it makes you laugh and pleases you, or else I never would have released it. At least it will be a change from the patty-cake Lowell and Jarrell play in print.

Here is the sequence about "dancing" which you suggested I send you. Hope you like.

I curse myself because I write so slowly. A play idea keeps torturing me, but I can't get the thing going. I curse you for having got one done: so much done that is good. It isn't jealousy: exasperation. I envy you the B.B.C. and of course am really wistful about what you mean to your own people—to say nothing of mine. After rave reviews, hosannas, dancings in the street, *Praise to the End!* sold 550 copies. Myself, I thought the book really did something new. Is it too far ahead or am I deceived?

I hope we can poop around this spring as we did in 1950. I'm tired of interruptions by jerks, well-meaning and/or pulchritudinous dames.

Break down and let me hear from you. I do hope you like the poems.

The "piece on *In Country Sleep*" was a review of Thomas's book of that title and it appeared in *Poetry* in December, 1952. It was in Ted's wild, "Elizabethan" style, somewhat like that of *The Last Class* or *A Tirade Turning* and it contained a fairly obvious comparison of Thomas to a pig. Ted had worried about this to Brinnin,

"The wallow pig reference, as you'll see, represents a serious point: he is taking a very old way of a type of mystic, embracing the flesh to escape it, etc." The review was entitled "One Ring-tailed Roarer to Another" and he signed it with his pseudonym, "Winterset Rothberg." But by this time, Thomas was too sick to care what was said about him one way or another.

The play he curses Thomas for having finished was, of course, *Under Milk Wood* but, actually, it was not finished and the anxiety of Thomas's frantic last-minute revisions for the New York production may have contributed to his death.

It is obvious from the sentence, "I hope we can poop around this spring, as we did in 1950," that Ted sees no reason why they shouldn't.

Ted left Seattle for the reading at the Poetry Center and arrived at Brinnin's place in Boston on December 2, 1952. He spent a day or two with Brinnin and then registered at the Hotel New Weston in New York on December 4, the day of his reading. Ted was always nervous before readings; he knew New York always hopped him up as it does many other people, and he probably had not wanted to come early and find himself involved with friends.

That night on the way to the reading, Beatrice O'Connell saw Ted crossing the street beside her. She said, "Remember me?" Ted said, "Hi, puss," and started going through his pockets to find a piece of paper so that he could write down her address. At last he said, "Where can I get in touch with you?" And, to see if he remembered her name, she said, "I'm in the book." She did not wait around after the reading as did many friends and former students and this puzzled Ted.

Beatrice had been in Ted's classes at Bennington, and, like many another, she had had a crush on him, but she had not seen him since she left college. While she was going to Columbia to get her teacher's certificate, she had been a dress model on Seventh Avenue for a while and John Powers, in the course of teaching her how to walk, had said he would hire her if she would lose ten pounds. As soon as she had her certificate, she began teaching art (she had been a Fine Arts major at Bennington) in Harlem at P.S. 101 at 110th Street and Madison Avenue, and she was sharing an apartment with two girls from Winchester, Virginia, her home town.

Ted's reading at the Poetry Center, a great success, was on a

Thursday. On the following Saturday, December 6, Ted called her in the afternoon and took her to some jazz uptown where a friend of Wilder Hobson's was playing. On Sunday Ted took her to the New Weston for a couple of drinks and she asked him for dinner at her apartment. She had some steaks which she thought were quite nice but Ted was not impressed—they weren't thick enough. After some drinks, Beatrice told him she had been in love with him since Bennington, thinking that Ted at forty-four was too ancient for serious consideration, but he surprised her by saying, "It's not too late now."

After that they saw each other every day and it was accepted by them both that they were soon to be married. When Ted wrote his mother and sister that his fiancée was teaching in Harlem, they had a moment of panic for fear Ted was marrying a negress.

Ted was very happy and his behavior resembled that of his manic periods. He was flinging money around and Beatrice remembers him giving an elevator boy ten dollars merely for bringing them downstairs. He moved into the St. Regis Hotel on December 18, and called Dame Sitwell at two in the morning and asked if she had a sleeping pill she could give him. It was exactly the right approach to the doyenne of English poetry. The old girl was charmed. "I was in my Aga Khan phase then," Ted said later.

Beatrice was going home to Winchester over Christmas and Ted had the loan of R. P. Blackmur's house in Princeton over the holiday. John Berryman, who saw it, tells of the debacle of Ted's meeting with Edmund Wilson.

Berryman was living in Princeton then and one day, meeting Wilson on the street, Wilson said, "This man Roethke—is he any good?"

"He's brilliant," Berryman said.

Wilson, whose enthusiasm for new poets has been less than tepid, said, "Humph."

"You asked me. I told you," Berryman said.

Out of this encounter apparently, Ted received an invitation from the Wilsons to a Christmas party. Berryman says that when he and his wife arrived, one wall of the Wilson's living room was a bank of flowers, dozens of them, bearing the card of "Theodore Roethke." It was a characteristic gesture. (When he was in New York Ted was always sending masses of flowers to his friends and running up big bills at Max Schling's which Doubleday would have to vouch for.) Mrs. Wilson was delighted and eagerly awaited Ted's arrival.

Around nine o'clock in the evening, Ted came in "aggressively sober," Berryman asserts. He paid his devoirs to his hostess and went at once into the dining room where a large collation lay ready. He was offered a drink but called instead for tomato juice. He took a large piece of cheese and a bunch of hothouse grapes in one hand and with his tomato juice in the other, went in to join the gathering. He found a chair next to a very handsome woman of about thirty-five and at once began a lively conversation. In one of those inexplicable lulls that sometimes comes over a party, Berryman heard Ted say vehemently, "But it only costs a hundred bucks to go to the Caribbean. Come on. Let's go."

This offer seems to have been promptly rejected and Ted got up, still carrying the cheese and grapes, and wedged himself in next to Wilson, who was sitting on a sofa. Ted said to him, "Come on Let's blow this and go upstairs and I'll show you some of my stuff."

"I can't do that. I'm the host," Wilson very properly replied.

Ted glowered at him. "You hate all contemporary poets, don't you?"

Wilson began to protest angrily and Ted reached over, seized Wilson's cheek, and said, "Why, you're all blubber."

"Get out of here, you half-baked Bacchus!" Wilson cried.

Ted got out.

He and Beatrice set their wedding day for January 3, 1953. It was her father's birthday and she thought it might be lucky. Ted had sent his sister some silver jewelry from San Kramer's, a designer on 8th Street and Beatrice went down there to buy the ring, a gold free-form ring that she says has always drawn comment.

They did not intend to tell anyone they were getting married but they went to a "roast beef" at the Bagster-Collins's and Ted told them.

They were married at noon in a little chapel of St. James's Episcopal Church on Madison Avenue. Wystan Auden was best man and Louise Bogan, matron of honor. Also present were Beatrice's father, mother, and brother, Irvan, a Marine who was about to go to Korea. Beatrice wore a knee-length champagne-colored taffeta dress with a veil, white bugle heads, and big white earrings, while Ted wore a blue double-breasted pinstripe suit not quite so big as some of his others. During the ceremony, Ted had a spot of trouble getting the ring from Auden and muttered, "*Gott im Himmel!*" but otherwise everything went well.

A wedding luncheon was served at the Alrae Hotel, a small hostelry on 64th Street. Ted had picked it instead of a larger one because he said he didn't want *The Daily News* to get hold of the story. (This seems to have been expression more of hope than of fear.) In a red Viennese décor an excellent luncheon was served with lashings of champagne, so good a meal, in fact, and so pleased was Ted that he sent the chef a $100 bill with his compliments. Ted and Beatrice did not then have many friends in common and only Mary and Jeremy Bagster-Collins and Chester Kallman were present beside the wedding party, although the Larry Pratts came in later. During the festivities, Auden offered Ted and Beatrice his villa at Forio d'Ischia for their honeymoon.

They did not leave immediately, however. Beatrice had to finish out her term teaching at P.S. 101 until February. Ted had moved into the Hotel Croydon on his return from Princeton and they lived there until Beatrice was free. Arrangements had been completed with the assistance of Wilder Hobson for Ted to give a reading with music at the Circle-in-the-Square on January 25, 1954. Ted wrote David Wagoner about it:

> There'll be a night-club song, music by me, arranged by Ben Webber, with Wilder Hobson on trombone, Larry Pratt on the accordion, Verna Hobson (for pulchritude) on the tuba, Decent Dengler (maybe) and Dirty Dengler on trumpets.

Beatrice said they never had a real rehearsal. They would meet at Larry Pratt's apartment in the village full of good intentions, have a few drinks, and forget about it. When it came to the actual performance, Ted carried it off with his energy. He seems to have been developing fairly definite ambitions to be a stage performer.

On February 18 he gave a reading at New Hope, Pennsylvania, and just afterward one at Penn State where the Astons gave a tea party for Ted and Beatrice. Then they went to Winchester for a wedding reception with Ted sweating in a suit of twenty-year-old tails.

Ted gladly accepted Auden's offer of his villa at Ischia for the honeymoon. He and Beatrice sailed on the *Saturnia* and docked at Naples on March 8, 1953. From there they crossed to the island, which Ted liked at once.

Auden's place was a little house in the Via Santa Lucia in the village of Forio, with high ceilings, white plaster walls, and a garden at the back with orange trees. With the house came a young Italian majordomo, Giocondo, who called Beatrice, "*Signora,*" and Ted, "*Professore,*" and he once said Ted had a "*ridere epidemia,*" an infectious laugh, which was very true. (Ted had no smile except a social bearing of the teeth.) Beatrice says, "Giocondo was good company. He was a painter and not particularly interested in cooking. However, we struggled with the menus. I say "struggled" because at that time there were few foreigners on Ischia and the available comestibles ran to olives, Provolone and one or two other Italian cheeses, salami, and spaghetti. There was good veal but the steak was freshly-killed cow. Our attempt to have the butcher age the beef was a disaster, refrigeration being what it was on Ischia. Ted and I scraped the "aged" tenderloin but even the cats, who were verging on starvation, wouldn't touch it. When we had unborn goat there was still some hair left on it: Ted ate in silence. In March, when we arrived, it was cold and only comfortable at mid-day. At night I read *I, Claudius* aloud while we sat in bed under a heavy rug to keep warm."

Beatrice was learning Italian and already had enough so that communication with Giocondo was not difficult. She bought a grammar and tried to teach Ted but he was recalcitrant and flung the book across the room. He was no linguist, did not try to be, and now, with Beatrice, did not need to be.

This simple life appealed to him.

He loved the brilliant sun, Auden's books, the little balcony looking down on the street where he could sit and watch the villagers driving donkeys, and lambs and goats to market, singing songs that seemed to have come from Arabia. They could take a bus a mile or so to a beautiful crescent-shaped beach with a castle at one end. There were seldom many bathers and they would take a lunch, swim, and lie around in the sun.

Soon, although he had not stopped taking notes, the old *Tuchtigkeit* began to spur him and, sitting on the balcony above the street, he began to work on poems. He had already done, Beatrice says, some lines for "Words for the Wind" and he finished the poem there. And he completed "The Dream," "The Storm," and "I Waited." The line in "I'm Here," from the sequence, "Meditations of an Old Woman," about the witch who slept with her horse was given him by Giocondo, who pointed out an old hag in the village and said she was such a woman.

It would seem to have been a pleasant time but it was only a few weeks after the wedding that Beatrice learned why he had married her—he wanted someone to take care of him. This, of course, is familiar. All the women who knew him well say that he liked someone to call him to meals, someone to have clean shirts and pajamas ready, someone to find lost articles, to buy tickets, pack, and remember train and plane times, someone to listen to poetry first, to talk to late at night, a woman to stave off loneliness. Before the marriage, they had agreed that she was to teach for several years. "I can't respect you unless you work," he said later, and during the bright days at Ischia, she was writing to the Seattle School Board offering her services as a teacher of French and art. She got a job at a school in Bellevue, a district of Seattle on the east side of Lake Washington.

They remained at Ischia until May 25, 1953, Ted's birthday. The boat to the mainland sailed at five in the morning. This was the middle of the night to Ted, so the day before they hired a two-horse carriage with a driver who was supposed to wake them in time to make the boat. He was late, of course. The boat put in at another port up the coast of Ischia and we have the auroral spectacle of the driver larruping his horses along the shore road, racing the boat to the pier with Ted and Beatrice jouncing behind him.

They went to Rome where they stayed at the American Academy for about a month. There they met a great many people, Rose and William Styron, Alexei Haieff, Eugene Walter, Ralph Ellison, Jessamyn West, Hortense Calisher, and Stanley Moss, who was working for Princess Caetani as one of the editors of *Botteghe Oscure*. At parties they often met Alberto Moravia. Robin White, the son of Stanford White, did a drawing of Ted which was used on the jacket of *The Waking*. Prince and Princess Caetani asked them for dinner at the Palazzo Caetani and there they met Eleanor

Creveri, Benedetto Croce's daughter. John Berryman and his wife were in Rome at the time and they saw them often. And Ted met Irwin Shaw and Lillian Hellman to whom he was to dedicate *I Am! Says the Lamb!* Ted saw a great deal of Leo Smit, who was an ardent ping-pong player, and they had many games. Smit was also a talented pianist and Ted loved to hear him play. (He couldn't stand the violin or records of people singing, "yowling." He hated string quartets, "Hee-haw." Once at a concert with Beatrice, Ted took a wide-nibbed pen, and as each number was finished, he ran a line through its title on the program and said, "Check.") He did not, of course, tell Smit he had ever played the piano himself.

In a strict sense of the word, Ted was not a tourist because he would not tour. Churches, galleries, the Colosseum meant nothing to him and he simply refused to visit them. It was people he liked to see.

From Rome they went to Geneva where Beatrice had stayed with an Italian Protestant family in 1946–1947. They took a train which Beatrice had often taken and stood in the corridor and watched people working in the rice fields. They took rooms at the Hotel de l'Ecu on July 6, 1953, and stayed there two or three days. If Ted was impressed by the lake and its scenery or the relics of Calvinistic Protestant culture that so intrigued Stendhal, he did not mention it. There were good restaurants nearby, and he liked that.

They left Geneva for Paris. Beatrice says that "any place you were supposed to like," Ted, before he had seen it, was certain to disesteem. He didn't like Paris. They stayed at the Hotel Continental on the Rue de Rivoli, but at that time they knew no one in the city. In spite of his university courses, Ted would not attempt French, and any talking that was done with the natives Beatrice had to do. Auden had suggested they visit the Café Flore and the Brasserie Lipp on the Boulevard Ste. Germaine. They did but they did not see Sartre or Mme. de Beauvoir or indeed any Existentialist. Ted wanted to leave for London but Beatrice, who liked Paris, sent his shirts out to a laundry and he had to stay. He did not visit the Louvre, Notre Dame, the Sainte Chapelle, or the Luxembourg. His dislike of Paris was not Prussian but unique and personal, for it was the Prussian General Staff who seized the Tour d'Argent in 1870 and told the management, "Keep everything as it is. We will see that you are supplied. We will eat here," and it was the Ober-Kommando Wehrmacht who seized the Tour d'Argent in 1939 and told the management the same thing. Prussians like Paris. Ted did not.

Beatrice took him to the Comédie Française to see Molière played, but with his deliberate blankness about the language, it is hard to see what he got out of it. On July 13, he wrote to Ernest Hemingway who was at Biarritz,

> Mr. Harry Burns, an acquaintance, said that you had written some poems recently. I mentioned this to Marguerite Caetani (La Principessa Caetani di Bassiano, blah, blah) who as you probably know edits and sponsors *Botteghe Oscure* to my mind the best of the international reviews. She was, of course, enchanted, transported at the possibility of something from you but is too timid to write. She suggested I do so.
>
> So I make bold to write and ask. Her Paris address is 4, rue de Ligne. Her Rome editorial address is *Botteghe Oscure*, via Botteghe Oscure 32, Roma.
>
> Also I thought enclosed doggerel in which you are mentioned might amuse you.
>
> It's my belief that you prose writers should look at the versifiers once in a while.
>
> I grew up in Michigan and have fished your country there; often have hoped to meet you in the flesh to exchange views on such subjects as What Greb-or-any-smart-hooker-could-do-to-Marciano, etc.

The poem Ted enclosed in which Hemingway was mentioned is "Song for the Squeeze-Box." No reply from Hemingway was found among Ted's papers.

After a week in Paris, he and Beatrice took the boat train to Calais, crossed the Channel in good health, landed at Dover, and arrived in London late in the afternoon. They put up at Berners Hotel, Berners Street, and Ted went out to dinner with Stephen Spender. It was the first of many meetings with the literary people of London. The BBC was negotiating with Ted to give a broadcast and its producer was a man after Ted's own heart, John Davenport.

He was perhaps the most highly educated man Ted had ever

seen, Balliol College, Oxford, Trinity College, Cambridge, and the École Polytechnique. He was a poet and critic. His family had founded New Haven, Connecticut, and he had visited the United States many times. He had met many of our best writers, Faulkner, Hemingway, Conrad Aiken, Malcolm Lowry, and he knew everyone worth knowing in London. He was probably the best friend Dylan Thomas had in London, and before the Second World War, being then quite rich, he had given Thomas and his wife a haven in his big house at Marshfield in Gloucestershire, which held thousands of books, two grand pianos (Davenport was also a pianist), Rouaults, Picassos, a great Tanguy now in the Museum of Modern Art, and a cellar full of fine wines. Together Thomas and Davenport had written what Thomas called "a fantastic thriller," *The Death of the King's Canary.*

In spite of all this and Davenport's real genius for friendship, it was by no means certain that Ted and he would have hit it off. One more touch was necessary—Davenport was a big man. He had boxed heavyweight at Cambridge and won all his bouts. In fact, just after he had gone down, Davenport came to the United States and he ran into old Jack Johnson, the former heavyweight champion, then sixty-three years old. Davenport says, "I was full of myself then, having won all my matches, and I thought I was pretty good." He asked Mr. Johnson if he would spar with him for three rounds and Mr. Johnson said he would. They put on the gloves and went at it. Davenport, of course, was nursing a private ambition to knock down a heavyweight champion of the world as old as he was. "But it was horrible, like a bad dream," Davenport said. Laughing all the time, Mr. Johnson picked off every punch Davenport threw with ridiculous ease, and frequently, just for show, he would snap Davenport's head back with left jabs. "I never touched him. In three rounds I never laid a glove on him." A friendly, literate, not to say literary man who had at least tried to exchange punches with Jack Johnson—he and Ted became friends at once, and through him he met a great many people, among them, I think, William Empson, the author of *Seven Types of Ambiguity.* From them he got a sense of the English literary establishment, which is much smaller than our own, only a large group, in fact, where everyone who is any good at all knows everyone else, a group filled with friendships, feuds, rivalries, puffings-up, undercuttings, all quite apparent to all who are in it. It was a new experience.

John Berryman was in London at the time. (He took Beatrice to the Tate Gallery.) And one night Ted and Beatrice were going to dinner at John Davenport's flat along with Berryman and Peter Duval Smith. They stopped at a pub on the way, and, leaving, they did not notice Berryman had already left. He did not appear at the Davenports, and next day Ted ran into him with Allen Tate, and Berryman, who did not know that part of London, said that he had got lost and wandered the streets all night long.

In preparation for his broadcast, Ted spent a lot of time with what Beatrice calls "BBC types" and he drank at lunch, which was rather unusual for him. He and Beatrice met Dylan and Caitlin Thomas one day at a pub near Broadcasting House, perhaps the George, the last time Ted was to see him. As Constantine Fitzgibbon says in his life of Thomas, at that period Thomas was drinking far too much and he often had blackouts and fell down in the street. He and Ted were delighted to see each other but Caitlin, true to form, having heard that Beatrice's maiden name was O'Connell, said belligerently, "Where's your Irish accent?" (If Beatrice has an accent, it is rather that of the Old Dominion than anything.)

Ted made his broadcast on July 30, 1953, *An American Poet Introduces Himself and His Work*. It was well-received and caused enough comment so that the BBC rebroadcast it later. The entire script is reprinted in *On the Poet and His Craft, Selected Prose of Theodore Roethke*, edited by Ralph J. Mills, Jr., University of Washington Press, 1965.

Ted was still anxiously persisting in his effort to get his children's book published and on August 5, 1953, he wrote to T. S. Eliot at Faber & Faber:

> This note is to corroborate the essential facts of my conversation with your secretary, Miss Fletcher, relative to an untitled manuscript of nonsense verse for children, with illustrations by Bobo Leydenfrost:
>
> 1. Last December W. H. Auden suggested that I approach Faber and Faber with this material, which at that time was without illustrations. He offered to write, but I thought that this was unnecessary.

2. A decision before I leave on Friday is not absolutely essential. It would interest me very much, of course, to know your reaction to these pieces and, possibly, to encourage the illustrator when I pass through New York.

3. Some of these pieces have been set to music by Gail Kubik, Ben Webber and by Bernard Wolfman.

4. Five were published in *Flair*, four in a double-page spread; four in *Poetry*, and some in the *Hudson Review*.

At some appropriate time I would very much like to have you consider my serious work as a possibility for your list. Doubleday & Co., Inc. is bringing out on September 7 a volume of selected poems, *The Waking, Poems: 1933-53*. This house paid an advance of $2000 for this book on the basis of the reviews the earlier books received in America and England.

If you would be interested in seeing the contents of the book or the notices, I would be happy to discuss this with you personally—since I may not get to England again. However, if you are too busy this week, I should like to have the book sent to you in September.

Yours truly,
Theodore Roethke

Eliot replied the same day:

Thank you for your letter of August 5. I was pleased that you should submit your manuscript of children's verse, with illustrations, to this Firm, and am sorry that it does not fit into our list.

I am, however, very much interested in considering your volume of Selected Poems, and wrote as much to Madame Bassiano, who had informed me that it was about to appear. So I shall be very glad if you will have the book sent to me for consideration in September. I put it this way, because unhappily I cannot possibly fit in a meeting this week, as my otherwise free time is at the moment entirely occupied with rehearsals. I am very sorry that you are leaving so soon, and should have been happy to make your acquaintance.

Yours sincerely,
T. S. Eliot

This reply seems not only polite enough but encouraging, yet it enraged Ted because it put another tether on the high hopes he had for the children's book, and it seems to have hurt him that Eliot would not take time from the rehearsals for his play, *The*

Cocktail Party, to meet him. He seems to have taken it as a sign that his reputation was, in spite of Edith Sitwell's praise, not high enough to make him a man that Eliot could not afford to ignore. Many times afterward he referred to Eliot as "Tiresome Tom."

Although the writing in the notebooks was constant, Ted finished no poems that summer except the ones he did at Ischia. However, he published six poems in 1953, and Doubleday's *The Waking* would contain eight new poems, "The Visitant," which had been published in the *Sewanee Review* (Winter, 1950), "A Light Breather," *Kenyon Review* (Summer, 1950), "Elegy for Jane," *Kenyon Review* (Summer, 1950), "Old Lady's Winter Words," *Kenyon Review,* (Winter, 1952), and "Four for Sir John Davies" of which the first one, "The Dance," had appeared in the *Atlantic Monthly,* (November, 1952), the second, "The Partner," in the *Partisan Review* (September–October, 1952), the third, "The Wraith," in the *Hudson Review,* (Winter, 1953), and the fourth, "The Vigil," in *New World Writing,* Fourth Mentor Selection.

For the fourth edition of *New World Writing,* Ted had sent Arabel Porter from Geneva a two-page introduction to a section, Five American Poets, by Stanley Kunitz, Jean Garrigue, Chester Kallman, David Wagoner, and himself. In it he says of the ordinary reader,

> He will not be afraid of feeling—and this in spite of the deep-rooted fear of emotion existing today, particularly among the half-alive, for whom emotion, even when incorporated into form, becomes a danger, a madness. Poetry is written for the whole man . . .

The truth of this observation seems to me to be immediately striking. A technological society like ours is based on logic. It cannot recognize emotion except as a disruptive force, and in offices, in factories, in laboratories, disruptive forces cannot be countenanced, and must be repressed. Yet a man has his emotions and, repressed, they can eat him up. The "half-alive" is Ted's recognition of those so eaten.

On July 12, 1953, he had written Malcolm Cowley from Geneva,

> Doubleday is bringing out that selected poems, Sept. 8. I'll see you get one. Honor me, old walrus, by sitting down and reading

it all through. Then if you don't feel inclined to run up a flag or something, I'll turn in my suit.

Ted does not seem to have felt the anxiety about the publication of *The Waking* that he had with his earlier books. There had been enough praise, enough prizes now for his work to give him—in his upper levels at least—a certain confidence in himself as a poet. He wrote no anguished letters to Ken McCormick or John Sargent at Doubleday about layout, typography, make-up, or jacket. He sent them Robin White's portrait of himself, stern and plump, for the back cover and he seems to have read the proofs in what for him was a casual manner in Europe.

At the end of summer Ted and Beatrice left England and returned to Seattle, he to resume, she to begin teaching there. Ted set down nothing on paper of his general impressions of his first encounter with Europe, and I am inclined to think they were not very deep. He met Princess Caetani, whom he loved and respected; he made many continuing friendships such as the one with Lillian Hellman, who fascinated him because she wrote plays, and with John Davenport, who knew as much about poetry as he did and more about art and music as well as being a real and not a shadow-boxer, but in the main, he was not overwhelmed.

On August 7, 1953, they embarked at Southampton on the *Ruysdam* for New York where they stayed a few days at the Chelsea Hotel on 28th Street, which once sheltered Thomas Wolfe and Dylan Thomas as the bronze plaques show, and now Léonie Adams and Arthur Miller. Then they went to Saginaw where Beatrice met Ted's mother and sister for the first time. He had left "The Flying Juke-Box" there and they drove across the continent to Seattle, arriving there about the first of September.

They took a house not far from where Beatrice was to teach in the Bellevue district of Seattle on the east shore of Lake Washington at 1219 96 Street SE. It was a stained shingled cottage, set about two hundred feet above the shore of the lake, the steep slope down to the water covered with wild jungly brush, ferns, and rhododendrons. They paid $75 a month rent for a big living room, kitchen, bath, and one small bedroom with an attic above. At first the only water in the place was lake water and they had to get their drinking water from a filling station. There were also fleas in the greenery and Ted complained that their bites left him covered with big red welts half an inch long. Ted had a kind of bower down the slope, a wooden platform where he worked in fine weather. What did he see in that calm, looking out over the water, scratching and swearing, hearing a wife in the kitchen of the house above?

Robert Heilman gave an English Department tea early every fall so that the old hands could meet the newcomers. It was Ted's first public revelation of his wife in Seattle. He was very proud of her, proud of himself, too, for having acquired this panache, a beautiful woman on his arm to display as one displays a Titian or a Rolls-Royce, to parade before his colleagues and the women he had known someone very lovely, very striking, very chic as if they should have known all along that only this kind of woman would do as a wife.

Marriage, obviously, permits a condition of the greatest intimacy. Ted had never lived with any woman very long and he always preserved certain reticences with his male friends. Hitherto, the only people he had admitted to that interior arena where his fears and his guilts were plain to see, where his rage struggled with his tenderness and generosity were his parents and his sister, and they more often as sources and objects of them all than sharers in them. After so many years with his beaver up, Ted could not let it down plump at the preacher's words, and say to his wife, "Come in." Incrustations of habit and feeling had to be dissolved first and it took Beatrice a long period of loving and trusting before he could let her know him and let himself love her.

Ted had to use what stock of patience he had right at the beginning. Beatrice's school started at 7:30 in the morning. They had only one car, "The Flying Juke-Box." This meant that Ted had to get up in what to him was the sheerest dawn and drive her to school. He had to do it because it was he who insisted that she teach. He would come back after dropping her at the school, doss down until noon, get up and drive himself to the campus, teach his classes from one until three, drive back to the school and pick her up. It was not what could be called a handy arrangement. In 1954 Beatrice bought a '49 Ford which she paid for herself.

It was at the Bellevue house that they gave their first dinner party. Beatrice had a *Joy of Cooking* and she made a dish of veal and mushrooms with sour cream, some sort of fish mousse, and a green salad. Their guests, she remembers, were the Heilmans, the Max Nicolais, and the Arnold Steins, and the dinner went off very well. Then Ted said that they couldn't ask people to come all that way just for cocktails—they would have to give them dinner as well, so they started competing against themselves, and every dinner had to be better than the last. She would submit several menus, Ted sometimes saying, "We can't have that—we had it last time," until he found one that suited him. But the dinners were successful, partly because Beatrice was a good cook, partly because she balanced the guests like many a hostess before her.

However, she learned in time that Ted's private tastes in food were not so much those of the *Feinschmecker* as he liked to give out. Food was important to him but he didn't eat much more than she did for all his size. (He weighed around two hundred and twenty pounds then.) Every morning he would ask, "What are we having for dinner?" and if, to tease him, she would shrug and say, "Oh, I don't know," he would shout, "Don't torture me!" Facetiously he graded her on every meal. (She never got more than a B.) However, she found that while he liked a *blanquette de veau* or a *coq au vin*, he was content if she gave him steak or lamb chops (always rare—every time Beatrice was cooking one of them, he would come into the kitchen and say, "Don't overcook the meat;" he realized that he was a nuisance and tried to find ways of saying it roundabout as if he weren't saying it; sometimes he would sing it) roast pork, rare hamburger, potatoes, beets, his mother's cuisine, in fact. He hated rice, was moderate about fish and he always wanted her to buy fish at the public market in Seattle, never at supermarkets—he said supermarket fish was tired. At breakfast he would grill his own bacon very carefully, and since he rarely did this before ten, he seldom ate more than two meals a day.

With people who counted, Ted was always secretive about his mental troubles. He had not told Beatrice anything about them and she had not heard about them from anyone. Quite possibly, until his marriage, he thought that each episode would be the last, that he would be able to keep himself under control. When he appeared one day late in the fall of 1953 at her school with a box full of assorted objects he had bought—she remembers glasses and a pair of scales—she thought it strange but the truth did not dawn on her. She did not yet know that a buying spree signaled a manic phase. He started keeping her up all night, talking incessantly, and it was then that her patience and everything she felt for Ted was tried. It was not bad talk; there were only moments of incoherence but in the end she realized that he was ill. Ted did not have a psychiatrist then, only a medical doctor. Beatrice persuaded Ted to call him and the doctor put him in Columbus Hospital and prescribed barbiturates which only sent him up higher. However, it was not a serious episode—he was in the hospital only two weeks and he was discharged, fairly well recovered, just before Christmas. And Beatrice had experienced the samples of what the marriage was going to be.

Dylan Thomas died on November 5, 1953, but Ted didn't hear of it until Stephen Spender cabled him, asking him to do the piece about Thomas. He wrote Lisa Dyer of the *Hudson Review*, "The Welshman is dead and, from here, it seems impossible to believe." He was working on the poem, "Elegy," about this time and when he had it finished, he cried. (Beatrice says he cried very easily.) Then he could not decide whether to dedicate it to Thomas or to his Aunt Julia. In the end, it bore no dedication. Arnold Stein believes that Thomas' death, the shock and grief Ted felt when he heard of it, stimulated Ted's mental attack.

Between Christmas and New Year's Ted and Beatrice took a trip to Vancouver and Victoria, B.C. They stayed at a famous old Victorian hotel in Vancouver with an indoor swimming pool. Ted wanted to take a swim, and in a vast red plaid bathrobe, talking volubly to the other passengers in a Scottish accent he affected— he was still slightly high—he lost Beatrice in the elevators going down to the pool. It was on this trip that he met Malcolm Lowry, the author of *Under the Volcano*, a friend of John Davenport's whom he liked at once. They called on the Canadian poet, Earl Birnie, who had a new book-length poem he wanted Ted to hear. Ted stretched out on a sofa—he hadn't slept for two or three nights. Birnie started to read. Ted shut his eyes and in a few minutes was snoring loudly. Beatrice was across the room and couldn't nudge him awake. After reading on gamely for a while, Birnie stopped and said, "There doesn't seem to be much use in going on."

During his Christmas vacation in 1953, Ted went to New York for the Modern Language Association meeting with Robert Heilman. On his way he stopped in Saginaw and saw his mother for what turned out to be the last time. His sister, June, had written him that his mother had been in an accident, struck by a car while crossing the street, and her recovery was slow. On the train, Ted, filled with anxiety, worked himself up into such a state that his mother and sister had to console him rather than he, them. In the pain and confusion caused by the accident, neither June Roethke nor her mother took steps to gain any redress, and in the end Mrs. Roethke got no compensation at all.

In February, 1954, Helen Roethke died of a heart attack. She had had a swelling on her neck and both Ted and June, perhaps recalling their father's death, had feared cancer. Ted, in Seattle, broke down in tears at the news but he did not go to the funeral. With his father and mother gone, the greenhouse gone, the proofs of his old life had dwindled but it still lay vividly, ineradicably in his memory.

It was a misfortune that his mother could not have lived a few weeks longer, for one day when Ted picked up Beatrice after school, his face was one big grin. "I got it, honey," he said. He had just been notified that he had won the Pulitzer Prize for Poetry.

XIII

The Prizes, The Awards

To chart the movement of an artist's mind is risky because trust-worthy information is hard to come by; you may misinterpret it, and what you say may be only partially or intermittently true. To those who look only at his work it will seem to move forward in a smooth progression if only because the artist himself has wisely suppressed his false starts, his mediocrities, and indecisions. Ted's work has been criticised for the narrowness of its range, for his constant concentration on the fluctuation of the state of his own soul, with the implication that he either selfishly or helplessly limited his vision or deliberately turned it inward, using his images of the nature outside himself merely as barometric signals of internal pressures, as if he found nothing worth writing about in the world around him or was blindly unaware of it.

In Ted's earlier poetry, before 1950, he often uses the word "rage." It occurs frequently enough to be noticed as part of the gamut of his poetic moods. Now it is possible to agree with Paul Valéry's remark that clarity and profundity are mere literary effects, and if they are, so perhaps is rage. But I am inclined to think Ted was more sincere than that, and less sophisticated. In short, the literary rage corresponded to a real rage in him, but what was he raging against? His situation, it would seem, the ambiguities of his life with his family, the dreary swing between love and fear of his father, love and hatred of his mother, and his angry stupefaction when he discovered that the greenhouse and the field where he had played happily as a child lay in a setting as banal and inimical as Saginaw, his slow realization that the rest of the world was as banal and inimical as Saginaw, and these pricks and irritations forced him to consider it.

The reconciliation with his family took him all his life to achieve (but he made it in the end.) But in the late 1930s and early 1940s when he was discontented with his first work and had not yet found what Kenneth Burke calls "his greenhouse line," he veered toward writing some poems about "people in a particular suburbia"—this is quoted from his 1941 Guggenheim application—and he wrote several of them. "Dolor" is one he allowed to see print, as well as "Highway, Michigan" and "Night Journey," but there were more he never submitted anywhere and rightly. They seem to have been written easily out of topical angers. They did not mature slowly—lines from them are not found scattered in his notebooks. It is always easier to condemn than to praise, and Ted, realizing that his best work came hardest, had the tact to let these poems vanish from his *oeuvres*. They represent a blind alley that he saw was blind—he had looked outside himself, had not been able to make much of it, even of his rage against it, and it was years before he tried it again.

As I have pointed out, Ted wanted each book to be new, and *The Lost Son* was, new entirely, but others, although he did not think so, were new only technically, in manner, in length of line, or in the different influences that gave him certain promptings. There was no change of vision or new profound poetic impulses at work yet his mind was changing privily, behind his work, so to speak, and in this way: some time—it is hard to say exactly when —after the fourth of his mental episodes, he comprehended that these were not casual ditches in which he happened to fall. He saw that the landscape in which he moved was full of ditches, and that, given certain pressures, even certain releases, he was bound to fall into them and be mired. Up until this time it had all been happenstance or an affair he could say he had arranged himself. Each episode might be the last and all together they had not represented an inevitable continuity, but now he understood. They were to be part of his life. This was the kind of man he was. In a notebook begun in November, 1955, he has the following entries:

> "Madness is closer than we know.
> And dare we assume its gestures,
> These movements take us over.

"I can't go flying apart just for those who want the benefit of a few verbal kicks. My God, do you know what poems like that cost? They're not written vicariously: they come out of actual suffering; real madness."

"I've got to go beyond. That's all there is to it."

"Beyond what?"

"The human, you fool. Don't you see what I've done: I've come this far and now I can't stop. It's too late, baby, it's too late."

Since these entries come fairly close to each other in the notebook, interspersed with lines of poetry, it seems clear that he was thinking about his own condition. The last entry is apparently a fragment of a play he never ceased working on.

Many people who suffer from periodic bouts of mental imbalance regard these periods, as Ted had hitherto, as interruptions of their normal life, regrettable but occurring like an infection implanted from the outside for which they are not responsible. Ted was different: somehow he accepted them. He seems to have said to himself, "This is the way I am," and he used these random, jarring intensities as sources for his poetry. To draw together the sanity demanded by his daily life and the "madness" of his periodic illnesses into a whole, to resolve these opposites in the being bounded by his skin was a heroic act, and it established for the rest of his life his tremendous dignity as a human being which everyone felt who met him.

It gave a fillip to his pride to put himself into the company of the "mad" poets, Blake, Christopher Smart, and John Clare, but this was defensive, perhaps even the summoning of surrogate fathers to protect him. And once he had made this total acceptance, his students and his colleagues accepted him also as a fine poet who was unfortunately sometimes ill, and they thought no more about it.

Ted had grown to know himself extremely well. He knew a great deal about the ambiguities of his life, the "dance of opposites" that beset him, and after he had recognized himself for what he was, he could begin reconciling them. His long studies of the mystics seem to have taught him the fatuity of flying from one extreme to the other, he wanted a wholeness in all, a "steady storm of correspondences" as he came to see it. From the middle 1950s onward, he seems to have been trying to achieve this quiet balance that is so apparent in his last poems. His attempt to resume a relationship with his cousin, Bud, shows, I think, that he was trying to exorcise a rooted lifelong hatred.

He was a religious man but he was not concerned with sin as might have been expected from his Presbyterian upbringing nor was he much interested in being his brother's keeper, although he performed many spontaneous kindnesses. Rather, he was troubled about the nature of God, not necessarily a Christian God, his own relation to Him, and his relationship to what he believed to be God's primary creation, nature. (There are remarkably few mentions of artifacts in his later poems and they are never presented as evidences of Man's accomplishment.) He did not completely achieve this sense of wholeness of communion in his personal life or he would have been a saint and nobody ever called him that. He reserved it for his poetry.

Late in February, 1954, Ted gave a reading at San Francisco State College. Ted had never visited San Francisco before and the place charmed him, the Palace Hotel where he stayed, and the restaurants, as they have charmed many another. At his reading, he announced from the rostrum, "I just married a Powers model," and he wrote to Beatrice about his performance,

> I didn't let you down—I really had them. They laughed plenty —were with me all the way . . . Toward the end (long over an hour) I stopped and said now just how much longer should I run & some guy yelled, 'Another hour!' . . . I did a longish recording of the first six long poems for this FM station . . . The radio guys want to send the tapes to Caedmon as well as use them for themselves. (Their idea) . . . You'd love this town.

This excerpt gives some indication of the notion Ted had of himself as a reader, one that is amplified in an essay by Robert Heilman in *Shenandoah*, Autumn, 1964:

> He had an equally goading conscience about readings. He wanted to be paid well; he had a Byronic disinclination to give anything away. But then he wanted to put on the best show the audience had ever seen or heard; he had in him none of the languid youth on the poetry circuit, listlessly dropping pearls before swine unaware of their good fortune, nor of the turtle-

necked sweatered-adolescents using unkempt mien and verse as
instruments of retaliation against an unheeding world. Roethke
wanted to delight, move, "send," overwhelm an audience. He
gave everything he had lavishly—of voice, variety of pace,
mimetic talent, gesture, of energy rushing out as it were over
and above its physical channels, as though he were forcing life
into an audience, bringing them to a new height of vital par-
ticipation and excitement. The strain was exhausting; he came
to know that he could not accept a third of the invitations that
kept coming to him. Weeks before a reading he would begin to
tense up. He told me that sometimes he vomited twice before a
public appearance. He planned the "show" carefully; he did not
drift around as though he did not know what was coming next.
He wanted to be the ultimate showman, to read as soaringly as
Dylan Thomas—or better—and to combine the reading with a
vaudeville or night club act. He strove to be a great public
entertainer, a combination of powerful, sublime reader with
comedian and humorist and even satirist. In the latter role his
judgment was unsure, and his consciously funny topical verses,
quips at the audience, topical references, and jokes about others
and himself often fell below his best level of private spontaneous
humor, not to mention his bardic performance. But whatever
faults of this kind he may have had, if faults they were, were
intimately attached to the extraordinary virtue of commitment
to the maximum excellence of the poet holding and enthralling
his audience.

Ted liked to give readings because of the live applause and the
money. (He made three or four thousand dollars a year from
them, he told me.) Many poets do not read well and Dylan
Thomas said he was the best reader in America, but it is vain to
compare him even remotely with Thomas, who was so far superior
to them all. Ted had a good voice, a tenor or a high baritone, and
he read clearly (many, snuffling and muttering, do not), but the
times I have heard him, I thought he read aggressively, as if he
were saying to the audience, "Take it, damn you, or else . . ."
    In 1954 Ted and Beatrice took a house took on Ivanhoe Place in
the University region, nearer the campus than the one on Lake
Washington. Beatrice visited her family in Winchester for a while.
She also took summer courses at the University to get her per-
manent teaching certificate—an odd mélange: Washington state

history, and Montesquieu's *L'Esprit des Lois.* Ted's sister, June, visited them and the three of them spent a vacation on the Olympic peninsula.

In the fall of 1954, Ted and Beatrice moved into Morris Graves' house in Edmonds, about fifteen miles from the campus. Ted and Graves had met socially several times, become friends, and Ted admired Graves's paintings. Graves was going to Ireland and he offered to rent Ted his beautiful house. No description can do it justice but Wystan Auden called it the most beautiful house in America. Graves had leveled the land himself with a bulldozer, had made all the plans, and helped with the actual building. It looks out over a long lawn with a garden running up one side to a stand of splendid first-growth timber, spruce or pine, immensely tall. Graves seems to have intended the place to have an air of peace and it has.

Ted found it easy to work there and David Wagoner remembers seeing him sitting out in a chair on the lawn with a clipboard on his knee and a little rickety table beside him with a pot of tea and a cup on it. The poems Beatrice remembers from this period are "The Slug," "The Siskins," "The Small," and "A Walk in Late Summer." They kept a goose there named Marianne after Marianne Moore and "The Happy Three" comes from an incident involving it. In the fall, field mice invaded the house looking for warm places against the winter. One night Ted was working in the house and a mouse ran over his foot, startling him. He threw something at it, hit it, and saw that it was still alive. Thinking that the kindest thing to do was to kill it, he hit it again and ran in to Beatrice, tears streaming down his face, to be comforted. Another time, he found a little mouse alone on the lawn, brought it in carefully, fed it three kinds of cheese, and gave it water from a bottle cap. Out of these two occurrences came "The Meadow Mouse." Morris Graves had done a picture entitled *The Bird of the Inner Eye,* and Beatrice believes that the lines in "I'm Here" from "Meditations of an Old Woman" where he mentions a bird singing in his grandmother's inner eye derive from the title of the picture.

Graves influenced Ted in another way. In 1956 Ted tried unsuccessfully to sell the *The New Yorker* a group of line drawings, done with a pen, mostly of birds. There is nothing compellingly excellent about them—they are merely clever, no more—but they show traces of Graves's style.

Some time during this year, Ted applied for a Fulbright grant for Italy. He was given one for the year 1955–1956 and in May, 1955, he was writing Peter Viereck, who had lectured in Florence, for advice as to the number of lectures expected, the nature of the audience, and how long he would be expected to remain in Florence. He arranged with Stanley Kunitz to take his place at the University while he was gone. He found living quarters for him and sent him information about the way he ran his courses. He used Bullett's *English Galaxy of Shorter Poems* and the *Collected Poems* of Yeats and sometimes an Untermeyer or Oscar Williams anthology, and he said that English 413, 414, 415, (fall, winter, spring) involved "a pretty close look" at four, five, or six people a quarter. In the fall he had "done" Kunitz, Louise Bogan, Auden, Hart Crane, with some works of Léonie Adams and Dylan Thomas. In the winter he had done mostly Yeats, and in the spring, Hopkins, Allen Tate, and William Carlos Williams. He makes a point of saying that he has never worked much with Eliot, Pound, Moore, or Stevens. He admired Wallace Stevens and Marianne Moore openly and Eliot, if we believe his critics, covertly, enough to imitate him somewhat in his last poems. I have never heard him mention Pound at all.

In May, 1955, the Irish poet, Richard Murphy, had written Ted from Galway, saying that he was producing a program of new verse on the BBC Third Programme in August, and asking Ted's permission to use some poems. It was Ted's first introduction to Murphy, who later became a good friend and took him to Inishbofin, the island off the coast of Connemara where Ted had some of the best times of his later years.

On September 20, 1955, Ted and Beatrice sailed on the U.S.S. *Independence*. They disembarked at Gibraltar and spent two days at Algeciras, a town I remember not so much for the famous conferences or that it was Molly Bloom's birthplace, but rather for a magnificent chocolate hippopotamus I saw in a store window. Their beds were infested with fleas and Beatrice was the one they bit. They went next to Malaga and then to Granada where they saw the Alhambra, a religious procession, and a bullfight which Ted liked a lot but Beatrice didn't. They went next up to Madrid where Roy Campbell had written to Aurelio Valls, a Spanish poet. Valls had been brought up in England, so he was easy for Ted to talk to. He and his wife, Carmen, had a small apartment where at dinner one night they began their engaging hospitality. They drove Ted and Beatrice out to the Escorial for a picnic—the poem, "The Thing," is taken from an incident that happened on that day. The death of a little bird clearly impressed Ted more than the gloomy pile that covers the graves of the Kings of Spain. The Valls drove them to Segovia and to the outskirts of Toledo but not into the town—Valls wanted them to see the town from the spot where El Greco painted it. In Madrid they often ate at the Méson Segoviana, a restaurant famous for its roast suckling pig, and Valls took them to a flamenco nightclub, the Caballeria. Ted was crazy about the dancers, especially one vivid little gypsy girl. He had asked her her name. She said, "Gloria." "Gloria what?" Ted wanted to know. "Gloria d'Espana," she said. It was a joke and everybody burst out laughing.

After Madrid, they spent a few days in Barcelona at a hotel near the Rambla, the Occidental, which Ted said was a dump. Valls had given them the address of a flamenco "pub," as he called it, and Ted was again entranced.

Ted loved to ride buses and they took a slow trip around the Mediterranean littoral. They stopped at Le Lavandou for a few days and sat on the beach. They stayed overnight at Marseilles and spent a few days at the Hotel Ruhl at Nice (where Ted deposited some money in the hotel safe) and they enjoyed some wonderful lobster, *grillé façon du chef*, at the Restaurant Puget whose chef had won a national prize for the recipe the year before. It was a day's journey from Nice to Florence.

In Florence they stayed their first fortnight in a *pensione* while looking for an apartment. It was there they found Gisella, a young, plump, pretty cook-maid, and they hired her.

They found an apartment near the Ponte Vecchio and the Piazza di Signoria, at Piazza Saltarelli 1. It was a district that had been bombed flat during the Second World War and restored to its prior state with American money.

Ted's term did not start until late in November, and the college was not the University of Florence proper as Ted always said it was; it was the teacher's college, the Magistero. His course was not offered for credit and the budding teachers wanted credit, so Ted never knew how big a class he would have. Worse, he said he couldn't get these Italians to "hear" the poems. In Florence at the time were Peter Viereck, the William Jay Smiths, Anne and Jack Phillips, and Tekla and Alberto Bianchini. They would come to his class sometimes and he attracted a few other students, but it was a frustrating experience and Ted didn't like it.

Probably the best insight into Ted's stay in Florence is in a letter to Robert Heilman in March, 1956:

> We seem to move (when I can be made to move) in a limited but fairly lively orbit of Americans and Americans married to Italians for the most part. One of the nicest people around is Mann's daughter, Elizabeth Borghese; and I've had a lot of fun going for walks with Peter Viereck, who is bright, and is perceptive on people like Beddoes, Swinburne, (the Vierecks live out in the country where walking is possible. And the Jack Phillips, a Boston couple with six girls—sets of two by different marriages—have been jolly. The feeling is quite splendid on occasion. For instance, the Phillips broke out with really good snails, squab, the works, since Beatrice had regaled them with chicken soup using a whole pressed chicken, tournedos, etc.
>
> But for the most part I have been sweating away at verse—making, or putting together notes for lectures. The dying-man sequence is up to five pieces now, three of which are in *Encounter*, and four will be in the *Atlantic* in early summer. The editors have been startlingly receptive, "as fine as anything poetic we have seen in a long time," wrote Ted Weeks—and then sent me a check for a lousy hundred bucks. And Michael Straight took time off for a "not since Yeats" note about a piece which I don't like much . . . And in England the *Times, London Mag., The New Statesman, Encounter* are running stuff, most that has appeared here already.
>
> (I regale you with these loathesome items just to assure you that I haven't changed.)
>
> I can't claim, alas, any great burst of production: one hundred-line thing which *The New Yorker* will run next winter, and four lyrics, one (enclosed) which is probably unprintable. Love and death, the two themes I seem to be occupied with, I find are exhausting: you can't fool around or be just "witty," once you start playing for keeps.

Teaching

Oddly enough, I have found the teaching no soft touch. During November and December the attendance, twice a week, averaged 21 people; during January, 14—considered very good by European standards, even for a credit course—which mine isn't. But I kept trying to draw the Italians out: make them talk. I thought I was getting somewhere; but once right in the middle of the exam period, during the fly-and-cold spell, only two people showed up. I got sore, knocked off classes for the duration of exams, and started over on a straight lecture basis: attendance has been good again.

Sometimes I think the fates brought me here for my own development: to see my contemporaries, and elders, in their true perspective. And some of the American biggies have dwindled a good deal in my sight. For instance, Hart Crane, whom I once thought had elements of greatness. Except for his early poems, he now seems hysterical, diffuse—a deficient language sense at work. Williams, for the most part, has become curiously thin, self-indulgent, unable to write a poem, most of the time, that is coherent.

Next Moves

We go to Rome for the American Seminar (a captive audience), in April. Mizener will be there, and that man, Campbell from Mississippi, also Rudolf Kirk. Two lectures, two seminars a week, Marguerite Caetani is putting us up for the first two weeks—which should be a pleasant bit of free-loading. In May, to Austria for some lecture-readings.

Friendship with Robert Heilman came slowly with the thawing of Ted's suspicion but it arrived at last.

Early in January, 1956, Ted and Beatrice were startled to receive a letter from Morris Graves in Ireland offering to sell them his superb house in Edmonds, together with the five acres of land surrounding it. His first offer seems to have been $50,000. Ted and Beatrice had been so happy there that they were naturally interested but they did not have the money. Ted's mother's estate was still being probated and he had hopes of getting about $10,000 from it (which he did, eventually) and there was the possibility of getting a bank loan on the property to cover at least the down payment or of persuading Graves to hold a mortgage himself. The next few weeks were spent in frantic negotiations by letter and misinterpreted cable with Graves, Max Nicolai, who acted as Ted's agent, with his sister, June, who had inherited two-thirds of the value of the house at 1805 Gratiot in Saginaw and whom Ted offered his third for $4500 in one of his efforts to raise cash. After concessions on both sides, however, the sale did not go through, and on April 29, 1956, Ted said in a letter to Graves,

> The only way I can fathom things is that you have been offended probably by some request or procedure for which I am not responsible.

Toward the end of the negotiations, the deal had looked possible, and if Ted had not been in Italy, Graves in Ireland, and the property in Edmonds, their difficulties might have been solved face to face.

While he was still in Florence, Ted applied unsuccessfully for an extension of his Fulbright for Bedford College, London, to succeed Arthur Mizener. The following statement of his proposed activity there is interesting because of the generosity with which he treats his poetic contemporaries:

> Even the informed English reader (or poet, for that matter, who has travelled in this country), is generally not aware of certain very fine American writers still unpublished in England: Louise Bogan, Léonie Adams, Rolfe Humphries, Stanley Kunitz, Yvor Winters. Then there are the writers that the English know *about* but rarely appreciate fully because their attitudes and rhythms are peculiarly American: William Carlos Williams, Hart Crane, John Crowe Ransom. And there are the American young like Elizabeth Bishop, Richard Wilbur, Rosalie Moore, J. V. Cunningham who have been published very little in England.
>
> It is these and various other writers, and their American ancestors, with which a course at Bedford College would be concerned. The poems would be *heard* and examined, certainly not a new thing to the English with all their programs on the B.B.C. But the material would be largely new, and welcomed, if I can believe the reception given a half-hour on the B.B.C. Third Programme, "An American Introduces Himself and his Poetry," which has been repeated four times.
>
> In twenty years of teaching I have become more and more convinced of the desireability of presenting minor writers as one

of the principal clues to an age. The "big" figures would keep coming in repeatedly by way of contrast: they would remain the background against which one plays another music.

A young architect, Martin Kermacy, who had once worked for Beatrice's uncle, had stopped with his wife to see Ted and Beatrice in Florence. It was he who arranged for Ted to read his poems and lecture at Innsbruck and Vienna. They entered Austria on May 6. Ted was pleased at his reception. He said the Austrians were most cordial. They all spoke English and had no difficulty understanding him. At Innsbruck he read at the University and in Vienna at the University there and at the Austro-American Institute. In Vienna he wrote out the list of common German words and their translation, in case, I suppose, he lost Beatrice somewhere.

When they came back from Austria, they returned to Ischia and stayed in the village of San Francesco, about a twenty-minute walk from Forio. Again Ted found the island congenial and worked hard. (He finished "The Lizard" there.) They had a little three-room house with bamboo curtains and a balcony where Ted sat and behind it a garden with grapes, chickens, and rabbits. Auden was there, recuperating from his Professorship of Poetry at Oxford, the William Jay Smiths, and Harry Craig, an Irish poet. Ted was beginning to like Europe.

Ted said he got "the Number One treatment in Rome, thanks to Marguerite Caetani." In July, 1956, they stayed two weeks at the Palazzo Caetani with occasional visits to Ninfa and Ted improved his acquaintance with Elena Creveri. "Her husband is a banker; hates it; was in the Resistance . . . Elena backs a magazine in Rome, very good, too," he said. (Ted always respected fighters of any kind, gloves or guns.) After the first fortnight, he and Beatrice stayed again at the American Academy. At lunch they met the Irish poet-diplomat, Denis Devlin, who was ambassador from Eire to Italy at the time. With him was Alberto Moravia. They spent an evening with Mario Praz, Professor of English at the University of Rome and the author of *The Romantic Agony*.

The American Seminar went well. Ted's students were a picked group from all over Italy. They understood English. He had to lecture nearly every day and he was delighted. They came to him afterward and told him his "lessons" were the hardest and the best.

If he needed any confirmation, and he always did, that he was a good teacher, these Italian students gave it to him.

On July 20, they left Rome for Paris by way of Nice where Ted stopped at the Hotel Ruhl to pick up the money he had left there. (I wonder why he left money there. Didn't he trust the Italians? Or did he like the feeling that he had cash safely stashed away where he couldn't get his hands on it? There is a faint resemblance —which would have charmed Ted—to W. C. Fields here, who kept money in banks all over the world against the rainy days of his youth. Even in Madrid.) In Paris they stayed first at the Hotel Saintes Péres on the Left Bank; then they moved into an apartment Jackson Matthews lent them. It belonged to Sylvia Beach of Shakespeare & Co. who printed Joyce. Princess Caetani was then in the city and she employed her customary hospitality to introduce Ted to a poet who became one of his translators, Henri Michaux, the author of *Exorcismes* and *Un Certain Plume.* At her house in the Rue de Ligne he also met René Char for the only time but immediately a certain profound rapport was established. He had admired Char's work and, he discovered, he admired him as a man, and it was rare that Ted could let himself admire both.

Char was from the Vaucluse, as big a man as Ted, a year older, and he had fought in the Resistance. One of his poems concerns the dreadful waiting in a field at night for an airdrop by the British. Ted did not quite realize it at the time but he paid Char his ultimate compliment—he admitted him to the domestic circle that was the source of his deepest emotions. He later told his psychiatrist that he saw René Char as the elder brother he had never had and, having said this, burst into tears. (Like Dylan Thomas, David Wagoner was another. Ted had helped and encouraged him ever since Wagoner was his student at Penn State in 1947. Wagoner came to teach at the University of Washington, and Ted told him there that he regarded him as a younger brother.) There seems to have been a sense of incompleteness, a sense of lack, in Ted's memories of his home or it may be that he could think of no higher honor to give a friend than to claim kinship.

In January, 1966, I received this letter from René Char:

> J'ai tardé à répondre à votre lettre et m'en excuse. Ce n'est pas par faute j'y avoir pensé. Les liens de lointaine maise de ferme amitié qui nous liaient l'un a l'autre, Roethke et moi, se

sont plus developpés dans le silence et des échanges muets que dans des rencontres et des correspondances. Nous ne sommes vu qu'une fois à Paris, après que chacun eut lu les poèmes de l'autre, leur resistant puis les aimant, et cela jusqu'au partage, a la réconnaissance qui ne craignent plus d'etre remises en question, comme il arrive souvent entre contemporains. Je ne crois pas qu'un quelconque abandon nous ait jamais menacés. Tout a été dit, et rien n'a été sur cet étrange et viridique accord entre deux hommes qui sont poètes. Joseph Conrad met dans la bouche de Stein dans *Lord Jim* ce propos expliquant tout: "C'était l'un des notres." C'est quelque chose comme ce grand laissez-passez dont nous avons éprouve la grace, Ted et moi. Et dans l'ombre de sentimentalité ou d'erreur gourmande. Nous tirions l'eau d'un meme puits et nos seaux en étaient joyeux! Nos malheurs et nos bonheurs respectifs—et leurs parts obscure et inévitable, ne se melerent pas d'en importuner le geste et le mouvement, de le contraindre à s'arrêter.

Voilà, cher monsieur, mon souvenir et ma dette à l'égard de Theodore Roethke. La mort n'a mis pas fin à sa vie, la mort n'a fait que le pousser un peu. Les quatre points cardinaux à present le tiennent dans leur régard, dans la convoitise merveilleuse et assurée de leur régard.*

In August, 1956, Ted and Beatrice went to London where they put up at Duke's Hotel. It was here that he arranged with the firm of Secker & Warburg to publish *Words for the Wind*, a collection

---

*The French is printed as it was in manuscript. A translation follows:

I am sorry to have taken so long to answer your letter but it was not for lack of thinking about it. Although we lived far from each other, the ties of friendship that bound us together, Roethke and myself, were strong and they developed more in silence and in mute exchanges than through meetings and letters. We saw each other only once in Paris, after we had read each other's poems, resisting them then loving them so much that we shared the recognition that we did not fear to question each other's work as contemporaries often do. The only think that threatened us was a certain outspokenness. Everything and nothing was said in that strange, green harmony that exists between men who are poets. Joseph Conrad in *Lord Jim* put into Stein's mouth the remark that explains everything, "He was one of us." It is something like that great passport whose grace we tasted, Ted and I, and without the least sentimentality or the mistake of greediness. We drew water from the same well and we were joyful doing it! Our respective ills and delights—even those portions obscure and inevitable, did not interfere by breaking out into gesture or movement or by forcing them to stop.

Such, my dear sir, is my memory and my debt in respect of Theodore Roethke. Death did not put an end to his life; it only pushed it forward a little. Now he is regarded by the four points of the compass, in the marvellous firm covetousness of their gaze.

of the poems he had written so far. He also taped another broad-
cast for the BBC. Now that he had friends in London like John
Davenport, Stephen Spender, and William Empson, he felt easy
there and he said he would like to live in London for a couple of
years. They took Davenport and Empson to dinner at the
Connaught. He had written Dame Edith Sitwell earlier in the
spring and sent her some poems. She asked Ted and Beatrice to
a cocktail party.

During their London peregrinations they often met a young
woman named Veronica Henriques whom Ted, as she says,
thought "a sweet kid." She dressed quietly and, although she was
a novelist, she was not well known but she was very nice and,
when she asked them if they would like to spend a weekend in
the country, they accepted very gladly. Weekends are often dull
for visitors in London because everyone goes to the country. She
gave them the address of a little railroad station in Gloucestershire
and said she would meet them. To them she was the kind of girl
who might have a little country cottage where she did all her own
work. They boarded a train full of commuters on a Friday after-
noon and it took them through the Cotswolds to their destination.
Beside the station platform stood a rank of cars, among them a
magnificent Rolls-Royce, gleaming and impeccable with a uni-
formed chauffeur beside it. The commuters would say jocosely,
"Ah, there's my car," and then cross the platform and get into
little MGs and Morris Minors. At last the commuters had all
tooled away. Only the awesome Rolls was left. The Roethkes were
feeling apprehensive, something had gone awry, when the driver
stepped up to them, touching his cap, and said, "Miss Henriques's
guests?" Dutifully they got into the back seat and Ted, to keep
the driver from hearing him say it, wrote Beatrice a note. It said,
"Don't act impressed."

Impressed they were, however. Veronica Henriques was the
daughter of Robert Henriques, the novelist, who was a very
wealthy man. He owned not a simple cottage but a large estate.
He was interested in the most modern methods of stock raising
and worked very hard at it. The Roethkes had a wonderful week-
end and Beatrice said she took a great many pictures "but they
turned out to be mostly of sows."

About the middle of August they embarked on the French

Line's *Liberté* for New York. As an example of the permanent floating muddle Ted lived in, the two of them had sixteen pieces of luggage when they came to the New York customs on August 22 —including cardboard boxes full of books, papers, receipted hotel bills, manuscripts, notebooks. Beatrice had bought a lot of perfume and they were so far out of cash that they didn't have taxi fare and they had to call Doubleday's, who sent a messenger down with the money. They stayed with Stanley Salzman and his wife at 92 West 10th Street. Stanley Kunitz also lived on West 10th and one day, quite by chance, they ran into him—he had just returned from Seattle where he had been teaching Ted's courses.

Now that he had moved through it safely and enjoyably, Ted began to appreciate Europe. While they saw many Americans on their travels, Ted had made friends with Italians, French, and English. He liked London the best of all the places he went, probably because he did not have to sit mute. He had found that he could be at ease with men like Empson and Spender whose reputations were still higher than his own and this pleased him but, aside from these social gratifications, it is, I think, safe to say that little in Europe impressed him so deeply as to make much mark on that level of himself where the sources of his poetry lay. If naïveté is an incurable state of permanent wonder, Ted was a naïf, lifelong and glowing, but the creatures he wondered at were the lives of the natural world, not men or monuments, and women only a little. Out of his European experience thus far only three poems had suggested themselves, one about a bird (apparently), one about a lizard, one about a storm.

Is this reluctance, fear, or a kind of myopia? None of these, I think. Except for these three poems, the sources of Ted's imagery lay at home, in the greenhouse, the field, the Saginaw Valley, its lights, its airs, its creatures. Merely beautiful scenery did not inspire him. He had lived in beautiful country in Pennsylvania and Vermont and he had seen the Alps from the shore of Lake Geneva but he made no use of these places. What he seems to have needed before he could even see, before any sight could burn in his mind, was a strong bond of love for some person, as if things were visible only in its light. And at home, of course, he had loved (and feared) his father. In his last poems in *The Far Field* he begins to introduce imagery drawn from the West Coast—all the birds mentioned in "Meditation at Oyster River" are native to Vancouver Island—and I believe the reason is that he had ceased to regard Beatrice as an acquisition whose beauty would enhance his reputation every time he appeared with her. It would have been a trial of anyone's affection to live with him, and their married life together often eroded her patience and raised the possibility of doubling her love for him. But finally, he came to see what she meant to him as a woman, how great his dependence on her was, and hesitantly, even reluctantly perhaps, he admitted her into those labyrinths within himself where his father still lived, and he began to love her, not in the same way that he loved his father but with a true love nevertheless. And from this time forward, she participated in his growth, encouraged and supported it. Then he could see the mountains, the siskins, the madronas, and begin to use them.

While Ted and Beatrice were staying with Carolyn Kizer they were looking for another house to rent. They found one in the University district and moved in early in September, 1956. Each room in this house was decorated in a different style. Ted's was Empire and his bed had swan's heads on it. They had learned *bocce* in Italy. Beatrice had brought back a set of balls and they used to play in the yard.

Ted resumed teaching and on December 5, 1956, he was at William and Mary College in Virginia as Phi Beta Kappa poet.

The strains of the marriage began to tell on Beatrice. She had learned to overlook Ted's behavior with women at parties and it was not so much that they disagreed seriously over the handling and spending of money any longer; rather it was more that Ted almost unconsciously demanded so much of her time and attention. He was, as I have mentioned, a finicky eater. At night he would not go to sleep until he had eight or nine blankets over him winter and summer, with a blanket or a pillowcase to wrap his head in. This made him sweat so much that it would wake him after an hour or so and he would want a clean pair of pajamas; then he would go to sleep, wake up again, and want another pair. There were often eighteen or twenty pairs of pajamas a week in the laundry. When he did sleep, he snored so loudly that no one could sleep in the same room with him. If he had finished a poem or a paragraph of good lines, she wanted to listen.

Of his parties, Robert Heilman, who was a guest at many, says in his *Shenandoah* essay:

He had a vast conscience as a host. Entertaining, I'd guess, was not easy for him but he was more than dutiful about it, more than generous. When he embarked on a party, he wanted it to go, or still better go off with a bang. Sometimes he supervised the cooking; he had some kitchen talents. He could bellow immoderately at his wife if things seemed to him not split-second, not spit-and-polish, according to the book as he pleased to read it at the moment. (He was immensely devoted to her, and she took his drill-sergeant shouting or sarcasm in stride: "Oh, dear, there goes Ted again.") He was a bartender of reckless elbow and overbearing insistence; he considered continuing sobriety among his guests a case of challenging bad manners, and he was prepared to grind it down; guests might well fear that, if necessary, he would hold their heads under pools of drinks, for he was big and strong and gave the impression of not bowing to petty inhibitions. Before dinner or in the early hours of an evening party he would be an unsmiling earnest pusher of drinks, which were always tanned in complexion, never pale; he was like a churchwarden rigorously and even harshly urging a bigger dose of the gospel upon backsliding Christians. With a mixture of unease and censoriousness he would anxiously demand that guests instantly shed their anxieties and break into boisterous gaiety. Eventually he would ease up himself and take the lead in genial noise, in guffawing, in frolicking fancies; and he loved to get a dance started. When guests began going home, he would look incredulous, aggrieved, hurt, unloved; for them to go before 4 or 5 A.M., before an early breakfast, was a blow to the host, a failure of respect, a vote of lack of confidence, an accusation of inadequacy. No doubt he never did say piteously, "What have I done?" but the image of his doing just that best describes his air of anguished disbelief as we weaker sisters took off.

At parties, I've heard women say, he was as good a dancer as he chose to be, light-footed and rhythmic; it depended on whether he wanted to yield to the music or seize stage, be a participant or a dizzying star—or toy with his partner in a jocose or even raucous elephantine amorousness that betrayed more a sense of spotlights than a Don Juan intentness on results. He liked looking like a naughty boy and was inclined to take looking for being; in any little enterprise a deux his eyes, registering delight at his deviltry, were as likely to be seeking applause from the observers as consent from the woman in hand. (Some women found him, with his unsubtle hands and mountainous verbal coynesses, bothersome and boring; some were charmed, some fascinated; some were matter of fact, some found the sparring fun; some dutifully disliked the passes, some hated to be passed over; and veterans of dining-table and parlor skirmishes could always be relieved by new volunteers, half-ready to bare a breast to the enemy charge, half-ready for the purple heart, and always able, if the pressure was too severe, to retire upon reserves of husbandly strength. The reserves had styles ranging from suitable indignation, fired from heavy batteries of propriety, to an insouciant, "You know your way around the course, dear. Don't lean on me."

And there was the pretty young faculty wife whom Ted was groping on the dance floor who said, "There's a bedroom right over there, Ted. Come on, let's go." Ted blanched and drew back.

Now if these parties be looked at from the point of view of the hostess, it will be seen how much patience and energy were demanded of Beatrice in addition to the daily drain.

In January, 1957, their former hostess, Veronica Henriques, was in the United States, and she paid them a visit in Seattle. In answer to a request of mine, Miss Henriques, now Mrs. Gosling, wrote me the following perceptive letter:

> I find it very difficult to answer your request because my impressions of Ted are so very much affected by his impressions of me. He thought me, at the time I knew him, almost ten years ago, a sweet kid. So that I had, to make any communication with him at all, to get through this barrier! As you have known him for so long I'm sure you know very well his tendency to paw women, and being somewhat intimidated by his size, his way of talking, etc. I never had the courage to say, "For God's sake, stop pawing," but finally, Beatrice said it for me while I was staying with them in Seattle.
>
> I found him constantly on the edge of being a pathetic man in his longing and need for approval, and very frightening in his outbursts of anger and intolerance. His range of interests so far as I could see (not very far, I'm sure) seemed exceedingly narrow. To do with poets, poetry, and his immediate world. He

talked so slowly I often couldn't hang on long enough. But I found him a most kind and considerate host when I stayed there; he was very proud of anyone he took up. Of Beatrice, he was always saying to me, "Don't you think she's beautiful?", of his students, (I sat through a class of his) and even of me because I was staying with HIM! I found him very sentimental on such subjects as mothers and babies: in the abstract, of course.

The best time I had with the Roethkes was in the evenings during my stay when we read poetry. He enjoyed hearing English poetry read in an English accent, and I was very startled by and interested in his way of reading poetry, which I have heard is not so startling in the States as it is here. This sudden way of rushing a sentence, and then stopping.

I was surprised by the delicacy of many of his poems. It was a side I never saw in his character which merely indicates how superficially I knew him.

Last time he was in England I hardly made any contact with him. I had just had a baby and my hours very limited in the Roethke world. I was exhausted by ten P.M. and he was just waking up after a bottle of whiskey at midnight. They were both having a very difficult time then anyway and I had a helpless feeling when with them that I could be of very little help.

He needed adulation badly, but I suppose no amount of it could counteract his fears.

It was shortly after Miss Henriques's visit that Beatrice was diagnosed as having pulmonary tuberculosis. It was a very light case but she entered Firlands Sanitarium at the end of January, 1957. She said, "I felt very tired." Since it is mental or physical strain or a combination of the two that causes these tubercular breaks, fatigue is naturally one of the symptoms. This was the first time Ted had ever been forced to be responsible for another person's welfare and he was shocked and frightened. On his visits to her, he hovered anxiously over her with the dreadful false cheerfulness such occasions evoke but he could not hasten her cure. All he could do was to pay the bills.

Ted lived alone in the house on 16th Street N.E. and gave many parties for students there. Robert Lowell came to give a reading at the University. Ted asked him to stay with him and so resumed a friendship begun at Yaddo many years before.

Beatrice recovered sufficiently to be discharged from the Sani-

tarium on May 23, 1957, but before she left, she and Ted nego-
tiated the purchase of their first house, a large ten-room place at
3802 East John Street on the shore of Lake Washington. There
was a certain amount of decorating and repair work they wanted
done before they moved in, and, during the summer, they stayed
in different motels and resort hotels while this was going on. Paul
Thiery, later the chief architect of the Seattle World's Fair, ad-
vised them on the color scheme (off-white) and fixtures. He was
a calming influence on Ted who characteristically called him
Papa—it is remarkable that Ted could express his admiration or
affection for anyone only in domestic terms.

In the May issue of *College English* appeared Ted's piece, *Last
Class*. It was written about Bennington and it had appeared first
in *Botteghe Oscure* in 1950. Eliot had told Princess Caetani that it
was the finest piece of invective since the Elizabethans, and Ted
often quoted this. An excerpt follows:

> A young girl, said Montherlant, what a dreary subject for a
> writer. And don't I know it now, me up to the armpits in quiver-
> ing adolescent entrails, still trying to find something I can save.
> Take it from me that's been hit over the head, still slug-nutty
> from those long years in the technique mines. I'm beginning to
> feel the mould creep over the noble lineaments of the soul. O the
> lies I've told my own energies trying to convince myself I was
> teaching you *something*. Twenty times a day I asked myself: Are
> you really worth it? And the more I asked, the more I lathered,
> vomiting before Thursday classes, chasing after examples like a
> greasy stack-rat, learning passages by heart only to forget them
> when I got there, beating my off-stage beat to death, schmalzing
> all day long—a high-speed pitch artist, a sixteen-cylinder Mr.
> Chips, wide-open Willie (Just look sad and he'll change the
> assignment), I ask you, is that the way for a grown man, and
> me past thirty-five, to make a living?

Its reception in the academic world was varied, as these two
letters, amusing for different reasons, to Professor Frederick L.
Gwynn, the Editor of *College English*, reveal. The first is from a
former editor of *College English*.

> Dear Professor Gwynn:
> This letter would be anonymous but that I always felt such
> letters to be a bit cowardly. You should read this as if it came

from a teacher, perhaps a department chairman, in some mid-
western teachers college. My concern is not personal but pro-
fessional.

The Roethke article in the May *College English* seems to me
very unfortunate. Will it not tend merely to widen the gulf be-
tween some college teachers and their students, to deepen the
pessimism of those who have aimed impossibly high or just do
not know how to reach students? In a lifetime of teaching I have
had a few classes that *seemed* lazy, and felt that I rather than
they had fallen short. I have never seen any who deserved the
vituperation that Mr. Roethke hurls at his students, apparently
mostly women.

His language, too, adds insult to injury. It seems to me to be
in bad taste. Everyone, including the author, would have been
better off if, after he had relieved his tension by writing the
screed, he had tossed it into the waste-basket.

The second letter is from a member of the English faculty at
Antioch College:

Dear Mr. Roethke (and Mr. Gwynn):

Congratulations on your deliciously unkind *Last Class*—and
to *College English* for having the courage to print it. (A few
years ago CE printed an article of mine, *The Wench Is Dead*,
but not without washing my mouth with soap. "Groin had to go,
and Marlowe's "fornification" was too strong. The editor was
queasy, even, about the title.) But the editorship has admirably
changed.

I hope *Last Class* gets reprinted in every freshman anthology
for all time to come. The poor dears will not understand it, will
be confused, hurt, and rejected. But it is high time students
learned that teachers, some of them, are people, capable of
honest responses. There is so much phoney about this whole
education business that from time to time maybe we ought to
lay our testicles on the table just to establish we are all there.

Needless to say, the renaissance prose was a joy and a model.

Since it was Ted who kept these letters, I think he was amused
by them also.

In her convalescence, Beatrice wanted to see the industrial
south end of Seattle and they stayed for a few weeks at the Angle
Lake motel. There was a lawn with apple trees and Ted liked to
sit out under them and work. Later they went up to Orchis Island

in the San Juans where they stayed at Bartel's Resort. Out walking one day they found three little kittens and over Ted's protests, Beatrice took them back to their rooms. (Ted hated to touch animals and he hated dogs entirely.) Two of them died and Beatrice, mistakenly thinking the survivor a male, named it Andrew and she still has it. From Orchis they went to Vancouver Island and stayed at a salmon fishing resort very near Oyster River. Ted wanted very much to catch a salmon and kept trying. He finally landed a seven-pound one. Beatrice, however, caught the season's biggest on her first day out, sixteen pounds. (This does something to a man.) They fished for crabs and one day there was a school of whales disporting themselves not far from the shore. Ted wanted to go out to them in a boat but was dissuaded. Later, they returned to Orchis Island.

On September 1, 1957, they moved into their new house, moved themselves and their baggage. They had no furniture, literally none at all; they had always rented furnished. A friend of theirs who lived nearby, Walter Walkinshaw, brought them a mattress to sleep on the first night, staggering down the street with it perched on his back. The house contained the usual stove and refrigerator, and when they had bought a bedstead to fit the mattress, Ted was satisfied—he didn't care whether there was any more furniture or not—he could work in bed, in fact, he pre-ferred to. Beatrice's parents sent her some furniture as a kind of belated wedding present. She says, "I had a thousand dollars in the bank, about one-eighth of what I had earned in two years of teaching. I did not expect to put my whole salary in the bank and let Ted pay the bills when we were both working but I was more anxious than he to furnish the house. I accomplished this by buy-ing old armchairs at the Salvation Army and Goodwill Industries and having them covered, by making the curtains for the kitchen and the room adjoining it, by refinishing an oak table that had been left in the house and by talking Ted into buying some Swedish tables and having draperies made for nearly the whole house. Our friends contributed paintings and drawings, and Rich-ard Gilkey lent us a rug for the living room. Perhaps the house was as tastefully furnished as it was because I had ample time to consider well what I wanted before I bought it. Later I used much of the thousand dollars for more antiques from Virginia, a phonograph, and landscaping. Ted contributed much more than that later for a chaise longue and sofa made in Ireland, ordered when he was in an expansive mood, and additional landscaping, not to mention a rather astounding sum for having the kitchen remodeled.

When Ted married he had $7000 which he kept in a checking account, but this was a reserve fund so that he would not be helpless when he was ill. He particularly feared being forgotten in some state hospital. So this money was quite properly unavailable to pay for furnishings. However, Beatrice persisted and, in the end, since she has great taste, the house was furnished and furnished beautifully.

In September, 1957, both Beatrice and his friends could see that Ted was entering a manic phase. He took a suite at the Olympic Hotel, the most expensive in Seattle. As he says in a letter to Jim Jackson, dated October 15, 1957, "I had set up a suite at the Olympic in order to rest & give Beatrice a rest; and be able to yack on long distance without umpteen explanations." This was a touch of *folie de grandeur* in itself because he could not afford such accommodations. His colleagues realized that trouble was ahead and they wanted him to meet at least one class of the fall term so that he could receive sick pay. He promised he would.

The day of his first class was October 2. The students gathered in the classroom but Ted was not there. At this period he was at the height of his power and reputation as a teacher. His students had the air of disciples; they waited half an hour. Suddenly the door burst open and Ted appeared, panting with exhaustion, his face grey and wet with sweat, his damp trousers clinging to his legs. He had walked or run all the way from downtown Seattle, a distance not less than five miles. He flung himself against the blackboard in a kind of crucified pose, muttering incoherently. His students knew that he was subject to such attacks and one of them ran to the English Department office and got the Secretary, Mrs. Dorothy Bowie. She and some of Ted's other friends, David Wagoner and Carolyn Kizer, led him into the English office. When a man as big as Ted goes off the rails, it is a frightening spectacle. In his letter to Jackson, Ted claimed that all he was trying to do was to get a cab so that he could get a dry shirt, but to his friends it did not seem that simple. Mrs. Bowie knew that something drastic would have to be done. She called the city police and said,

"This is a very distinguished man and he is ill. All we want you to do is take him to a sanitarium. No rough stuff."

Ted feared and hated cops. When he saw them, he made one lunge at them but they seized him and smoothly handcuffed his hands behind his back. There wasn't any rough stuff. They were gentle but firm. And they led old Ted, the distinguished man, the poet and friend of poets everywhere through the corridors of Parrington Hall just as classes were changing, with his head bent nearly to his knees and the cops sedately around him. David Wagoner said, "The tears ran down my face and everybody who saw it felt soiled, a little ashamed."

Ted was taken to Harborview Hospital and later admitted to Halcyon House Sanitarium, where he spent three months. He was admitted in the spring of the next year because of the paralyzing side-effects of a new drug that had been prescribed. On that occasion his symptoms were those of Parkinson's disease.

It was a period of intense worry about money. Aside from the payment for the new house and its decoration, there were Ted's bills, often running over $1,000 a month, inflated by Ted's orders for prime steaks and cases of ale to be sent in, and after January there were Beatrice's bills. Ted was fully aware of the problem, sick or not, and the numerous letters he always wrote in sanitariums were now attempts to deal with it. In October, 1957, he wrote Stephen Spender at *Encounter* a jocosely threatening letter, asking when *Encounter* was going to print (and pay for) "The Sensualists," which he had accepted over a year before. He wrote a facetiously stern letter to Howard Moss, the poetry editor of *The New Yorker* about the same time, asking about a "grave Donnesque-like thing, a sombre, terrible piece" he had submitted and a "first-look" contract that was in the works. (It was mutually signed August 11, 1958, for a consideration of $100 for "all poems, fiction, honor, reminiscences, and casual essays" and they were to pay him 25 percent more than his current rate for poetry which was $2.10 a line.) Ted also mentioned that he was beginning his autobiography to sell to *The New Yorker* but he was worried about a possible libel suit from his cousin, Bud. (The autobiography was barely begun and never finished.) He ends by asking if the magazine can advance him two or three thousand dollars on account. On October 19, 1957, he wrote Mark Schorer at the

English Department of the University of California to see if there was a possibility of a post as a permanent poet-in-residence, teaching two quarters a year. "I am, I realize, hardly the Berkeley type," he says. "But then, I can play it stuffy, too, if need be."

Not all his news was bad. In October, 1957, Ted received word that the English edition of *Words for the Wind* was the Christmas choice of the Poetry Book Society. He continued to work, as usual, completed three poems, one of which he sold to *The New Yorker*. Beatrice's younger brother, Irvan, back from Korea, had enrolled in the University of Washington to do an M.A. in classics. He often visited Ted and they hit it off very well.

Ted had intended to do readings, and had made the arrangements through Elizabeth Kray at the YM-YWHA Poetry Center, at Loyola, Harvard, and the Poetry Center, but in March, 1958, these had to be canceled.

On May 28, 1958, Beatrice received a note from the National Institute of Arts and Letters,

> Your good friends, Lillian Hellman and Richard Wilbur, have informed us about your husband's illness and we hasten to send you the enclosed check for $500, the maximum we can send to anyone from our Artists and Writers Revolving Fund.

This was very helpful but more substantial aid was in the offing. Archibald MacLeish wrote to Ted suggesting that he approach the Chapelbrook Foundation for aid. (This was kind of MacLeish because it does not seem that he knew Ted personally.) On October 16, Ted replied. He said he was out of the hospital but over three thousand dollars in debt; that his present medical expenses were running over four hundred dollars a month; that his doctors estimated that ten thousand dollars would be necessary to "effect a complete cure." (It is hard to tell what Ted means here. It is very doubtful if he believed he could be "cured.") He says there are no further family resources to be tapped, that, in fact, his sister has put forward "a considerable amount of her savings" to help him. MacLeish had suggested that Ted apply for three thousand dollars. Beatrice said they hoped they might possibly get five, but they were astounded when the Chapelbrook Foundation sent them ten thousand. To have a poet of MacLeish's stature befriend him and then to get much more than he expected naturally enlarged

Ted's ideas of his own stature, but immediately he was hounded by fears that he was unworthy of it. Princess Caetani also wrote the Foundation in Ted's behalf.

Ted resumed teaching in the spring quarter of 1958. On May 23, he endured his fiftieth birthday. According to Arnold Stein, it was a climacteric and a pall of gloom seemed to descend on him. He had remarked beforehand that the half-century mark was a crucial time for him, yet he was not a professionally youthful man like Scott Fitzgerald. But after it, his walk changed, and, seen from behind, he looked like an old man. He seemed to lose his bounce, much of his humor, even his hope except for his poetry. His jolly intervals came more seldom and lasted a shorter time. In the years preceding he had often told Stein he expected death, but from this birthday on he never mentioned it. His father had died at fifty-two but whether Ted felt that he should go when his father did can only be conjectured. Beatrice says she did not notice all this but men often try to look better to their wives than they do to their friends out of some sort of male pride, and, as practiced as Ted was in the use of a mask, he may have worn one before her.

Beatrice had been taking lessons in painting and Ted took a good deal of husbandly pride in her work. In the sanitarium Ted had showed Arnold Stein a painting on cardboard he had done himself. (Ted told him all about his painting lessons in his boyhood.) It was an abstraction, a little crabbed design, the center of which, Ted insisted, contained all the secrets of the universe. Later Ted painted some more, all abstractions (one titled "S. Matuna"; "Samoots Matuna" is the name of a character in "Song for the Squeeze-Box"), but he had little talent and they were not very good. Nevertheless, he hung them all in his house and one night invited some wealthy people of artistic tastes, the kind who buy paintings, to view them. View them was all they did; they bought none. He thought poets should be rich, good ones, that is, like himself—they worked harder than the rich.

About this time Ted came to depend quite a bit on Arnold Stein for criticism of his poetry but he showed him only the poems he had doubts about. Stein was always being surprised by finding a poem in print he had never seen. And he soon discovered that for Ted criticism did not consist in making pronouncements. It was rather an exchange, an arguing back and forth over lines and the purpose was to clarify his own ideas. He used to call Stein and read him poems over the phone. It became a kind of game. "I found I couldn't talk to Ted as I talked to students, 'Well, this is pretty good . . .,' you know the kind of thing. I had to be spontaneously acute. I never suggested words or phrases. I merely said, 'I think it's wobbly here,' or some such phrase." Stein once told him, "You're all soul," a penetrating remark since it had to go through Ted's bear-like exterior, and Ted quoted it approvingly many times. "He made a marvellous use of his own weaknesses," Stein said. "He had to have impossible aspirations, that is, to become 'all soul.' "

Ted had arranged with Mrs. Ruth Witt-Diamant of the English Department for him to come to San Francisco State College for a fee of $1800 for the period from June 23, 1958, to August 1. It was money he could have used but he had to cancel the engagement for he was in "deep therapy" conducted by Dr. Ian Shaw six times a week. One of the things that came up during these sessions was the character of Otto Roethke and Shaw seems to have suggested that he was not quite so god-like a figure as Ted believed, but it is doubtful if he convinced Ted. Ted was not in the least awed by psychiatrists. He once said to Shaw, "Come on, get hot. You haven't had a new insight in weeks."

In May, 1958, Ted started the usual string of anxious letters to Doubleday about his next book. They had accepted *Words for the Wind* for fall publication, and a letter to Ken McCormick asks for an increase in his advance on the book of $500 or $1,000 because of his hospital bills. He says, "The book should, at the very least, unless the judges are completely mad or incompetent, win the National Book Award. Of course, I think it should win everything but that's impossible." Then he worries about the subtitle: shouldn't it be "The Collected *Poems* of Theodore Roethke" rather than "The Collected *Verse*"? He continued to fidget right up until publication date as this letter, one of many, to Miss Kate Steichen at Doubleday shows:

> I keep thinking: who is doing the jacket copy and has he or she the necessary material? I sent in some excerpts from English reviews, but on the chance they weren't filed, I'm sending them (and some others) in again. I trust this is not presumptuous.
>
> Damn it, I want to win something with this book—for the

house and for myself. I think the book should, but I'm convinced most of these committees don't go much beyond the jacket. Hence this concern.

When *Words for the Wind* came out in the fall, the book contained the poems Ted wanted to keep from *Open House, The Lost Son, Praise to the End!*, and *The Waking* as well as forty-three new poems under the headings of "Lighter Pieces and Poems for Children," "Love Poems," "Voices and Creatures," "The Dying Man" sequence, and "Meditations of an Old Woman." It was very widely reviewed as the work of a major poet, in the *New York Herald-Tribune* by Babette Deutsch, among many others, by Richard Eberhart in *The New York Times*, who said, "The collection of Theodore Roethke's work is a major achievement in the Romantic tradition of American poetry," and by W. D. Snodgrass in *Poetry* who said, "Roethke seems here to have accomplished (or, at the very worst, to be on the verge of) a language which many of the best poets of his age and younger, among them Lowell and Berryman, have been dreaming about and working toward."

And in recognition of his excellence, he was fairly pelted with prizes and awards: the first of his Borestone Mountain Awards, 1958 ($1250); the Edna St. Vincent Millay Award, 1959 ($200); the Bollingen Award, 1959 ($1,000)—the year afterward it went up to $2500, which Ted regarded as sheer bad luck); the Longview Award, 1959 ($300); the Pacific Northwest Writers Award, 1959 (Ted wrote in a letter, "No money, alas"); and, as he had hoped, the National Book Award, 1959 ($1,000).

It was all very gratifying, both the acclaim and the cash, and Ted seemed to be fleetingly content but there were still his "impossible aspirations." He had to become "all soul."

XIV

The Last Years

The last years of Ted's life, as we look back on them knowing they were the last, seem to have a strange air of unconscious preparation. As the fabric of his body begins to give way, the best part of his mind, his poetry—seeming to have forgiven everyone everything, demolished its hatreds, and solved all its discords—strives toward a mystical union with his Father. But this *was* unconscious. I don't think he was at all aware that he was getting ready to go. He had too much work in hand, too much projected, yet the last poems seem prophetic: they read like last poems.

His arthritis grew worse and became more painful in Seattle's damp climate. (He kept trying to get a job in California for the winter terms where he could be in the sun. He liked the sun.) He seemed to have a permanent bursitis in his elbow, and what he called "spurs" in his shoulder for which he often got cortisone injections. When I saw him last in 1962, he was swaying from side to side more than ever when he walked and he said, "My goddamned knees are gone. Tendons are shot. Too much tennis on clay courts." He played no more tennis; only a little badminton on his lawn. But he could say to Tom Kinsella when they were sitting on top of a cliff on Bainbridge Island, overlooking the water, in the summer of 1963, "You know how I've stood all I've gone through?" He thumped his chest. "Got a strong ticker."

And in the last two years of his life he was frequently in a state of manic excitement. He seemed to have a feeling of exhilaration, of great freedom—too great, he realized, for he drank a good deal to control it. (Of course, that was what he had always tried to

251

do in his manic states, to control them.) He often took a glass of beer the first thing in the morning and later in the day drank whiskey—not like medicine exactly, for he always liked a drink —but as a depressant.

Whether this exhilaration stimulated his writing or whether, as he believed, his creative energies caused the exhilaration is impossible to say; but these were prolific years. From 1959 until his death in 1963 he published sixty-one poems, and both Beatrice and Arnold Stein say that the long poems like "The Rose," "Meditation at Oyster River," "Journey to the Interior," and "The Far Field" came easily with an unwonted confidence—he knew what he wanted to say and he was sure of his means.

In the first few months of 1959, Ted was in Halcyon House Sanitarium. As usual he continued to work at poetry, and, free from the burden of classes, he wrote a great many letters, full of extravagant proposals and complaints about his career, seriously intended but too extravagant to be taken seriously.

About the middle of February, he sent McCormick a perfectly rational complaint. He included a clipping from an English newspaper about John Betjeman's work (which Ted admired greatly),

> Today, a first edition of 9,000 copies of his *Collected Poems* has been exhausted, a second printing has been ordered, and the book is reported to have been selling at the rate of 1,000 copies a day.

Next to the clipping, Ted wrote, "This is what I mean, Ken. Am I selling 1,000 copies a day, with all my honors, etc.?" (Ted neglects to say that the reason for Betjeman's phenomenal sale was that his book had been mentioned publicly by Princess Margaret as one of her favorites. Any doubt that England is still a monarchy should be dispelled by this statement.) He then pointed out bitterly and in detail how publishers' sales departments refused to bother with poetry, and, although he got more attention from Doubleday's than any other poet, he was right.

Unknown to Ted, something was happening to threaten his whole position at the University of Washington. Apparently some enemy of Ted's (and he had them) complained to one of the Washington state legislators that Ted was on sick leave again. Vice-President Frederick Thieme, a graduate of the University of

Michigan, was at Olympia, the state capital, to present the annual university budget for the legislature's approval. The legislator approached Thieme and said, "Say, who's this professor you've got down there that's some kind of a nut?" To a university official with a budget in his hand this was like a firebell in the night. Thieme was alarmed and called Robert Heilman. He said he thought that the English Department was right in giving Ted sick leave, that they should not be apologetic, but that he would like a strong statement to make in rebuttal.

On January 27, 1959, Robert Heilman wrote the following extraordinary letter to Thieme:

> Dear Mr. Thieme,
>
> I am replying to your inquiry about sick leaves for Professor Theodore Roethke of the Department of English. In order to give you a complete picture, I shall list *all* the leaves that he has had. This should forestall any possibility of confusion.

Leaves without pay	Leaves with pay
WQ and SQ, 1949–50	WQ, 1953–54
—illness	—illness
Year, 1952–53	FQ and SQ, 1957–58
—Ford Fellowship	—illness
Year, 1955–56	WQ, 1958–59
—Fulbright Fellowship°	—illness
(lecturer in Italy)	

> Roethke joined this faculty in the fall of 1947. Therefore he is now in his 12th year of service to the University of Washington. In that time he has a total of four quarters (including the present one) with pay. In 11½ years, this is not an exorbitant number. He has never had a sabbatical leave. Actually, the sick leaves amount to very little more than the sabbatical leaves that, as we normally count these things out, would have accrued during that period.
>
> However, I do not want to justify the sick leaves in these terms. Even if Roethke had had the sabbaticals, I would still have recommended the sick leaves with pay during his periods of illness. I feel that this is not only defensible policy, but in this case *is in the University's own interests*. The rest of the letter will be on this subject.
>
> First, one piece of clinical information. Roethke has a nervous

° Received the usual $1500 travel grant from the University.

ailment of the "manic-depressive" type. Periodically he goes into
a "high" or "low" state in which he is incapable of teaching. It
is in such periods that he has been on sick leave. (His illnesses
are well-known throughout the University and the local com-
munity. I have always been pleased that they have been ac-
cepted as would any other illness and regarded as the terribly
sad lot of an extraordinarily gifted man; his genius has been
valued, and his work admired; and all informed people have
been eager to have us take every step to save him for the
University.)

Under any circumstances, the University has some obligation
to staff-members who become ill. Surely this obligation is in-
tensified in the case of individuals who have rendered extra-
ordinary services to the University. But quite aside from obliga-
tion, there is a real sense in which payment during sick leave is a
payment for services *which continue to be rendered* even if the
individual is unable to meet classes. In this sense, Roethke may
be almost in a class by himself. He is, I think, one of the most
valuable of all our faculty members. Surely few people have a
reputation comparable to his in twentieth century American
literature. Although it is risky to guess about the future, I think
he will be a permanent figure in American literature, and what-
ever place he has, this University will always have a share in it.
He is an investment in history such as many a university would
be glad to have.

But whatever happens in the future, what he has done for us
in a little over a decade is an extraordinary service. I believe *he
has done more to make us known favorably as a university than
any other single person on the staff.* He is known nationally and
internationally, and wherever he is known, we are known.

First, there is the *sheer quantity of his writing.* His illnesses
seem to have almost no effect on his creativity; he is utterly de-
voted to his craft, he keeps writing poetry all the time, and he
never relies on the illnesses as an excuse not to write. I enclose a
formal bibliography, which will give you a good picture of how
much he has done. (As you can see, his work is so extensive that
making a record of it has been deemed suitable for an M.A.
thesis in librarianship.) You will note that it takes over thirty
pages simply to list what he has published! Note also that it
takes another six pages to list works about him! Here is the con-
crete evidence of the attention being paid to him.

Second, there is the *quality of his writing.* The numerous poets and students of poetry in the University and in this section automatically think of him as one of the great American poets. But the objective evidence of his status is the number of awards and grants he has won. It is a truly extraordinary list. (Since he is ill, and I cannot consult with him now, the list below may be incomplete or slightly inaccurate in detail, but in the main it is right.)

Guggenheim Fellowship (before coming to U.W.)	1945
Grant to Yaddo Writers Colony (before coming to U.W.)	
Tietjens Prize	1947
Guggenheim Fellowship	1950
Grant ($1,000) from National Institute of Arts and Letters	1952
Levinson Prize (highest award by Poetry Magazine)	1951
Ford Foundation Fellowship	1952
Pulitzer Prize	1953
Fulbright Award (To lecture in Florence, Italy)	1953
Borestone Mountain Prize (2nd)	1958
(Annual Stanford volume of Best Poems of Year)	
Bollingen Prize	1958
Edna St. Vincent Millay Prize	1959

In summary, there are about ten distinguished awards that he has won since he has been here, and at every such announcement *the name of the University of Washington has won national attention.* Let us put it into the most materialistic terms: no one else has given us so much free public relations of the most excellent sort.

One note on the Fulbright appointment to the ancient University of Florence. Roethke, conscientious as always, worked himself almost ill interpreting American poetry to the Florentines. The result was a special letter to President Schmitz from an official of the State Department, of which I enclose a copy.

Finally, to close the record with another kind of evidence. Aside from his own writing, Roethke has been a phenomenally successful teacher, with the most devoted following of gifted creative students that I have ever known a teacher to have anywhere. He does not use his teaching for subsistence in order to be able to be a poet; he always works hard at teaching, and it is possible that the intensity of his teaching work helps bring on his attacks of illness. The results of his teaching may be described in the following objective terms:

1. The University of Washington is nationally known as one of the great centers of poetic study and creativity in America.

2. Young people interested in writing poetry come here to study from all over the country. Just this week I answered an inquiry about the "Roethke seminar" from a young lady now studying at Bard College in New York.

3. Writers want to come here to teach. Research scholars who have the Ph.D. but who are also interested in poetry make many special applications here.

4. Most of all, the students in the Roethke courses have done a great deal of writing for publication. As a member of another department said to me, "You can't open any literary journal nowadays without seeing poems by at least one person who teaches or studies at the University of Washington." I know of no English Department in the country of which this can be said. All of this stems from the work of Roethke.

5. Need I say that poetry is one of the oldest creative arts? For us to have a flourishing local "movement" or "school" seems to me to indicate that we are performing one of our educational functions in an unusually successful way. We are helping develop a certain type of creative human being, and this is in some way related to the health of a society. In this connection, I enclose a clipping from a recent Seattle *Times*—a story which tells of the great scope of poetic activity here. And, appropriately, at the center of the story, is the name of Roethke.

In all of these ways—teaching, developing interest in a great literary form, training writers who themselves go on to become known, and doing his own distinguished writing which has won all kinds of acclaim—Roethke is performing what I call a *continuing service to the University,* which goes on whether he is ill or well. When we keep him on the payroll when he is ill, we are not merely helping a sick man or aiding a fine artist; in realistic terms, we are simply continuing to pay a great University debt. I shall without hesitation continue to recommend we continue with this policy whenever he is ill.

Sincerely yours,
Robert B. Heilman

There are three things remarkable about this letter. The first is that it is the strongest, and, in humane terms, the finest support of a staff member I have ever heard of any university department making anywhere. The second is the evidence of Robert Heilman's loyalty, affection, and admiration and this in the face of Ted's initial suspicion of him which was enough to have killed most friendships at the start. The third is that Ted had acquired a position of the greatest prestige in an academic community entirely on his own terms. He had made no concessions, had buttered up no one. He had followed his private interest, what he did best. He wrote and he taught, and out of them he made the reputation which Heilman described. With this letter, Provost Thieme was able to allay the fears of the legislators that they might be throwing away the state's money on some kind of a nut.

Knowing that he could not be present at the National Book Award dinner in New York in February, 1959, Ted prepared a long comic essay, totally unsuitable, purporting to be an account of the career of "Winterset Rothberg," which he suggested be read by Louis Untermeyer. However, other arrangements had been completed, and at the dinner Professor Daniel Hoffman of Swarthmore College accepted the award in Ted's place with an able and moving speech.

In January and February, 1959, Ted wrote two letters to Hans Sahl, his German translator. Sahl had turned *The Lost Son* into German and Ted urged him to submit it to Princess Caetani for *Botteghe Oscure*. In passing, Ted says,

> I suffer from a guilt about Germany. I wont go there for a lot of reasons. To Stettin I may go sometime, or to Enrico von Hesse's estate next to the Bismarck estate (if the little princeling asks me ever.) . . .

Since he does refer elsewhere to the kind of guilt he suffered about Germany, it is hard to tell what it was. He had so many.

He had applied for a second Ford Foundation grant and he had submitted the following statement of projects:

> If I were given a grant-in-aid freeing me from other occupations, I would complete, not endeavor to complete, the following works, (listed in their order of importance):
> I. A sequence of serious poems beginning with a long dirge which will express through suggestive and highly charged symbolical language the guilts we Americans feel as a people for our mistakes and misdeeds in history and in time. I believe, in other words, that it behooves us to be humble before the eye of history.

Obviously such an attempt would, indeed, must bring into play great boldness of imagination, poetic and spiritual wisdom, in order to reveal some of the secrets of our enigmatic, vast, shrill, confused, and often childish nation. Obviously, this would not be chronological, yet would expose some of the lies of history; our triumphs of rage and cunning; our manias, our despairs; our furtive joys. And it would attempt to expiate some of our collective mistakes.

General Design of this Proposed Long Poem:

I. Three dirges of increasing line length (two already partly written)

II. A lament and two songs (possible more)

III. A sudden break into a kind of euphoric pure joy.

II. To finish and publish a book of songs and rhymes for children, with illustrations by Robert Leydenfrost. Musical settings already composed by Ben Webber, Gail Kubik and others may be included in a slip-case in the back of this book. These poems have already been widely published in America and England, danced to all over this country and broadcast (without payment) over all major networks.

III. (For Second Year) Help European translators with editions or sections of anthologies in progress:

a. Italian: to be first in a new series; editors, Salvatore Rosati, University of Rome, and Agostino Lombardo of University of Bari.

b. German: Hans Sahl. Mr. Sahl is incomparably better as a translator of my work than any that appeared in *Perspectiven.* Three poems of mine have been read by him over at least a dozen German radio stations, and he has done the best critical article in German.

c. German-Swiss: Elizabeth Schnack. (This may be abandoned since she is ill.) She has done a good deal of work, and has a publisher in Zurich "most interested."

d. French: Alain Bosquet, René Char, perhaps Henri Michaux.

The "proposed long poem" was never finished in the form he outlined it here but it shows that after nearly a full career as a lyric poet, he was beginning to exercise a historical imagination and to look outside himself for material. He was awarded this grant by the Ford Foundation in February, 1959—one of eleven made that year—and he took a leave of absence without pay after September, 1959.

In March, 1959, still in Halcyon House Sanitarium, he received the check for the Longview Award and a request from the National Director of his college fraternity, Chi Phi, who was anxious to run an article in the fraternity magazine "all about yourself and your many accomplishments." However he may have felt about these attentions, grateful or guilty, Ted could not feel neglected, a fear that always obsessed him that he might be thrown into some institution and forgotten.

Ted resumed teaching the spring quarter of 1959 but his doctor, Ian Shaw, restricted the amount of work he could do, and he kept Ted under regular treatment for several months. Ted had hoped to go to New York to meet Hans Sahl and during August to teach at Breadloaf but he canceled both these engagements at his doctor's advice and remained in Seattle.

He and Beatrice went to San Francisco where he gave a reading at San Francisco State College on July 9. He was popular there and he liked the city. (I remember recommending The Blue Fox restaurant to him.) He also gave a reading at the University of Washington on August 20, but in the main the summer was quiet. He wrote constantly as was his habit and continued his therapeutic interviews with Dr. Shaw.

He intended to go abroad in the spring of 1960 and in the fall of 1959 he wrote many letters to arrange for readings before he left— he was anxious about money as usual—letters to Naomi Diamond at Wellesley, Harry Levin at Harvard, and Elizabeth Kray at the Poetry Center in New York. He had been asked to make the Hopwood Lecture at Ann Arbor in the spring and he wrote Professor Warner Rice complaining of the flat fee of $500. He wanted $500 and expenses or a flat fee of $700.

Ned Rorem, the composer, had asked his permission to set some of his poems to music, and in October, 1959, Ted replied that he was delighted to have this done, but he set the following conditions, with his customary eye for business, that all royalties be split fifty-fifty, that any publisher provide him with a separate contract and royalty statement, and that any listing of the work whatever include his name as lyricist. He was particularly pleased when, on April 3, 1960, Alice Esty, the soprano, gave a program at Carnegie Hall which included eight of his poems that Rorem had set to music.

His presence had been sought as far away as India and he wrote to Shawn Mandy, the editor of *The Illustrated Weekly of India* in Bombay, to say that there was no chance of his coming there unless some agency of the State Department decided to send him. However, if Mandy would like to give some of the U.S. Information people a prod, he believed that the State Department paid special attention to suggestions originating within the country itself. He also wrote a letter of thanks to Mihir Gupta in London for translating "The Longing" into Bengali. Ted was very proud of this.

It cannot be stressed too often how persistently Ted kept working—he published eleven poems in 1960—and the work continued during this year uninterrupted by hospitalization, teaching, psychiatric treatment, honors received, and preparation for his European journey.

In January, 1960, he approached many of his friends and acquaintances in New York to help him find a two-room apartment to use for his stay there but nothing came of these efforts. Finally he put advertisements in the classified section of *The Saturday Review of Literature* and *The New York Times* and eventually he was able to rent one at 15 Washington Place.

In March the *Chicago Review* contained a very favorable essay-review of his work by Ralph J. Mills, Jr., and he wrote Mills to ask if he could meet him when he came through Chicago. He says he will arrive at the Union Station in Chicago on the *Empire Builder* at 2 P.M. on March 29 and will be leaving for New York at 6:45 P.M., "so it will make more sense to meet the train. Besides, I have a hell of a time getting around Chicago all by myself." Ted's stories about gangsters always made it seem as if he knew the town like the palm of his hand but I believe they were, as I have said, mere moonshine. This letter sounds like the truth.

One of the last letters he wrote before leaving Seattle was directed to Matteo Lettunich at the Institute of International Relations in New York,

> On June 3 we intend to sail for Antwerp and will possibly be in Denmark, most certainly in London, Paris, Rome. If there are any writers you think might be interested in meeting me, it would be a kindness to let me know. I am a good friend of René Char and Michaux.
>
> Please understand that I am not trying to be pushy about this. I'm simply interested in people. Incidentally, I'm a bad linguist, but my wife, a very pretty woman, is a good one.

Out of this came their meeting with Hugo and Elly Klaus. Klaus, a Belgian novelist, had visited the United States in a cultural exchange program sponsored by the Institute. In an interview in *The New Yorker* he had said that the two Americans he wanted most to meet were Ted and Frank Sinatra.

On March 27, 1960, Ted and Beatrice left Seattle by train, met Ralph Mills briefly in Chicago on March 29, and arrived in New York on March 30 where they put up at the New Weston Hotel for a couple of days because Ted was reading at the Poetry Center the next day. Then they moved into their flat on Washington Place.

In the next few weeks he gave many readings: at Columbia, April 12, at Wellesley, April 25 (he stayed with Robert Lowell in Cambridge), the Morris Gray Lecture at Harvard, April 27, at New York University, April 30, and May 12 at Wesleyan. On May 19, he gave the annual Hopwood Lecture in Ann Arbor and the next day he took part in a writers' conference there. Before an audience composed largely of students and little old ladies he read and discussed poems by contemporary poets but none of his own. One of the old ladies asked him if he would read some of his own work. "I will if they'll get up three hundred more bucks." (Laughter) "I'll tell you what I will do—I'll give you my Nixon poem." It will be remembered that the Kennedy-Nixon campaign was beginning then and he recited a very funny but libelous poem that cannot be reprinted here.

As he finished one of the old ladies went, "Boo! Boo! Boo!" Ted burst out laughing and said, "I love ya, doll." On the typed copy of the Nixon poem left in his papers, he has written, "Example of American gutter poetry."

The next day he and Beatrice were driven to Saginaw where they stayed in his old home at 1805 Gratiot with his sister, June. The greenhouse had been torn down by then and it must have seemed strange and unnatural. On May 24, 1959, in a ceremony at Arthur Hill, his old high school, he was named "10th Honor Alumnus" with this citation, "For his outstanding ability as an educator, his recognized genius in the field of creative poetry, and his dedication to the furthering of the arts in America, Theodore Roethke, '25, is proudly welcomed as Arthur Hill High School's 1960 Honor Alumnus." (He must have ground his teeth at the redundancy of the phrase "creative poetry." He always hated to hear it called "creative" writing.) There was a good clear picture

of Beatrice and him in the *Saginaw News,* standing with some of
his old teachers, and in the high-school newspaper they had re-
printed two old photographs of Ted when he was a senior, one
smiling, the other sober, a small slender youth with wavy blond
hair.

At the time it was the best Saginaw could do. It was the slender
youth they remembered, the good student who was sometimes
caught drunk, the boy who used to deliver flowers and work in
the pickle factory. It was reported out of New York and such
places that Ted Roethke had somehow turned into a great poet
and there was this long list of prizes with totally unfamiliar names
to prove it. No one, or at best, a few had actually read any of these
poems (and at his death there was not a book of his to be had in
any Saginaw store), but it was claimed that he was making a
reputation and so they honored him the best they knew how.
After all, it was good advertising, as it was for the University of
Washington—whenever Ted's name was mentioned in all these
reviews and magazines, Saginaw's name was mentioned, too, so it
was probably all right to have a poet come from there.

He spent the day with Buzz Morley, hashing over old times.
They had a few drinks and Ted found his old coonskin coat hang-
ing in a closet. He also turned up some of the jazz records he had
collected in college. It was the last time he went home.

They were nearly ready for their European journey but they
were uncertain of their itinerary. He wrote me that they were
going to "the isles of Greece," and he had written René Char at
Isle-sur-Sorgues in Provence that they were going to Paris, to tour
Brittany, and then come down "to your beloved country." On
June 3, 1960, they sailed for Antwerp on a Norwegian freighter.

They docked in Antwerp ten days later and were met by Hugo
and Elly Klaus. Mrs. Klaus was a former model and, Beatrice says,
"very glamorous." The Klauses took them to Bruges and Brussels
where Ted found some excellent restaurants.

In July they went to Paris where they stayed at the Regent
Hotel in the Rue Madame. They bought a small Peugeot and
drove through the chateau country of Touraine and they saw
Chambord, Chenonceaux, and the others. It is hard to believe Ted
would have gone there on his own if Beatrice had not cajoled him,
for, as she says, "He liked people, eating, and drinking. He would

rather see a beautiful beach than a beautiful building any day."
After Touraine they went to a beach, at La Boule in Brittany. It
was beautiful weather and they swam every day. They stayed a
week in a pension but ate their meals at a restaurant, La Duchesse
Anne. This miffed the proprietor of the pension and he went to
great lengths not to speak to them. Then they toured all of
Brittany. Ted left no record of his impressions of the dolmens and
the manhirs or whether he was aware of the old poets of the region
or the Breton Nationalist movement. What he liked was driving
through a beautiful countryside in fine weather, the feeling of
health and well-being it gave him. He did not care to pick the
gems out of the setting. They stayed at St. Malo for ten days, and
picnicked and played *bocce* on the beach.

Ireland had run through Ted's life like a fine thread, probably
green, ever since Rolfe Humphries had suggested he go there on
his first Guggenheim Fellowship. He had studied her history more
than that of any other country; he had read her old folk poetry;
he had studied Yeats and Joyce thoroughly enough for them to
influence his work; he had even conned travel books of the island,
and now through the solicitations of Richard Murphy, one of her
best contemporary poets, and fearing that accommodations might
be hard to find elsewhere at the height of the tourist season, he
arranged with Murphy to go to Inishbofin, one of a group of small
Atlantic islands off the coast of Connemara.

On July 20, leaving their car in France, they flew to Dublin by
way of the Island of Jersey. They were met there by Beatrice's
father and they found quarters up several flights of stairs at Fox's
Hotel in Upper Leeson Street. Morris Graves was in Ireland,
rebuilding another beautiful house, and through him they met
Michael Scott, Ireland's leading architect, who designed the
present Abbey Theater and who had once owned the Martello
Tower which is the setting of the first chapter of Joyce's *Ulysses,*
and also met Mrs. John Huston. Scott had built a fine house for
the Hustons at Athenry, where John Huston, when not busy with
movie work, is joint Master of the Galway Blazers. Richard
Murphy was in Dublin and he introduced Ted to his fellow poets,
Tom Kinsella and John Montague, and to Liam Miller, the pro-
prietor of the Dolmen Press. Irish hospitality is incredible, vocifer-
ously splendid, and the ubiquitous bottle of John Jameson's or

Paddy's or Tullamore Dew helps it speed. Even in London, Ted had not fallen into a literary circle he liked better.

Mrs. Yeats, the great poet's widow, was living alone in her house in Palmerston Road and Ted wanted to meet her, naturally. John Montague and Liam Miller, who knew her, offered to take him to pay a call. As he always did when he wished to do someone, especially a woman, a courtesy, Ted took her flowers. They stopped at a flower shop on the way and asked the girl to see some roses. He was shown some but they didn't please him. "Bring me your best ones," he said emphatically. "Roses are something I know about." A large bouquet, at last eminently suitable, was arranged, and Ted carrying it, the three started out again. In the taxi Ted got more and more nervous—thirty years of study and admiration were obscurely involved and perhaps some magic. He may have felt that Mrs. Yeats, when he touched her hand, could endow him with some of the Master's powers. They arrived at the house. They rang the bell but no one answered it. They rang and rang. Was it to be a fiasco? At last Mrs. Yeats opened the door herself. In a frenzy of nerves, Ted incoherently presented her with the bouquet. "Such lovely roses," she said cordially. "W.B.'s favorite flower." And she showed them into a drawing room.

Then she disappeared for such a long time they feared she was gone for good but eventually she came back with the flowers in a vase. Conversation as it is apt to be in such circumstances was bumpy until the first note of comradeship was struck: Mrs. Yeats complained of a pain in her back. Ted responded feelingly with the tale of his arthritis, hip and shoulder and knee, and offered to rub Mrs. Yeat's back. Kindly, gratefully she refused but she did lie down on a sofa to be comfortable. After that talk was easy. She showed Ted Yeats's books, and, better, some of his notebooks, and it turned out to be a pleasant meeting.

When Ted returned to the hotel afterward, Beatrice says he was gloomy and dejected by the amount of work Yeats had done, the sheer area of paper he had covered. (Probably no more than Ted had but then he had seen all his own notebooks in one place.) And he complained bitterly that Beatrice could not do the kind of automatic writing Mrs. Yeats had done for Willie.

When I was on Inishbofin in the summer of 1965, I was walking down a road that led to a ruined abbey. A fine rain was falling. A little wee old man was sitting on a stone fence. As I passed he said, "So yer from the States."

"I am," I said. (You never say "yes" in Ireland.)

"And did ye know Roethke, then?"

"I did."

"Ah, he was a grand mon, a dear mon." The old man was a sailmaker.

This was the impression Ted made on the island, the impression he obviously left. When Ted and Beatrice came to leave Dublin for the west, Beatrice went by train to Galway, and Michael Scott drove Ted in his car. The trip turned into a pub crawl; the native whisky is only about 60 proof and seems mild and harmless. Scott had met Ted only a few days before but he said he seemed a sick man. Ted complained of his legs, how hard it was for him to walk. "But I liked him very much, a vivid, candid man," Scott said.

They picked Beatrice up at the railroad station in Galway and drove on to Cleggan, the little port for the three islands offshore, Inishshark, Inishturk, and Inishbofin. From Galway to the coast it is a strange country, almost treeless, worn grey mountains covered with a shawl of green here and there, a string of fresh-water loughs running beside the road to the sea, a rare white cottage, and men digging peat out of bogs, a few black-faced sheep with dabs of red or blue paint on their wool to brand them, and at the shore, the mountains falling down into the sea and the clouds with them. A month there, and it would not be hard to believe all the old tales.

At Cleggan they were met by Richard Murphy, who saw them across the six miles to the island. Murphy, who has introduced nearly every living poet to Inishbofin, spends his summers sailing tourists along the coast and among the islands in the *Ave Maria*, the last of the Galway "hookers." He sees that the tourists patronize Day's Hotel on Inishbofin where one of the handsomest couples in the world, Michael and Margaret Day, dispense their inimitable hospitality.

The island is usually shrouded in mist. Going into the little harbor, you pass the ruins of a stone fort, reputedly built by a Spaniard at the time of the Armada. The channel is barely forty feet wide and you tie up at a stone pier with grass growing over it, and pick your way among empty Guinness Barrels, lobster pots, and small boats careened for caulking to get to the hotel.

Two or three hundred people live on the island, fishermen who, since the disaster in 1927 when nearly thirty men were laid out dead on Cleggan pier, seem to fear the sea and go out (and never out of sight of land) only when the mackerel are running to get a few for their families' winter. They farm small hillside plots of potatoes, cabbage, and onions, and they receive a small dole from the government. They sit in "The Shop" when it is open, drinking Guinness, and when I asked Michael Day what they do in the winter, he said, "Stare tranced into the fire."

It is a place for talk and song and it is easy to see why Ted loved it. He did not walk out over the barren hills because his legs hurt him. He sat in The Shop with the fishermen, talking, listening, and drinking. To find a whole community where language was respected, where any brave deed, every odd occurrence passes at once into a song or a tale, exhilarated him immeasurably, and knowing no other immediate way to express his delight, he would fling his arms around some old fisherman's neck and cry, "I love this place. I love you people." This was not specially appreciated at the time; later.

A man who can sing a song is honored here. There were two whom Ted was vastly fond of, Desmond O'Halloran and Bernard Tierney. O'Halloran was about twenty-three when Ted knew him. He has a high baritone, a large repertoire of ballads and revolutionary songs, the true Irish ballad singer's tone, a kind of horn-like note drawn out on certain words. Ted wanted him to come to the States. "I'll make you bigger than Presley," he said. Tierney was older, with a loud clear voice, good in pubs, and he was a composer. He had made up a song about the Island, "Oh, don't come to Bofin. It's shaped like a coffin . . ." with dozens of verses. Singing, he would look around The Shop to see who was there and weave all the listeners into his song by name. When Ted was projecting his musical comedy ("me and Hellman") he gave parts in it to both O'Halloran and Tierney.

The children put on a little program at the school of songs and dances, jigs and reels, and Ted was entranced. He told everyone he would fly the children to New York where they could accompany his next reading with their performance. After these high windy promises, Richard Murphy drew him aside and said, "It's

a cruel thing to do to promise these kids New York. Every Irish-
man, man or boy, wants to go to the States." But, of course, in his
excited condition, Ted believed his promises were true.

Ted realized he was getting ill and he wanted treatment. He
entered Ballinasloe, a hospital not far from Galway, and spent a
month there on a mild regimen under the supervision of Dr. Liam
Henniffy. The assistants and sisters at Ballinasloe remember him
as a big burly man, full of energy, kind, generous, and, above all,
uproariously funny. Beatrice stayed with friends in Dublin and
made several trips to Ballinasloe to visit Ted and to bring him
back to Dublin when he was released. Beatrice says, "We stayed
at the Hibernian Hotel for some days and then Morris Graves
kindly invited us to spend a few days at his house at Rathfarn-
ham. Ted was talking of spending Christmas on Inishbofin. How-
ever, I knew the weather there would be cold and rainy in the
fall and winter. The only way I knew to get Ted to leave Ireland
was to leave myself and hope that he would follow me, mean-
while letting him have a taste of Inishbofin rain in early October.
My plan worked: he arrived in London ten days later."

Ted's second visit to the island was more quiet. He was writing
more and drinking less. (He had written "Song" just after his first
arrival there, and he wrote "The Shy Man" and "Her Wrath" on
the island.) He asked Mrs. Day if he could go to church with her.
He knelt and crossed himself as he entered but she said he got
restless during the service. Ted's pleasure in the island was un-
diminished. It was quiet—aside from the wind, the clucking of
hens, and the pump-like "hee-haw" of an ass, the only sounds
were those he made himself. And there was always someone to
listen to, speaking the exuberant speech of the region, and to have
a jar of Guinness with when he had finished working.

Until early November they lived first in the Alwin Court Hotel
in Gloucester Road, and next in the Aban Court Hotel in South
Kensington. Ted did not like the accommodations at either one
but this is not surprising. He had other things on his mind. He was
disturbed about himself and he was going for supportive therapy
to Dr. William Hoffer, a pupil of Freud's, and, something not all
psychiatrists are, a man of wide knowledge of artists and the arts.
Ted liked him better than any other psychiatrist he had ever had,

and in the few weeks he saw Ted, he was able to tell him many
things about himself, and, characteristically, about his ties with
his father and mother. Ted was also disturbed about Beatrice and
he began the series of poems, "The Young Girl," "Her Words,"
"The Apparition," "Her Reticence," "Her Longing," "Her Time."

Early in November, 1960, they moved into a flat in Lyall Street,
Chelsea, which they rented from Cyril Conolly's former wife. It
was here that he was interviewed by Zulfikar Ghose for an English
newspaper syndicate and the interview was widely printed. In it
he reveals the picture of himself he wanted to show to the public
then. The title is *Roethke: I Ran with the Roaring Boys*. After a
few introductory remarks, there is the subtitle *Cherubic Image*
and following this:

> Roethke is a large man with an attractive head, round-
> cheeked, and thinned greying hair. He has a deep sonorous voice
> with an incantatory ring about it. He clarifies each point he
> makes in his talk, leaving no doubt about his meaning: his
> readiness to explain any point at length is probably due to his
> work as a professor.
>
> He is conscious that his stature as a poet might give the im-
> pression in his speech, that he is being condescending, and with
> striking humility turns round in mid-speech and says, "I hope
> I'm not pontificating." He has a tremendous sense of humor
> which is so infectious that, meeting him for the first time, you
> think you've been his friend all his life.
>
> We met in his fourth-floor Chelsea flat. He threw the key
> down from the window in a white envelope which floated down
> like a feather, and his head suddenly appearing as I looked up
> at the grey London sky seemed to be a cherubic image painted
> on the ceiling of an Italian church.
>
> The walls of the large room in which we sat were painted
> green and skirted all round with books. He poured drinks and
> sat in a sofa by the window, a table littered with papers and
> periodicals in front of him.
>
> But he is restless and kept getting up, sometimes to go into the
> next room to get some more drink, sometimes just to walk up
> the room, or to pull out a book: going out of the room, he would
> stop in mid-sentence and returning would continue as he opened
> the door, his voice entering always before him . . . We talked for
> three hours. First he was a little formal, but soon relaxed.

The North-West

We began with his early days. "I was translated into 26 languages when I was 13," he said, laughing. This was a vigorous speech in praise of the Red Cross. He seemed to blush remembering it and said, "Hell, it was better than Eisenhower."

At college, he said, he "ran around with roaring boys mostly," and at that time, he wanted to write plain poetry which would appeal to many people.

What were the early influences? Did he model himself on any particular poet? "I don't like to talk of influences," he said, but Louis Bogan had been an important mentor. He knew a lot of Wordsworth by heart then and could recite whole chunks of it at the time, as well as Blake and Herrick.

It took him ten years to prepare his first book, *Open House*, (1941) which received very good notices. But his first book to come out in England was *The Lost Son and Other Poems* (1949) I asked him if he had any remarks to make on his own development. After *The Lost Son* he had become more formal, he said, learning from Yeats and Blake.

"My imagery is coming more out of the North-West rather than the whole of America." It is not like driving a car across America, but an exploration of the North-West.

He had always tried to write in rhythms which were close to prose, "yet rhythms which are not *slack*." He stressed the importance of rhythm in poetry. "To make a poem, you must have a rhythm that is an entity. Rhythms themselves can't be too coarse or too banal: otherwise it's nothing. But it is possible to have good poetry based on power of imagery and power of thinking, and not rhythm."

One-Man Band

He showed me some poems that he had written recently. A quick glance showed that he had gone back to the ballad form with its basic and powerful speech rhythms. They would be most effective read aloud, which Roethke prefers.

Which of the poets did he admire? Auden and Elizabeth Bishop came first to his mind—the latter for her "wonderful eye." But he did not want to make public pronouncements on his contemporaries. What about Stanley Kunitz? I asked. Yes, Kunitz was fine. "I was a one-man band for Kunitz," he said. Of the younger English poets he admired Ted Hughes but preferred not to comment on some of the others.

Were there any young American poets who showed promise? Again, and understandably, he did not want to make pronouncements, but he had high hopes of James Wright and W. D. Snodgrass.

How did he co-ordinate teaching with writing poetry? He thought that for the purposes of teaching the lyric was a better discipline than the essay for some students, and this was a good reason for classes in creative writing.

The English, he knew, tended to deride such classes, but the idea was not to manufacture poets, no more than essay-writing is to produce essayists. To make people write poetry was to give them an insight into poetry which could be more profound than learning about poetry through critical writing. Although the aim was not to produce poets, three poets who have shown promise have been under him: James Wright, Carolyn Kizer, and David Wagoner.

The teaching, he said, is "Damn hard work. Makes emotional demands which a lot of ordinary teaching doesn't make. Every class I approach with a sort of terror."

Soul Projected

He had once read his poetry with an orchestra. He thought that it was perhaps worth experimenting with poetry and music, but added, "If poetry needs music, then it is less poetry." And with Roethke poetry is all; he has hardly written any creative prose.

It is not with every poet that one's enjoyment of his poems increases after meeting him; it is with Roethke. The poems, one feels, are a part of him, they are the soul of the man as he has projected it into the language. For I came away with the feeling that I had met someone I had known for a long time previously, ever since first reading a poem of his; which is a tribute to his poetry as much as to him.

In Ted's papers, written about this time, was found a paragraph about René Char. It does not seem to be part of a letter or an essay, perhaps it was something he wrote for himself,

> I remain unconvinced by meditations which become maundering, by poems which are anthologies of other men's effects. But Char, for me, is something else: he possesses both the inner and outer fortitude, the great and final courage. Beside him, a hero like Hemingway seems an oaf and a lout; Eliot a doddering vicar.

During the winter of 1960–1961, they stayed at the flat in Lyall Street, Ted writing, Beatrice painting. In February, he gave a reading at Oxford, not an easy audience, for the undergraduates are quite used to the great and are not at all respectful, but Ted received great applause and afterward he was complimented by Sir Maurice Bowra, a scholar and critic of immense learning and at that time, I believe, Warden of Wadham College.

The perspective afforded by Europe throws America into high relief and apparently Ted had begun to use it, for in February he wrote Louis Untermyer a letter that shows him looking outside himself in his poems. He refers to "some longer pieces, 'Meditation at Oyster River,' and 'Journey to the Interior,'" where he says he is "trying to say something about America that I don't believe has been put down yet."

He also told Untermeyer of a BBC appearance in February on "live telly-vision," a panel composed of Peter Ustinov, Hugh Trevor-Roper, the historian, and himself. The announcer called Ted a remarkable poet with a steadily growing international reputation and Ted said it was lovely stuff to listen to.

He and Beatrice continued to see their London friends and about this time Ted lunched at Charles's Restaurant in Jermyn Street with Eric White, the head of the Poetry Book Society and the author of the great biography of Stravinsky. He told Ted about the plight of Ted Hughes and Sylvia Plath. They were living next door to W. S. Merwin and his wife. Merwin had to go to America and he had asked White to keep an eye on them. Hughes did not keep accounts and at that time was nearly destitute—Sylvia Plath was in a hospital for an operation and Hughes was trying to keep house with their year-old child. White called him and told him not to worry, that money would be forthcoming from the BBC and the Arts Council. Ted, who admired the work of both Hughes and Sylvia Plath, was immediately concerned and wanted to send her flowers but, he said, he was leaving England and would not have time, so he gave White some money and asked him to do it for him. Later he tried to get Ted Hughes a job at Washington.

On March 5, 1961, Ted made his first transatlantic flight with Beatrice. He seems to have been afraid of airplanes heretofore. He had arranged several readings and from New York they went directly to Williams College for the first one. Afterward William

Jay Smith met them at Albany. Beatrice had the flu and she stayed with the Smiths about a week while Ted went ahead with his program. He spent a night at Bennington and renewed his friendship with Kenneth Burke and Howard Nemerov; then he gave readings at Trinity, at the University of Connecticut, at Yale, and at the Poetry Center in New York.

On March 26, he and Beatrice arrived in Seattle by air in time for Ted to begin teaching the spring quarter. After his arrival, his book of children's poems, *I Am! Says the Lamb,* was published by Doubleday. It was dedicated to Lillian Hellman and very cleverly illustrated by Robert Leydenfrost. It was arranged in two sections, the first containing twenty-two nonsense poems and the second, the greenhouse poems. The reviews were enthusiastic and compared Ted to Lewis Carroll, Edward Lear, and Hilaire Belloc as a writer of nonsense verse, and many reviewers, among them, W. D. Snodgrass, noticed a disturbing, even frightening element characteristic of all good verse in the genre. None of Ted's earlier hopes for movies and comic strips to be drawn from the book were realized but he was pleased with the reception of a book that publicly extended his range.

It may be thought odd that Ted should write a book for children. He liked them, found them amusing and informative, and he would play with them—as long as they were other people's. In the early years of his marriage, he wanted none. He was too childlike himself to bear the rivalry of another in his home. However, in his last years his mind was changing. In his work he began to look outward in space and away from the present in time, and, perhaps the clearest sign of this change, he came to want a child.

In August, 1961, Ted and Beatrice went up to the San Juan Islands to visit the summer place of their friends, Walter and Maggie Walkinshaw. Ted spent his time lying in the sun or fishing for salmon. There is a photograph of him sitting in a boat wearing the old Borsalino hat he never parted with.

On the weekend of September 8, Ted was in Monterey, California, to receive a "Golden Plate Award," and he enjoyed himself. He said champagne flowed like tapwater, that he had a police escort at times, and a lovely chick to drive him around. The principal banquet was entitled, "Salute to Excellence," the first annual celebration of the Academy of Achievement. Among the winners were Dr. Edward Teller, Thomas Hart Benton, Quincey Howe, Dr. Charles Mayo, Ralph Bunche, Wernher von Braun, and General Nathan F. Twining. Each received a golden plate with his name fired on it. "They had misspelled not 'Roethke' but 'Theodore.' Ah, California!" Ted wrote.

The weather in Monterey impressed him, for on September 25 he wrote Ken McCormick asking if he or John Sargent knew any people around there. He says his arthritis is giving him a good deal of trouble and he must eventually get further south into a better climate, not that Washington wasn't treating him wonderfully. They had given him a $700 raise the year before, "more than the football coach (whose teams won the Rose Bowl two years in a row)," but he feels he could do more and be happier in a warmer climate.

Then he asks McCormick why "we" shouldn't start wooing the Swedes, if it can be done adroitly. "Why shouldn't we begin mending and weaving and doing whatever is necessary to bring the Nobel in poetry to America? Certainly I'm a vastly better poet than Quasimodo, and this last French man is good but does the same thing over and over. I think Wystan Auden should be next, then Pablo Neruda, then me and that's a cold, considered objective judgment." It is clear that Ted did not believe that a Nobel Prize descended like a bolt from the blue; the lightnings could be managed.

His growing concern for his reputation as well as the possibility of winning a Nobel Prize is apparent in this charming account of a visit paid him in December, 1961, by Rikutaro Fukuda, one of his Japanese translators. It was written for publication in Japan, the fourth in a series called *Poets I Met in America:*

> At the station I saw a big man carrying a newspaper-like material under his arm, whom I recognized as Roethke. He wanted to go to his office at the University first to get the manuscripts of his poems which he wanted to show me. He started for his car. I noticed something strange about his way of walking. He moved his shoulders up and down as he walked . . . He had a hard time finding the key of his car in his pocket but finally found it and started the car. He whistled whenever other cars

were in his way. I thought he was very young and energetic at
his age. It seemed that he was not so good at finding his way. He
lost his way a couple of times. In the car, I asked first of all, how
to pronounce his name, which was discussed so often in Japan,
too. He explained that his name is of German origin and pro-
nounced as (retki). Also I found out that he used to play
tennis but now enjoys just coaching it. In the meantime, when I
mentioned the numerous poles in Seattle as compared with other
places, he said, "Oh, it's ugly."

As that day fell on a Saturday, the campus was so quiet. After
he took his manuscripts from his office in Parrington Hall, we
went ahead to his residence. His house was situated on a hill,
commanding a beautiful view of Lake Washington through the
garden and surrounded with a heavy cluster of trees. I was led
to his study-room, which was furnished with grey book-shelves
set in a white-grey wall, three chairs, and a long bench attached
to the wall.

As he had proposed beforehand, we talked privately in com-
plete quietness from ten o'clock in the morning till three-thirty
in the afternoon. I had never experienced talking so closely and
so long with others. Sometimes he himself brought something to
drink from the kitchen. The tree with pretty small red fruits
planted beside the verandah was somewhat impressive to me.
When I asked whether he wrote poems in that study-room, he
answered, "No, mostly in bed," and smiled significantly.

He talked about his experience as a teacher in Florence when
he came to Italy as a Fulbright scholar several years ago. "But it
was a failure," he said. For he is a man whose nature is being
too much involved in the students. He expected too much from
his students, the result of which made him disappointed con-
trary to his expectation, it seemed to me. He moved from
Florence to Rome. In Rome he had the opportunity to teach the
best students in Italy, he said. Here at the University, his passion
and kindness for his students have been well talked about among
the students.

Then he showed his new poems to me. They are neatly type-
written and filed. The anthology, entitled *Motion* had several
other poems with the title poem in it . . . This *Motion* is going to
be published at the same time in England and in the United
States . . . Many of the subjects of his poems are taken from
animals and plants. When I asked where he made these poems,
he said they were memories of his childhood in Michigan, his

native state, where there were beautiful farms and greenhouses around his house. The nature he had seen there at that time, he said, still remained in his mind. He also told me about his wonderful father. He was so good a person that he lost his farms to others one after the other. Later, he was hit by a train and seriously injured and later died of cancer. The last part of his life was tragic. I do not have space enough to write about the details of it.

During the interview with him, Mrs. Roethke came downstairs in the afternoon and was sorry I could not stay the night with them, for I had reserved a room in a hotel downtown, having known Mrs. Roethke had been sick a long time. She had to be in bed even in the afternoon at least two hours a day, she said. She served me a lunch she cooked. The dessert was a sweet-tasting banana concoction that she cooked herself, having consulted a cookbook. The warm kindness of the couple was felt deep in my mind.

Mrs. Roethke is quite a well-known linguist and is also versed in Italian. Her hobbies are painting and music. She showed a deep interest in Japanese art. Lots of her paintings were seen on the walls in their house.

Roethke graduated from Harvard with outstanding grades. Among the professors he learned from at Harvard was I. A. Richards. He said he learned from Richards "how to look into language." Last year when he was invited to Harvard for his poem reading, he met Richards after some ten years. He was also a close friend of Dylan Thomas. Thomas stayed in his house when he came to Seattle a few years ago, he told me.

After we finished lunch, we started to talk about various things again. I picked up one poem called "Snake" from his newly published collection, *I am! Says the Lamb* and translated it into Japanese. I wrote it down in Japanese on the back cover of the book. I also read the translation, as he wanted me to. He gave me his first published collection, *Open House,* (1941) which was out of print, and which he had bought for 50 dollars, having tried hard to find it. By the way, it is said that the collection costed 2 dollars at the first publication, so we can guess how precious his works are now.

He said, "There are two countries I want to visit now, and they are Greece and Japan." Meantime, he mentioned that he was going to New York in January in order to be presented the Shelley Memorial Prize. "Oh, I have been awarded so many

prizes such as the Pulitzer Prize that I do not remember exactly
all of them, but I have not obtained the Swedish prize yet." I still
remember his voice when he said at one occasion, "I am very
glad you have come," which was so warmly and deeply ex-
pressed from the bottom of his heart: it is very seldom when we
can realize that human words can be pronounced with such a
deep sincerity.

When I went to the hotel that evening, I saw a vase of beauti-
ful chrysanthemums on the table and found a white card beside
the flowers saying, "Welcome to Seattle. Mr. and Mrs. Theodore
Roethke." I felt the poet was endowed with great and deep sin-
cerity, and his wife with pure and delicate beauty, with which
they created in their life a special atmosphere detached from the
world. Though I met Roethke only once, I am possessed with the
feeling that I could devote my whole life to this poet.

After he had failed to keep a speaking engagement at Johns
Hopkins in November, Beatrice, at his doctor's advice, accompa-
nied him to the Shelley Memorial Award Dinner given by the
Poetry Society of America at the Waldorf Hotel in New York on
January 18. The honorary president, Robert Frost, was presented
with a bronze bust of himself, and Ted with a check for $1250.
Time magazine said, "Then came the airy dessert, a morsel
whipped up by Shelley Award Winner, Theodore Roethke; a
poetaster:

> "I like New England men
> Their women now and then
> Of poets they've the most
> But mostly Robert Frost."

As fruit of Ted's efforts to find a job in the sun for at least the
winter terms, he received a letter from William Van O'Connor
who was teaching at the University of California at Davis offering
him a year at Davis for $15,000 or a semester at the same rate. And
ten days later, April 3, 1962, the offer was raised to $16,400 but
Ted did not accept it. He was making that much at Washington
and it is an axiom of academic life that you make no change unless
you can better yourself.

On May 4, he gave another reading at San Francisco State
College, whose students were becoming one of his favorite audi-

ences, and in the middle of June, he went to Ann Arbor to receive an Honorary Doctor of Letters degree from the University of Michigan, his alma mater.

He arrived the day before the ceremonies and my daughter, Laura, and I had dinner with him in a big student restaurant downtown, steaks and a pitcher of beer. The place was full of alumni wearing class blazers and funny hats, sporadically bursting into drunken song. There was a long table full of them next to us and their antics made Ted sore. Except for half a pitcher of beer, which was nothing to him, he was quite sober but he kept swearing and muttering about the self-degradation of the middle class all through dinner. At last he started heaving himself to his feet, saying, "I'm gonna bust one of those bastards just to show him."

I said, "Sit down, you big boob. It would look good in the papers, wouldn't it, HONORARY DEGREE CANDIDATE SPENDS NIGHT IN HOOSEGOW?"

He sat down reluctantly, still muttering, and finally subsided. After dinner he stood Laura, who was then fourteen, up against a lamppost outside and recited poems to her for twenty minutes. "Some day I'll tell you some of my own stuff, kid," he said. (Ten days later, she received a copy of *I Am! Says the Lamb* with the inscription, "To Laura, my latest and eternal love, Winterset Rothberg." Naturally, she thinks he was one of the greatest men in the world.)

The next morning I looked in on him in his room at the Student Union. He was restless and kept getting up and sitting down. He did not seem happy. At intervals of a few minutes he took about half a dozen pills.

"What are the pills for?" I asked.

"Ah, I'm nervous."

Uselessly, I said, "What's to be nervous about? You stand up there. They give you the degree. It's in the bag."

He growled contemptuously as if nervousness were China, a place I'd never been.

Robert Frost was receiving a degree also. He, Ted, Carleton Wells, his old teacher, and I all had lunch together. Frost was in fine form and he talked about the old days in London before the First World War, Pound and the Vorticists, Eliot, Ford Madox Ford, and T. E. Hulme. Ted, who had long since lost his respect

for Frost as a poet, saying that his New England was a mere
literary convention, had kept his respect for Frost, the ancient
oracle, and he did not try to shine.

The ceremony in the football stadium went off without a hitch
and Ted became a Doctor of Letters along with Frost, Cantinflas,
the great Mexican clown and humanitarian, Robert McNamara,
Secretary of Defense, and a host of scientists.

After a dinner given by President Harlan Hatcher for the new
doctors at Inglis House, the party went out onto a flagstone terrace
to enjoy the summer night. Now that it was all over, Ted seemed
relaxed, pleased, in fact, honored.

Ted had become a public figure. It was not that his name was
known on every street in the republic (I suppose Mark Twain is
the only American writer who ever achieved a popularity as
pervasive as that), but among writers and serious readers all over
the world, his name would be recognized. It was about this time
that Max Nicolai, who was legal adviser to Governor Rosellini,
gave a dinner party. The Governor was one of the guests and so,
among others, were Ted and Beatrice. Nicolai was introducing
Ted as "Professor Roethke" when Ted broke in, "I'm a poet."
Charmed as he was by meeting a governor as a social equal, he
could still insist that his true vocation be acknowledged. It was as
if he were saying, "You're a governor. I'm a poet. We're equals,
see? The hell with that professor stuff." Ted was on his best be-
havior, quiet, mannerly, engaging. Nicolai says that he drank
along with everyone else but he didn't show any signs of it. The
Governor was planning a hunting trip and seemed to be about to
invite Ted to go along, and Ted seemed willing to accept. It is
quite possible that Ted, remembering how his father went hunting
with a well-known political figure, Congressman "Sugar-Beet Joe"
Fordney, believed in a fit of euphoric emulation, that he could
shoot, too. But of course he couldn't—he was too tender-hearted.
He did not go.

Ted's reputation, his burgeoning fame, did not come as a sur-
prise to him as it had to Lindbergh when he landed in Paris. It
had spread slowly and he had worked hard for it, but when it
arrived, he was dismayed to find people reverential, even awed.
They spoke to the public figure, not to him, and he complained
vehemently to Beatrice and Arnold Stein about how hard it was

to get in touch with people any more. Yet, with his usual inconsistency, he reveled in it, and he felt it only proper that a poet of his stature should associate with the great and even intervene in their affairs.

In the privacy of his notebooks, however, there was no fame. The statements about God and personal humility, present from as early as 1942, come very frequently in the 1962–1963 notebooks, and there is one entry where he acutely assesses his own condition,

"Am I sick? Am I well?

Not even God, I think, could tell."

If his external life in these last two years sometimes gives an impression of speed-up, like an old movie, it was all calm within. He continued working on the poems that went into *The Far Field* and he seems to have been mulling over a work whose subject matter (if the phrase is permissible) would have been fresh and new, a sign of a change in the set of his mind from the long contemplation of self to a world outside himself and past. He had referred to the "guilts" of American history in his last application to the Ford Foundation, but the poem he projected there did not get written, at least in its projected form. Some of his last notes spoke of an epic dealing with the injustices done to the Indians and based on an automobile journey across the continent where he would pass the site of each tribe's final defeat or betrayal. He had been reading history about the Indians, for there are references to Custer, Crazy Horse, General Crook, Black Elk, and Chief Joseph. If we think in terms of the growth of Ted's mind, it seems to have taken nearly his whole lifetime to come to terms emotionally and spiritually with the presences of the Saginaw Valley, his father, his mother, the greenhouse, the field and its creatures. Only on the eve of his unexpected death was he ready to leave home, and even then, the epic he had planned may have started from the memories of what he had heard there of the debasement of the Chippewas and the extinction of the Sauks.

In 1962 Seattle was the site of the World's Fair which drew, of course, thousands of tourist visitors. It is a gauge of Ted's standing in the community then, his value as a civic asset, that he was asked to give a reading, which he did on October 14. Whoever reviewed Ted's performance for the *Argus,* a Seattle weekly, either knew him very well or had unusual critical penetration:

ROETHKE: VOICE OF BALDER
THROUGH MOUTH OF GROUCHO.

When Theodore Roethke made one of his rare Seattle appearances at the Playhouse last Sunday, he served up an odd dish of 90% Showman and 10% Bard. Joe Gandy, who was given the honor of introducing Roethke on the curious grounds that they were college chums at Michigan, proved that he understood awards and prizes better than any poem.

Then Roethke appeared on the stage waving and grinning, straining out of his tux like a precocious panda. For the next two hours he regaled a capacity audience with gags and asides, a juggler tossing up a dazzling repartee of balls and bellows and baubles.

Occasionally, in case anyone should forget, he would read one of the poems which have won him a reputation as perhaps the finest lyricist in the English language. But why the voice of Balder through the mouth of Groucho Marx? One sensed a secret, cunning dialogue between the Poet and the Clown.

The Clown, for example, spent a good deal of time buttering up his bosses. He went so far as to write a special little poem, far below his form, punning with the names of assorted University personnel—whom he repeatedly referred to as "the boys up ahead"—forgetting Marianne Moore's admonishment: "A poet should *always* work at the top of his form."

He kidded his mother-in-law, "A woman about two and a half years older than I am who spends her time between Episcopal retreats and national bridge tournaments."

He drank water right from a yellow pitcher when his glass disappeared. He burst into song with one of his Irish shebeen chanties. He liberally sprinkled his reading with commercials for books, friends, students, presses, colleagues, and the heavy population of the Roethke alliance.

He attacked Eliot's bloodless pedantry and Kazin's ivy opportunism. At one point Roethke burst out, "You see, what I really want is power!" proving once again that poets should stay out of politics.

Like Crazy Jane, Roethke can be guilty of "tremendous spiritual arrogance," but like Yeats's "other self," Roethke, too, redeems himself by attacking with love. All this is done in the style of a tough but lovable Detroit mobster running booze during Prohibition:

"If you find an old copy of *The Waking*, latch on to it. It's worth a hundred skins if it's worth a quarter." To what end? Roethke seemed to be saying this, "Love me, love me. I worked in a pickle factory. I labored in greenhouses, I know business deals and 'scratch.' I've been there, I'm great, but I'm helpless and afraid."

Any man who exposes himself that way *must* be all right. After all the Bard's first duty is to entertain. Roethke's balding dome gleams in the single yellow spot. His audience knows he is working, sweating, by God, doing all this for *them*. At least they can see why Roethke is one of America's great teachers, why he can whip a class into a frenzy of creative adoration. But how many could hear the voice behind the act?

Could they hear Roethke saying, "My poems were written in blood and sweat and anguish. How many of you can understand that? I have spent the torments of a life working free of the libidinous muck of worm and bat and lust to a ringing vision of God. How can anyone who has lived safely, suffered less, know this terror or this joy? It's too hard, too much to ask. So all right. If you can't love my poems, love me."

Roethke baits us on laughter and hooks us on pain. Love or no love, that is the meaning of the silent dialogue between the Showman and the Poet.

The trouble is, this is only part of the story. For about ten minutes last Sunday, something else happened. The mask of the Showman-Clown-Politician dropped and we saw the suffering face of the Poet. Then the great lines would ring out from "The Adamant," "The Bat," "Elegy for Jane," "My Papa's Waltz," "Once More the Round."

The voice would grow quiet, controlled, reverent, and poetry would happen. "I knew a woman lovely in her bones . . ." "I swear she cast a shadow white as stone . . ." "I measure time by how a body sways . . ." "Madness is nobility at odds with circumstance . . ." "The right thing happens to the happy man . . ." And suddenly one knew why Roethke was up there and what it had cost.

For ten minutes the audience became the poet. To use one of his own phrases, these poems are "in the language," singing out as clearly, painfully, inevitably as an infant's first cry.

Then one knew that those ten minutes alone were worth the price of admission. That's what it was all about.

It didn't even matter that the Clown was off somewhere in the wings, guiltily chastising himself for mugging. Even Joe Gandy must have felt the Poet was worth waiting for.

Later in October he gave three readings at colleges of the University of California at Davis, Riverside, and Occidental. On February 8, 1963, he appeared at Northwestern University at Evanston and on April 26 at the University of Illinois at Urbana. The review of his World's Fair reading shows the change that had come over his public style of behavior: a consuming excitement not justified by events but enveloping them nonetheless, a manner simultaneously and paradoxically more free and relaxed as if he feared no consequences, and more intense in the urgency of what he had to say as if he was obscurely convinced that he was not going to have time to turn his present vision of the world into poetry and so he had better say it off-the-cuff. Consciously, as he says in his notes, he wanted to live to be a hundred but actually, it seems, his vitality was burning him up.

After his reading at Urbana, he had a letter from the Department of Speech there,

> You provided us with the challenge we had hoped for. And you've given a real challenge to the guest poet at our next Workshop: it will be difficult for him to top the very best, for it was our privilege to have the very best this year.

On the evening of February 8, he gave his reading at Northwestern, and the evening after, he appeared on a panel with William Barrett, S. I. Hayakawa, Waldo Beach, and Arnold Toynbee, a program called "A Spectrum of Perspectives, perspectives on personal identity, perspectives on attaining knowledge, the challenge of global perspectives." The student newspaper's account of the evening made it clear that Ted was the most impressive of this distinguished group. (He spoke openly of God.) And a little later he received a letter from two students, Carolyn Burrows and Tom Bracken,

> You came to Northwestern because you were struck by the student plea for a spiritual unity with self and nature. We want to tell you that when you spoke, we felt we were that unity. You held us not just as a speaker but as a concerned, undefeatable,

loving spirit. It's so good to know you're in the world, Mr. Roethke, so good.

You've shaken us free. We will learn by going, God damn it, we will.

Ted always reached his students by his love and sincerity, but to evoke this kind of response, he had obviously given them much more.

Another evidence of the profound affection Ted drew from students is the making of the film *In a Dark Time*. The students who heard him at San Francisco State chipped in and gave most of the money, nearly four thousand dollars, and David Myers who directed it put up the rest. It is a unique and moving presentation. Ted can be seen and heard reading many of his poems and interspersed are scenes of the appropriate natural growths that he loved. Most of it was taken on Bainbridge Island, in Seattle on the campus and in his house on East John Street. One day Arnold Stein was standing at the top of the steps in front of Parrington Hall and he saw Ted swaying toward him all dressed up in a dark suit and a Homburg hat, carrying an attaché case. Ted did not greet him but Stein, seeing the Homburg, an unusual feature of the Roethke wardrobe, suspected something was up and tried to stop him to talk. Ted seemed reluctant. He kept going and at last said, "OK. You're in it." Stein was mystified but he found out later that David Myers had a camera on Ted all the time. In the finished version, Stein is not "in it"—they cut him out.

After Ted had finished teaching the spring quarter, he and Beatrice took a small house on Bainbridge Island in Puget Sound. From it a steep winding path led through an almost tropical greenery of ferns and trees down to a beach where they used to gather oysters. They became friends with their neighbors, Bagley and Virginia Wright. Through Mrs. Wright they met her parents, Mr. and Mrs. Prentice Bloedel, who also lived on the island. Bloedel is an extremely wealthy man and his French Provincial house is more beautiful than any I ever saw in the French provinces, with a broad lawn on which a few sheep graze sweeping down to a small lake where a few swans preen themselves. During the early summer, the Bloedels often had Ted and Beatrice over for dinner or a swim. On one part of their estate they have a beautiful Japanese guest house overlooking a Japanese garden on one side and facing a swimming pool on the other. Beatrice said, "Ted adopted Bing Bloedel as a spiritual father as he had adopted Marguerite Caetani as a spiritual mother," and it is a revealing remark.

As had become his custom, Ted enticed the best poets to read at Washington. (He tried very hard to have both René Char and Ted Hughes hired by the University.) In July he arranged for Tom Kinsella, whom he had met in Dublin, to give a reading and to stay at his house. Kinsella brought with him all Ted's memories of Ireland, and he was very glad to see him. Kinsella is a magnificent talker and they stayed up late every night, drinking and listening to each other, and this very likely did Ted some harm. Beatrice said he had been "high" ever since the term had ended and it showed in Ted's eager hospitality and verbal exuberance.

His old gangster fantasies returned with hallucinatory force. Early one evening, Ted was driving Kinsella down a long straight road on Bainbridge Island. Half a mile ahead they saw a car standing crossways in the road. Ted stopped his car at once.

"That's how they come to get you," he said.

"Who?" Kinsella asked innocently.

"Ah, the Mob," Ted snarled, and turned his car around and started back the way they had come. They found a filling station and Ted got on the phone to the Bainbridge police, a force of only two or three men. He said, "The Mob's got a road-block down here. You better pick me up. You need someone who knows how to use a Tommy gun," and he gave his name and the address of the filling station. The police must have thought someone was kidding them, for they did not show up. I do not believe Ted ever saw an actual Tommy gun outside the movies; much less did he know how to shoot one.

The evening came for Kinsella's reading. Ted sat in the front row. The reading was well-received and afterward Kinsella permitted a question-and-answer period. Someone asked, "Mr. Kinsella, who do you consider the greatest living American poet?" With Ted in the front row at the high tide of his renown, this was not, in a way, a genuine question but a solicitation of a compliment.

But Kinsella, helplessly candid, hypnotized into tactlessness by his honest opinion, said, "Robert Lowell."

Ted did not explode, but at the party he and Beatrice were giving for Kinsella later that evening, he grumped to his other guests, "That bastard, damn him. Did you hear what he said?" until Beatrice told him it would look better if he just shut up, and, oddly enough, he did. Later, calmer, more sober, Ted realized that Kinsella had a right to his opinion, forgave him and they parted friends.

Ted had been working hard every day getting the body of *The Far Field* poems ready to submit, changing, pruning, and polishing. He was also contracted to do a preface for the American edition of the collected poetry of Constantine Trypanis, who was professor of Byzantine and modern Greek at Oxford. He worried a good deal over this and he got a first draft finished which he intended to improve. (Later, it was published as it stood.)

On Sunday, July 28, Ted put in a phone call to John Sargent, president of Doubleday's, at his place on Long Island. Sargent had to be called in from the tennis court to receive Ted's excited demand for an advance of $15,000 on his next book, an unheard-of figure, to be forwarded immediately because, as Ted explained, he and Beatrice wanted to buy a house on Bainbridge Island. As an old friend who knew Ted well, Sargent was able to allay Ted's rapacity and ring off amicably.

The following Thursday, August 1, Ted went over to Bainbridge to see the Bloedels while Beatrice stayed in downtown Seattle shopping. Mrs. Bloedel, her daughter, Mrs. Meadowcraft, who was visiting her parents from Switzerland, and the Meadowcrafts' governess were all at the swimming pool. Ted joined them and made some mint juleps which he put into the refrigerator. It was still hot at five in the afternoon and Ted said he was going to take a swim. The women were sitting at the edge of the pool talking, and, since they knew Ted swam well enough, paying little special attention to him. He dove in and swam to the shallow end. A moment or two later, they noticed him floating face down. The three women got him out of the water, his face blue, and Mrs. Meadowcraft tried mouth-to-mouth resuscitation while the others called Beatrice and a doctor. The doctor arrived, examined Ted, and pronounced him dead of a coronary occlusion.

Ted's ashes were buried beside the graves of his mother and father in Oakwood Cemetery in Saginaw. As part of the memorial service there, one of Ted's favorite passages from Sir Walter

Raleigh was read to his friends and kinfolk, "O eloquent, just, and mighty Death! whom none could advise, thou has persuaded: what none hath dared, thou hast done; and whom all the world hath flattered, thou only hast cast out of the world and despised; thou hast drawn together all the far-stretched greatness, all the pride, cruelty, and ambition of man, and covered it all over with these two narrow words, *Hic jacet!*"

Appendix to Chapter IX

The treatment at Albany General Hospital in 1946 was different and more drastic than that given Ted at Mercywood during his first attack. At Mercywood there had been the easy lolling in the hydrotherapy tubs, reading and writing, and what to Ted were the real pleasures of table tennis. At Albany General the shock treatments terrified him.

However, it may be possible that the experience of the whole second episode from the first manic excitement through the strains of the treatment until its final subsidence in the spring of 1946 was beneficial to the composition of *The Lost Son* and not a purely morbid or destructive period.

In a recent book, *Positive Disintegration* (Little, Brown, 1964), the Polish psychiatrist, Casimierz Dabrowski, against the teaching of Freud and his followers argues that some neuroses, even psychoses, may be benign. Personality, Dabrowski says, develops primarily through dissatisfaction with and the fragmentation of one's existing psychic structure. Stimulated by a lack of harmony in the self and in adaptation to the strains of the external environment, the individual "disintegrates." Anxiety, neurosis, psychosis may be *symptoms* of the disintegration and they mark a retrogression to a lower level of psychic functioning. Finally reintegration occurs at a higher level and the personality evolves to a new plateau of psychic health. Dabrowski points out that these new integrations at "higher" levels seem to happen to people of high intelligence and marked creative powers.

Thus the Albany episode might be regarded not as an interruption in his life but perhaps as a spur to a new psychic synthesis of Ted's creative energies that enabled him to push forward and break new ground in his work.

The episode was a profound emotional experience, probably the most intense he had undergone in many years. In the greenhouse poems he had already turned back to the memories of his childhood. The terrain had already been set, so to speak. Following Kenneth Burke's hint, a plausible assumption can be made that the props of the structure and something of the content of *The Lost Son* was supplied to Ted by the whole episode.

Some confirmation of this is given by his own words in *Open Letter*, " 'The Flight' is just what it says it is, a terrified running away with alternate period of hallucinatory waiting (the voices, etc.) the protagonist so geared-up, so over-alive that he is hunting like a primitive, for some animistic suggestion, some clue to existence from the sub-human."

It would be ridiculous to suggest that *The Lost Son* is a mere poeticized version of a bout of mental illness, but I am suggesting that the pattern of the poem follows the pattern of the episode. The flight seems to be his retreat from the normal behavior of everyday existence into the phase of manic excitement, ("so geared-up, so over-alive") and this is followed by "The Pit" and "The Gibber," which may well express the terror, the physical and psychic exhaustion of his stay in the hospital. "Section IV is a return," Ted says, "a return to a memory of childhood that comes back almost as in a dream, after the agitation and exhaustion of the earlier poems. . . . After the dark night, the morning brings with it the suggestion of a renewing light, the coming of Papa." It seems that the memories of stability are the ones that heal, that the coming of Papa as if in a dream can rescue the lost son. "In the final section, the illumination, the coming of light suggested at the end of the last passage occurs again, this time to the nearly grown man."

The stages of this second episode, the manic flight from reality by paradoxically sharpening an awareness of it; the terrors of the shock treatments at Albany General and the resulting despair and exhaustion; and the slow but ultimate recovery bear sufficient resemblances to the spiritual journey from darkness to light dramatized in the poem to be regarded as its substructure. After the "disintegration" of his illness, if we follow Dabrowski here, comes the "reintegration at a higher creative level" which enables Ted to write the poem.

Stephen Spender seems to have approached this view in his essay, *The Objective Ego* (in *Theodore Roethke, Essays on the Poetry*, edited by Arnold Stein, University of Washington Press, Seattle and London, 1965):

> Entering into his world—indeed becoming it—his world *la-bas* where words become loam and roots and snails and slugs lying along some bright chips of jangles from nursery rhymes and gashed childhood memories—Roethke is forever on the edge of Rimbaud's goal of the systematic *dérèglement de tous les sens*. One does not know whether to rejoice with the poems or sympathize with the poet: for the disintegration which bore strange and marvellous fruit in his poetry caused tragic breakdowns in his life.

Ted himself in an amazing burst of self-perception comes very close to Dabrowski's ideas. These insights are from *Open Letter*,

> Any history of the psyche (or allegorical journey) is bound to be a succession of experiences, similar yet dissimilar. There is a perpetual slipping-back, then a going-forward but there is some "progress" made . . . Dissociation often precedes a new state of clarity.

I may point out that his illness certainly did not paralyze his poetic abilities then or even render them lethargic for he was writing Catherine De Vries from Saginaw on April 1, 1946,

> Me, I've been pooped and bothered somewhat by arthritis in this wet spring. But now have begun a second longer piece in a projected sequence. (The first called *The Lost Son*, some 8 or 9 pages long will be in the *Sewanee Review*).

I am not trying to offer here a general theory that artistic creativity depends in some measure on mental illness, nor am I saying specifically that Ted was always stimulated by it; rather I am pointing out in this one instance, the composition of *The Lost Son*, how closely Ted's remarks paralleled those of Dabrowski's. Speaking of the years of their marriage, Beatrice Roethke says, "When Ted and I were first married he thought it (mental illness) might be a requisite, but over a period of years he revised his thinking about this, I believe. What are generally thought of as his best poems were written when he was well and out of the hospital."

Index

Index

ALLAN SEAGER was a Rhodes scholar. After taking an Honours degree from Oxford, he returned to the United States and joined the staff of *Vanity Fair,* perhaps the most influential magazine of its time, where he worked as an editor. Turning his attention to teaching, Mr. Seager joined the faculty of the University of Michigan at Ann Arbor where he became, in time, Professor of English. Besides being one of the most important and influential teachers in the Midwest, he was the author of a number of highly praised novels including *Equinox, Amos Berry, The Inheritance* and *The Death of Anger.* He also wrote a collection of short stories, *The Old Man of the Mountain* and a fictionalized memoir, *A Frieze of Girls.* After a prolonged illness, Mr. Seager died in Ann Arbor, Michigan, on May 10, 1968.

Printed and bound by CPI Group (UK) Ltd, Croydon, CR0 4YY

13/04/2025

14656533-0003